The Digital Producer

The Digital Producer

Getting It Done with Computer-Based Tools

Curtis Poole

Ellen Feldman

**Focal
Press**

Boston   Oxford   Auckland   Johannesburg   Melbourne   New Delhi

Focal Press is an imprint of Butterworth-Heinemann.

Copyright 2000 by Butterworth-Heinemann

 A member of the Reed Elsevier group.

Recogizing the importance of preserving what has been written, Butterworth-Heinemann prints its books on acid-free paper whenever possible.

 Butterworth-Heinemann supports the efforts of American Forests and the Global ReLeaf program in its campaign for the betterment of trees, forests, and the environment.

Library of Congress Cataloging-in-Publication Data

Poole, Curtis, 1958–
      The digital producer : getting it done with computer-based tools / Curtis Poole, Ellen Feldman.
         p.   cm.
      ISBN 0-240-80395-7
      1. Video tapes—Editing—Data processing. 2. Video recordings—Production and direc-
      tion—Data processing. 3. Motion pictures—Editing—Data processing. I. Feldman, Ellen,
      1948–   . II. Title.
      TR899.P66   1999
      778.5'2'0285—dc21   99-41045
                                                                                                       CIP

British Library Cataloguing-in-Publication Data

A catalogue record for this book is available from the British Library. The publisher offers special discounts on bulk orders of this book.

For information, please contact:

Manager of Special Sales
Butterworth-Heinemann
313 Washington Street
Newton, MA 02158-1626
Tel: 617-928-2500
Fax: 617-928-2620

"Buddy's Truck Stop" footage provided courtesy of Richard J. S. Gutman, Boston, MA.

Portions of this text used with permission from *Media Composer® for Producers*, ©1995 Avid Technology, Inc. All rights reserved.

Avid, Film Composer, Media Composer, and OMF Interchange are registered trademarks and AVIDdrive and MediaLog are trademarks of Avid Technology, Inc. All other trademarks contained herein are the property of their respective owners.

For information on all Focal Press publications available, visit our World Wide Web home page at: http://www.focalpress.com

Printed in the United States of America

10 9 8 7 6 5 4 3 2 1

Dedicated to my wife, Gonca — a "digital producer" in training — and my children, Barish and Elif, who will own this digital future one day.

Curtis Poole

For my mother, Evelyn Feldman, and in memory of my father, Jack Feldman

Ellen Feldman

Acknowledgments

We are very grateful to the interviewees for generously sharing their time, expertise, and most of all their real-world perspectives and practical tips.

Paul Sampson co-wrote (with Ellen) much material in Chapters 6 and 7, for a course formerly offered by Avid Technology, "Media Composer for Producers." We are grateful to Paul for sharing his considerable knowledge of the nonlinear post-production process.

Thanks to our colleagues Tim Vandawalker and Joanne Izbicki of Avid's technical publications group for initiating Avid Press as a vehicle for encouraging writers to pursue projects like this one. Thanks again to Tim, Joanne, and also Doris Hathaway for their patience with the occasional on-the-job distractions this project entailed. Thanks to Jim Melvin, Steve Noyes, Glen Seaman, Steve Bayes, and Joe Wadleigh for reviewing the book.

Ellen thanks her colleagues in the Avid Educational Services department, a knowledgeable, creative, and adventurous group of people from whom she has learned much about digital technology in general and Avid nonlinear post-production in particular. She would especially like to thank Franco Sacchi, for reviewing portions of the book, and Mary Torgersen, her manager, and John Poulos, the manager of Avid Educational Services, for their support and encouragement.

We would like to thank the following colleagues for their help along the way: Jane Gillooly, independent filmmaker; Joan Kaufman, Joel Krantz, Leila Garcia, Ira Sarver, Iftach Shavit, and Richard Tilkin.

About the Companion CD-ROM

The companion CD-ROM included with the book has the following contents:

- The Digital Producer: The entire contents of this book are provided in PDF (portable document format) that you can open, view on any Macintosh or Windows system with Adobe Acrobat Reader installed.

- Advanced Project Templates: These templates allow you to integrate all the tasks of developing projects from beginning to end into a single-integrated-database approach that makes it possible to eliminate duplication of effort. You'll need FileMaker Pro to use access the templates. To install the 60-day trial version included on this CD, follow the directions included in the Readme file on the CD-ROM.

- Focal Press Catalog: The Focal Press Catalog has been created in Adobe Acrobat and supplied here as an interactive PDF file. Follow the instructions provided in the Readme file on the CD-ROM to install Acrobat Reader 4.0 onto your computer.

- Software and Readme file with installation instructions.

Contents

Chapter 6   **Preparing for Digital Post**

CHAPTER 1

Introduction

"Producer" is one of those titles that creates an immediate impression, and yet is difficult to define. Enter the "digital producer," a master of high-technology who is an even tougher animal to pin down.

This chapter attempts to bring some understanding to what we mean by "digital producer," and how this book can help if you are one, or would like to become one.

Chapter Topics

- What Makes a Producer

- Why Digital Matters

- Who Should Read This Book

- How to Use This Book

What Makes a Producer

I was an associate dean of students at a large university for many years.

Documentary essay producer

I started out as a copywriter for an advertising agency.

Broadcast television producer

I used to be a businessman in the oil industry.

News-magazine producer

I started out as an alternative education teacher in a junior high school.

Corporate video producer

I taught English as a second language.

Multimedia producer

Producers — like sky divers, short-order cooks, and possibly drag car racers — can come from anywhere. This is not to suggest that the average producer appears suddenly at the studio doors like Bigfoot emerging from the wilderness, badly in need of a haircut and a job — although after a rough 12-hour day he or she might look the part. In fact, most producers are highly educated with years of training in fields that have nothing at all to do with digital television production methods at the turn of the millennium.

This book is for you.

Unlike the trained technicians with whom they often spend their hours, producers require no particular certification to do the job. The successful producer is, in many cases, a talented generalist with some basic communications skills and an ability to coordinate the personalities and resources of others to convey the message of a script, a storyboard, or a general manager.

Until a few years ago this dynamic worked just fine. The fundamentals of videotape technology and technical union structures remained relatively stable for some twenty years, until the hyperkinetic engineers of the high-tech industry began touting the wonders of digital video in the late 1980's. Now the revolution is well under way, with the old above-the-line/below-the-line division of labor gradually being erased — and there's no turning back.

Why Digital Matters

Digital technologies are changing every aspect of production, not only the tools and techniques used to capture, prepare, and deliver video, but in some cases the entire structure of production environments and the very content of the television medium itself.

The Slow March of Digital Television

With their stunning pictures and equally stunning price tags, high-definition television sets have been slow to catch on with consumers. Yet digital television continues to march toward acceptance, at least at the distribution end.

Under the government's plan for rollout, affiliates in the 10 largest markets in the U.S. are to begin digital broadcasts by May, 1999, and in the top 30 markets by November, 1999. Digital technology is expected to allow broadcasters to squeeze as many as six signals through an existing channel, or TV stations could offer a single high-definition signal.

If you have no particular interest in computers, this book is not meant to sell you on the virtues of digital media, but simply to raise awareness of the important role these technologies play in the process. More and more the job will require, at the very least, a knowledge of how these digital technologies change the workflow of the various players in production — camerapeople, editors, directors, designers. At best, a true "digital producer" can use this book to gain mastery over these technologies and shorten the cycles of production. You might even discover completely new ways to communicate your message.

The Second Coming of the Superhighway

You might recall all that talk about the "information superhighway" and the "500 channel universe" in the mid-1990s. For a while it seemed like somebody pulled the plug before the construction even started.

Although the marketing lingo has changed considerably, the dream of the information superhighway has found new life, this time as a kind of re-paving of that meandering cowpath of the global village, the World Wide Web.

Services like @Home Networks and Microsoft's WebTV have already brought the World Wide Web together with conventional television for hundreds of thousands of subscribers. New systems from WebTV and a service called Wink use the trusty VBI (vertical blanking interval, traditionally used for closed-captioning and other types of information transmission) to provide web television users with direct hyperlinks from specific moments in the flow of television programming to closely-related web pages.

If the ever-merging communications power-houses have their way, those numbers will grow exponentially in the next few years. Currently, the WebTV set-top box has approximately 800,000 subscribers, and has also taken control of the navigational front end for the EchoStar/Dish satellite-TV box. @Home Network, the cable modem service with approximately 400,000 subscribers, is now part of the vast merger of TCI and AT&T.

It seems more and more likely that in the not-too-distant future, we might very well end up with a "5 billion channel universe."

Who Should Read This Book

The specific techniques and examples we use throughout this book are oriented toward the development of audio-visual scripts for documentaries, news-magazine pieces, corporate video projects, and to some extent short-form commercials, promos, and public service announcements.

If you are a filmmaker, or more specifically, if you develop dramatic scripts for feature films, television drama series, television movies, and sitcoms, this book is probably not for you. Producers and directors of dramatic or feature film projects who are interested in learning more about digital technologies should consider the book *Digital Filmmaking* by Michael Phillips and Thomas Ohanian (Focal Press, 1996).

For the generation that will come of age in the next millennium, the technologies discussed in these pages will probably seem ordinary, even quaint. The truth is, they won't need this book.

For those of you who are managing to get by with the typewriter and the telephone while insisting that computers are the producer's nemesis, you probably don't *want* this book.

This book is really for the "in-betweeners" — producers who are currently making the transition from analog to digital with enthusiasm, those who are straddling the fence with uncertainty, or those who are having the transition foisted upon them by changes in their production environments.

If you fit into one of these categories, chances are you already use a word processor to manage some area of content development, whether it's budgets, outlines, scripts, or logs. That means you already have a base. If you think about it, producers are the original "desktop editors," hammering source material into edit plans that might include narration, shot descriptions, tape and timecode information, and sound-on-tape. That blueprint of the program is, for all intents and purposes, a "rough cut" without the play button. With the latest computer-based tools and techniques, the distance from that script on your laptop to the finished program on screen is shorter than ever. This book will help you get it there safely and effectively.

How to Use This Book

As the digital era in the media reaches full steam in the next few years, computer-based tools covering the entire production process – from scripting to shooting to finishing – will become commonplace. This book will help you answer the following important questions:

- How are new digital production tools affecting the producer's budgets, schedules, and production plans?

- What are the advantages of computer-based production tools? What are the pitfalls?

- How should a producer prepare scripts and edit plans for effective nonlinear post-production?

• How can a producer best use computer-based tools to avoid duplication of effort?

Each chapter covers a different phase of the production process,
and begins with general information regarding the role of new digital
technologies along with advice and technical details for the producer.
We also include sidebar information and advice regarding current and
future trends.

You will find insightful comments from professionals who are grap-
pling with digital issues and workflow sprinkled throughout. These
interviews are also provided in full in Appendix A.

A number of chapters also describe off-the-shelf (or off-the-Web)
software tools that producers can purchase to make some aspects of
the job easier.

Sprinkled throughout the chapters you will find "do-it-yourself"
workshops that tell you how to use the Advanced Project Templates
provided on the companion CD-ROM. These templates allow you to
integrate all the tasks of developing projects from beginning to end
into a single, integrated database approach that makes it possible to
eliminate duplication of effort altogether. You'll learn more about
these advanced project templates in the next chapter.

Finally, some chapters end with a Producer's Checklist that you can
copy or print and use as a reminder of specific details during production.

Using the Companion CD-ROM

The Digital Producer companion CD-ROM attached to this book
includes a number of useful extras. For example:

• The entire contents of this book are provided in the form of a PDF
  (portable document format) file that you can open and view on
  any Macintosh or Windows system with Adobe Acrobat Reader
  installed. The book in PDF form is in full color and uses hypertext
  links for easy navigation between topics, as well as links to the
  World Wide Web.

- The Advanced Project Templates are provided in a folder by the same name, which you can copy and use in your own projects.

- The CD also includes a catalog of titles from Focal Press.

- A self-running title program on the CD-ROM labeled "Start Here!" The program introduces all of these items and allows you to open the PDF files and the web links file directly.

If your system meets the minimum system requirements and you have QuickTime 3.0.2 or later and Acrobat Reader or Acrobat installed, you can simply double-click the icon labeled "Start Here" to start the program.

Additional information regarding system requirements and installation of the software is available in the Readme file provided on the CDR.

CHAPTER 2

The Digital Landscape

Before launching into project development, this chapter provides the digital producer with some background information on the transformations that digital production methods and distribution architectures are making in the world of communications.

Chapter Topics

- The Future of Television
- The Lay of the Land
- What Computers Can Do for You
- When Computers Aren't So Great
- The Language of Digital Production
- The Database as Lingua Franca
- Introducing Advanced Project Templates
- Producer's Checklist: Digital Production Vocabulary

The Future of Television

Hollywood luminary Michael Crichton predicted that in the not-too-distant future television as we know it will cease to exist. Five or six years ago such an observation would have been laughable. After witnessing the rapid growth of the World Wide Web in recent years, we can begin to believe his prediction.

We've all read about the gradual breakup of the monopoly that the three big television networks have held for some 30 years in the battle for eyeballs. The first splintering of the television audience began with cable and the development of niche programming. But it was still the same television experience — millions of viewers glued to the march of interlaced images on television screens. Crichton's prediction was inspired by the more fundamental shift now underway as more and more "media consumers" spend their time away from the television set entirely, navigating through progressively scanned images on the computer monitor. Audience share at the big three television networks has steadily declined in the last few years while the numbers of subscribers to the internet has mushroomed.

Watching these trends, you might think that television is doomed. Scary thought for a television producer. But producers of video content should not fear for their jobs. The fact is, video and all forms of full-motion imagery figure very prominently in the digital future.

Cooperative efforts among engineers from the television and computer industries will ensure the integration of video into the digital future, whether it is delivered to a computer or through the home entertainment unit. Much is promised in the way of digital television as well as "webcasting," but the first real-world success in these cooperative efforts already exists in the form of DVD.

DVD and Your TV

A form of digital television is already well under way with the DVD (Digital Video Disc). Cleverly disguised as a sleek new video appliance, the DVD player uses much the same digital technology used in DVD-ROM drives now shipping in personal computers. DVD has experienced one of the best new product introductions in the history of media appliances.

According to the market research firm InfoTech, 230,000 DVD-Video players were sold during 1997, and over 500,000 were sold in 1998, with sale of over a million units projected for 1999. According to Microsoft, DVD-ROM sales topped 2 million in 1997 while the final tally for 1998 should exceed 15 million.

DVD-Video allows viewers to interact with their programming in completely nonlinear ways, by skipping through "chapters" of a movie, for example, as they might do with a multimedia CD-ROM. The success of DVD as a cross-over medium is effectively creating a new audience for interactive multimedia content delivered to both the television screen as well as the computer monitor.

Engineers and industry leaders are also working hard to bring about some form of DTV (digital television) that would combine access to the web with digital transmissions. When this so-called "convergence" finally takes place, there is the very real possibility that just as viewers are now turning from television sets to spend more time at their computers, digital television sets and web-enabled set-top boxes might one day draw many web enthusiasts back to the family room. At that point television as we know it will indeed cease to exist. What replaces it will be something completely different.

To track the evolution of digital television, visit: digitaltelevision .com

What does this mean for producers of video content? If we can believe the plethora of seers and market forecasters sounding off these days with millennial fervor, the television production industry will be changing as rapidly as the California coast over the course of the next few years. Here are a few more predictions:

- The trusty VCR will eventually bite the dust, while sales of DVD players will continue to increase.

- Digital cameras will continue to replace analog ones, keeping step with a steady increase in digital broadcasts.

- New digital TV set-top boxes and DTV-enabled computers will begin to enter the market.

- Cable television providers will broaden their competition with the phone companies through broadband World Wide Web and even telephone services delivered through cable lines.

- Phone companies, in turn, will increase their efforts to provide broadband World Wide Web services using a technology called DSL or Digital Subscriber Line.

- The major networks will in all likelihood continue to thrive. Increasingly their merger partners will be the new crown kings of the World Wide Web.

- Clearly, video will not go away (though video*tape* very well might).

We don't know at this time exactly what digital formats will win out, or what new distribution technologies will emerge in the years ahead. But we do know that computer technology will increasingly provide solutions at every stage of the production process. The time is now to learn as much as possible about the unique qualities of the various forms of digital media and the means of their production.

The Lay of the Land

If you haven't spent much time working inside the high-technology industries, some of the terminology used in the previous section might be entirely foreign to you. Before proceeding, it might be useful to take in a bird's eye view of the media industry landscape heading into the digital future.

Trends in Publicly Distributed Media

The following chart presents a brief visual history of the various forms of media that are predicted to "converge" at some point in the digital future. Specific histories of these various technologies are certainly more complex than they appear in this chart, which is designed merely to highlight general trends.

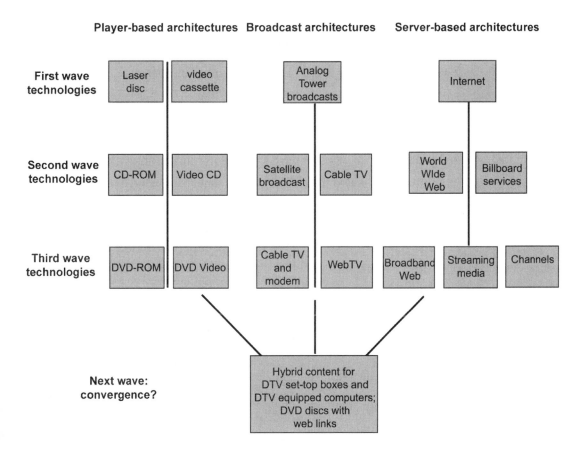

Acronym City

Now that you've taken in a map of the landscape, here's a brief key to understanding those garbled signposts of the industry, the acronyms.

The high-tech industries love acronyms. That's probably because it's impossible for anyone to remember all the names of these new technologies. Here are a few of the more prominent acronyms you might want to review.

The Big D's

They are: DTV, DV, SDTV, HDTV, DSL, and DVD. Try to say that five times fast. Here's a clue (as if you hadn't guessed): most of the D's stand for "digital." So what's the difference between them all?

- DTV stands for digital television, plain and simple. This is a more general term encompassing all forms of digital transmission, and might include any number of the more specific digital television technologies described below.

- SDTV stands for standard-definition television. This is television delivered in the traditional 4:3 aspect ratio. SDTV can be either analog or digital.

- HDTV stands for high-definition television. This is the digital television of the (near) future: the type of video that plays on those big expensive television sets in the 16:9 wide-screen aspect ratio.

- DV stands for digital video. There are two uses for this term: it can be used generically to refer to all forms of digital video; or it can refer to a specific format, the DV digital recording and play-back specification that has taken hold as a low-cost alternative to the professional Betacam format. DV cameras and equipment come at a fraction of the cost of traditional Betacam, and can produce nearly the same quality of recorded video. And because the video is recorded digitally, there is virtually no generation loss when transferred and edited under optimal conditions.

- DSL stands for digital subscriber line, and refers to a new technology that allows conventional telephone lines to carry much more data, resulting in broadband World Wide Web delivery — the kind that is currently available only along cable television lines.

- DVD stands for Digital Video Disc, or Digital Versatile Disc. DVD is the next generation of the now-familiar CD-ROM and audio CD technologies.

The Difference Between DVD Video and DVD-ROM

In the same way that CD audio and CD-ROM are two different implementations of similar disc-based technology, DVD video and DVD-ROM are very different. In some respects DVD video does for video recording what CD audio did for music and sound recording: it provides a digital consumer platform for distribution and playback of material previously delivered in analog form. DVD video is slated to replace VHS rental and purchase the way audio CDs have replaced records.

Likewise, DVD-ROM might one day replace CD-ROM as the medium of choice for interactive computer-based multimedia titles.

What Computers Can Do for You

You might wonder sometimes if computers are more trouble than they're worth. When the hard disk fails, when the software freezes, you might ask yourself, why do I bother? Certainly maintaining computers involves some frustrations, but on the whole, if used effectively, computers save you even more time and effort by helping you get through tedious jobs more quickly, leaving more time and flexibility for the creative work. The trick is knowing what tasks computers handle best, and what tasks are better handled by using other means.

The primary goal of this book is to provide you with a solid understanding of the three major ways in which computers can help you work more effectively as a producer. The methods and tools presented in this book will help you to:

- Eliminate the producer's traditional nemesis: duplication of effort

- Eliminate the need to perform time-consuming calculations

- Eliminate the incidents of error introduced by repeating information in many places

A secondary goal is to provide you with real-world tips for interacting more effectively with those technicians who are handling digital equipment, whether it's a nonlinear editor or a digital camera.

The following is a general overview of the specific advantages these methods, tools, and tips can provide at each stage of the producer's workflow.

The Producer's Missing Links

Traditional methods of project development and production involve a considerable amount of repetitive tasks and duplicated effort. These time-honored methods are so commonplace that we take their inefficiencies for granted.

In the traditional workflow a producer might begin with a proposal, followed by some kind of treatment or design document. These are usually accompanied by a budget and rough schedule and production plan. In the minds of production team members, these two complementary paths of development — imagined content and practical logistics — remain closely interlinked and continue to develop in an unbroken chain as the project progresses.

And yet, how many times is the chain broken on paper? The pages produced during a project, particularly a large and complicated one, can often fill several binders, with various facts and details repeated throughout. That means one or more members of the team had to type those facts and details repeatedly at various times. The cut-and-paste capabilities of a word-processing application help, but even then the proposals, budgets, storyboards, production plans, and schedules are all produced separately — often in completely separate applications.

During the crucial post-production stage video producers go through a grueling process of logging the source footage and noting timecodes, printing and marking up the pages and then reproducing portions of it on a clean page, continuing with the cycle for several drafts, and then finally transcribing timecode and source tape notes from the original logs onto a final draft.

A word processor can alleviate some of the duplication of effort, but one big duplication still remains: in almost all cases the producer carries a box of tapes and a pile of papers (along with a laptop) into the edit bay and proceeds to translate the entire content of that script to an editor, one edit at a time. The process is time-consuming and sometimes frustrating for all involved.

There are productions in which time constraints, style considerations, and the skills of the editors have given rise to a workflow where the scripts are handed off to editors who sometimes work alone for long periods of time with very little guidance. But in most environments the editor is not prepared to interpret the producer's script and notes, and the producer feels a need to "babysit" the project.

Most video producers see no separation between logging clip information and transcribing the audible content of the shoot — whether it is interview text, narration, or sound-on-tape. Many logging tools allow you to capture clip information without the text that a video producer usually associates with it in the normal workflow.

These are the producer's missing links — minor or sometimes major annoyances that complicate the "unbroken" chain of development of a concept that occurs in the imagination.

Computer-based development tools, or specifically the tools and methods we provide in the chapters ahead, including the Advanced Project Templates, attempt to fill in some of these gaps and allow the producer to develop a project more organically by taking the same material that begins in the first draft proposal and plans and continuing to reshape it, add to it, delete from it, and present that information in various useful formats along the way.

The following table summarizes the advantages of digital production methods at each stage of the producer's workflow (depending on the structure of your organization, some of these jobs might be performed by others on the production team).

Table 2-1: Field Producer's Workflow

Stage of Production	Traditional Workflow	Digital Workflow
1. Write an outline, notes, and standup text.	Type up with a word processor or typewriter on separate sheets (in separate files).	Create an outline and beginning script, then print out a customized list of standup text and notes directly from the file.
2. Develop budgets and production plans.	Type up with a word processor, typewriter, or spreadsheet program on separate sheets (usually in separate files).	Continue to develop production details directly from the outline and beginning script, then print out customized budgets and shoot plans.
3. Field produce on location.	Refer to hardcopy notes and text, or sometimes bring a laptop. Changes in the field are often handwritten.	Bring a laptop or personal assistant on location to make notes or changes. Logging can begin in the field in some cases.
4. Log/transcribe footage after shoot.	Type up with a word processor or typewriter.	Transcribe and log tapes simultaneously into a database, with various automated tasks for repetitive information like tape names and duration calculations.
5. Write the script.	Assemble from logs/notes by retyping text with a word processor or typewriter.	Shot log information can be imported directly into the script template using the Advanced Project Templates and some logging applications.
6. Time the script.	Requires frequent timing of narration tracks and calculation of shot lengths (done manually).	Clip durations and running time can be calculated automatically.
7. Submit script for approval.	Deliver script (typed or printed).	Deliver script or storyboard printed out directly from the same database.
8. Rework final draft.	Rewrite and re-transcribe any new log information.	Rework script within the same database file. Timing changes are automatically recalculated.

Table 2-1: Field Producer's Workflow

Stage of Production	Traditional Workflow	Digital Workflow
9. Submit requests for required elements such as graphics, stills, or titles.	Type up or handwrite requirements in separate forms.	Lists can be printed out directly from a script development database like the Advanced Project Templates.
10. Record the narration.	Photocopy or rewrite narration tracks, or highlight them on the script for the talent to follow.	You can also print out a customized list directly from the Advanced Project Templates.
11. Add timecode/tape notes from logs.	Transfer from logs to the script manually or in a word processor.	Automatically added.
12. Import shot log information directly into the edit controller or nonlinear editor.	Not possible.	Output tab-delimited text files in various formats directly from the script database for import into various systems.
13. Sit with the editor and convey the script.	The producer remains in the edit room throughout the editing phase and keeps track of script and running time.	With a complete and detailed script, the editor can work alone for long periods.

When Computers Aren't So Great

A study conducted in the early 1990's determined that despite the advent of desktop computers the level of productivity in the work place remained pretty much the same. Why? Having spent many years wrestling with endless upgrades, software bugs, and hardware failures, we can only guess. Not to mention the guilty pleasures of gaming and web-surfing.

There is a certain amount of time and effort that goes into operating and maintaining computers and software effectively. But there are a few ways you can get the most out of them, lessening the more time-consuming tasks. Here are a few snippets of "counter-marketing" wisdom you won't read on the back of software packages:

- Avoid new products when you can. Yup, you heard it here first. Despite the hype, often that whiz-bang new piece of software will end up providing you with only a small incremental improvement in your work methods while costing you hours of re-education.

- The second rule, very closely related to the first, is to "go with what you know." If you've learned how to use a piece of software or hardware, and you use it well, and it does the job you need to have done, then stick with it as long as possible.

- If you do take on some new software or hardware, do it when you have some down time. In other words, leave yourself plenty of time to learn the tools before coming under pressure with deadlines.

- Read up. Trade magazines are full of articles about new products and developments that will help you make educated purchases and plot out your future strategy. But also learn to read between the lines — or between the pages of text. Remember that those flashy ads that take up 60 percent of the average trade magazine are the life blood of that publication.

- If your computer breaks down, be ready with a backup. In other words, don't throw out your electric typewriter just yet. And keep a supply of standard forms around that you can fill out at the drop of a hat.

- Every now and then just for kicks try writing a letter by hand. No kidding, a good old fashioned letter. You'll be amazed at how quickly your writing muscles atrophy, and how physician-like your handwriting becomes, after years of nothing but keyboard.

The Language of Digital Production

No, this is not some rehashing of your most boring computer programming class from freshman year. Our intention is not to review information about computer technology that you can find readily at the local library, or more appropriately, on the web.

The language we speak of here is the new lingo of the production industry moving forward into the 21st century. The tables that follow provide a quick rundown of the major concepts and buzzwords in the digital production process. Many of these will be touched upon throughout this book.

Table 2-2: Digital Development Tools

Type of Application	Example	Uses
Word Processor	Microsoft Word, WordPerfect	Text formatting and manipulation of scripts, logs, proposals, etc.
Spreadsheet	Microsoft Excel, Lotus 1-2-3	Budgets, program run-downs, timing sheets
Database	Filemaker Pro, Microsoft Access	Creation and manage-ment of data records for invoicing, phone lists, sto-ryboards; collaborative production environments
Paint or illustration program	Adobe Photoshop, Adobe Illustrator, MetaCreations Painter	Image creation and manipulation for story-boards, pre-visualization

Table 2-3: Digital Production Tools

Type of Application	Example	Uses
Field logging applications	Shot Logger, e-trim, The Executive Producer	Usually using the data-base model for managing records, scripts, logs, pro-posals, etc.
Disk-based digital cameras	Ikegami Editcam	Direct-to-disk field cap-ture and nonlinear editing in the field
Tape-based digital cameras	DV cameras	Field capture in digital form onto tape

Table 2-4: Digital Post-Production Tools

Type of Application	Examples	Uses
Logging applications	Avid MediaLog, Log Express, Scene Stealer	Often using the database model for managing multiple records, creation of logs and storboards
Paint applications	Adobe Photoshop, MetaCreations Painter, Quantel Paintbox	Used for bitmap[a] image manipulation, creation of 2-dimensional graphics elements
Illustration programs	Adobe Illustrator, Macromedia Freehand	Used for vector-based[b] image creation and manipulation, creation of two-dimensional graphics elements
3D modeling and animation	MetaCreations Infini-D, Alias/Wavefront, Lightwave, Softimage 3D	Used for creating and animating three-dimensional graphics elements
Compositing applications	Adobe After Effects; Discreet Flame; Avid Illusion, Quantel Harry	Used for combining 2D graphics, 3D graphics, and video elements into a seamless presentation
Nonlinear editing systems (NLEs)	Avid Media Composer, Media 100, Adobe Premiere	Replacing tape-based systems for combining video and audio into edited programs of various lengths
Digital audio workstations (DAWs)	Avid Digidesign Pro Tools, Avid AudioVision	Used for audio sweetening and mixing of multiple tracks
Nonlinear Finishing systems	Avid Symphony, Avid Softimage	Replacing tape-based online suites as all-in-one finishing solutions for high-quality programming

a. Also known as raster images, bitmaps use a grid of small squares known as pixels to represent images.
b. Vectors are images composed of lines and curves defined by mathematical objects.

In their continuing evolution, nonlinear editing systems continue to bring together more and more of the technologies described above into single systems. For example, hidden in each nonlinear editor is a database system; some nonlinear editors use motion jpeg technology adapted from the time-honored jpeg image format used for years in programs like Photoshop; some of the more advanced nonlinear editing systems are adopting more and more of the paint and animation capabilities used in graphics and 3D animation applications; and audio editing and manipulation capabilities are always improving. There's even an option available for nonlinear editing systems from Avid Technology that allows you to import and mark up script text for the editors (see "Scripting Tips and Tricks" on page 160).

In fact, one of the primary goals of the developers of nonlinear editing systems, stated over and over again at trade shows like NAB (National Association of Broadcasters convention in Las Vegas) is to one day provide a seamless environment for the creation of full-motion imagery of all types. And they're getting closer every year.

The Database as Lingua Franca

As previously mentioned, almost all nonlinear editing systems have a database system in some form hidden within their software. This database system can be seen most readily when viewing and editing with the source footage in the bins or windows that organize them.

If you've ever used a logging program, or created an EDL in offline and imported it into an online edit controller, you've witnessed firsthand the fact that the database continues to be the producer's first and most direct point of entry into the workings of an editing system. Successful development and conversion of shot logs and offline EDLs can be a huge time-saver in post-production, allowing you to move successfully among systems. Even as developers of computer-based post-production products continue to strive for improved inter-operability, the database remains the one true lingua franca of the post industry.

What about the rest of the production process? These days the database is also gaining importance in collaborative production environments, where various members of a production team can access shared resources and information in a database structure made available over a network or even across the World Wide Web. This collaborative process often takes place throughout the course of production.

As a development tool for producers, the database is clearly one of the most versatile and underused resources. Most of us are accustomed to using word processors such as Microsoft Word for much of the work. Some might use the Excel spreadsheet program for tasks that require calculations, such as budgets and timing sheets. These are great tools, but they still require some duplication of effort, if not a lot of copying and pasting.

It is possible to extend the virtues of the database one step further. What if it were possible for the producer to begin work on a project in a database from the very beginning, then continue to build up that database while generating all the necessary paperwork along the way, and finally bring their database output directly into a nonlinear editing system? We've attempted to take a step in this direction with the Advanced Project Templates provided on the companion CD-ROM.

Introducing Advanced Project Templates

While we mention in these chapters many of the most popular off-the-shelf tools available for project development, we've also provided a low-cost alternative on the companion CD-ROM. Our Advanced Project Templates are designed to work more like the way you think during all phases of project development.

To access the Advanced Project Templates:

   1. Load the companion CD-ROM into your CD-ROM drive.

2. In the window that appears, click on the folder labeled Advanced Project Templates and drag it to a location on your hard drive (some central location, for example, where you can copy and use it frequently in the future).

3. To view the templates, double-click the folder labeled Advanced Project Templates.

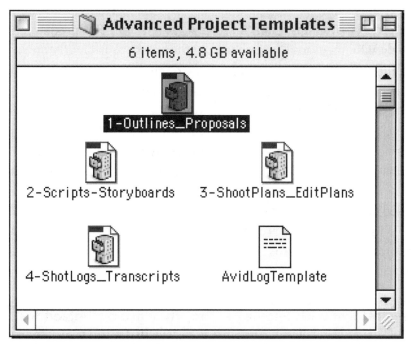

These templates consist of five interrelated files that were created using the "relational database" capabilities of Filemaker Pro, an application that provides great flexibility in storing facts and details, then displaying and printing out that information selectively based on a specific need. There is a file called AvidLogTemplate used in generating log files compatible with Avid systems, as well as a file labeled B-Roll that is used by the database. Do not remove these files.

Because the information remains in one source during development, there is less room for error. And because they allow you to build up the content of the project within one source, these templates effectively eliminate all duplicated effort from the project. Finally, because you are working directly in a database model, you can easily output tab-delimited text files for direct input into nonlinear editing systems.

Your work with these Advanced Project Templates parallels the way a concept begins very simply and develops in complexity during a project. We've designed these templates to allow you to begin with a very simple set of information, and then add layer upon layer of detail as the project progresses.

Requirements for Using the Advanced Project Templates

To download a demo version of Filemaker Pro, visit filemaker.com

To use the Advanced Project Templates straight off the CD-ROM, you will need a copy of Filemaker Pro Release 4.0 or greater for either the Macintosh or the Windows operating system.

We've used Filemaker Pro because of its versatility (Macintosh and PC versions are available, and files are cross-platform), ease of use (you can customize or adapt any layout to your own needs), and networking capabilities (Filemaker Pro Release 4.0 databases can be deployed across networks and can also be made available on the World Wide Web). If you are more comfortable with another database application, such as Microsoft Access, you can use the basic concepts presented in these templates to build your own system.

While the Advanced Project Templates files can be used cross-platform with Filemaker Pro, they are optimized for use with the Macintosh version and might require some adjustments when using them in the Windows version. See your Filemaker Pro documentation to customize the templates.

Throughout this book you will find topics labeled "Advanced Template Workshops." These topic form a guide to using these templates effectively. We do not provide training in the use of Filemaker Pro, however. For more information on Filemaker Pro consult the documentation or help system that came with your application.

Producer's Checklist: Digital Production Vocabulary

Some new words and acronyms to remember:

Distribution technologies

- Broadband Web delivery, including DSL and cable modem

- DTV (digital television) including SDTV (standard-definition) and HDTV (high-definition)

- DVD video and DVD-ROM

Development tools

- Word processor, spreadsheet, and database applications

- Digital Field Production (or Digital News Gathering)

- Paint and Illustration applications

- Effects and Compositing applications

- Nonlinear editors (NLEs)

- Nonlinear finishing systems

- Digital Audio Workstations (DAWs)

CHAPTER 3

Computer-Based Project Development

You can speed the development of project documents — such as outlines, scripts, and storyboards — by using a computer and the right software. In addition, with the right tools you can make the process of developing concepts and logistics more like the way you think, while avoiding some of the duplication of effort that occurs when working on paper or with a word-processor. These methods are described in the following sections.

Chapter Topics

- Setting Up a Project

- The Starting Point: Outlines and Proposals

- Project Template Workshop: Preparing Proposals and Outlines

- Storyboarding

- Project Template Workshop: Preparing Storyboards

- Scripting in Advance

- Project Template Workshop: Preparing a Script

- Producer's Checklist: Development Resources

Setting Up a Project

For most of us the hard drive of our personal computer is more like a closet than a desktop: we use our folders like a hodge-podge collection of boxes into which we throw things — documents, memos, plans in various shapes and forms — as we rush through our work with the hope of one day making sense of it all. Unfortunately the "closet" that seemed so big in the beginning fills up much faster than we expect. When it becomes unbearable we might pull some related files together and throw a few things away, only to find ourselves searching through the "boxes" a few days later trying to remember where we put that all-important document, hoping that we didn't trash it without realizing how useful it could be as we begin the next big project.

The following are a few simple organizational rules that will help you conserve space, speed your tasks, and make it easier for you to find things. This is just one way of organizing that you can adapt to suit your own particular needs and work habits.

This method of organizing project folders and files attempts to take advantage of the unique capabilities of the computer desktop, and works similarly for both Macintosh and Windows-based computers. By using this method you can create your set of project folders just once, and never create them again.

Creating a Master Set of Folders

First, create a master set of folders that are generic enough, yet specific enough to cover every potential type of production you will undertake in the future. You should place these folders along with the Advance Project Templates you can copy from the companion CD-ROM (see "Introducing Advanced Project Templates" on page 24) in some central location on your hard drive where you can access them easily and copy them for each new project.

To structure the folders, consider that for today's production environments there are only a few major types of media you can produce: disc-based (CD-ROM, DVD), print materials (documentation, marketing materials, advertisements, etc.), video-based (corporate programming, broadcast programming, etc.), and World Wide Web sites are the most common.

The following illustration shows this top level structure.

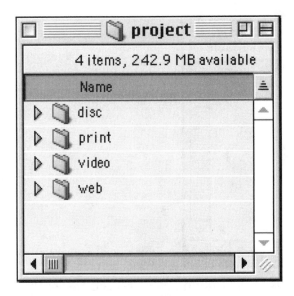

Keep in mind as you name folders that you can use the alphanumeric capabilities of the operating system to navigate quickly by making sure that all folders at each level begin with a different letter. For example, in the structure above, when you first open the project folder you can press a single letter, such a "v" for video, to instantly select that folder. You can then use keyboard shortcuts to open the folder, then press another letter, such as "b" for backup, to select that folder, and so forth.

Independents or producers in small production houses may very well find themselves called upon to work on any of these media types, and therefore might want to have all of these folders available at the start of a project. In this case "project" stands for "client" and all the possible jobs you might end up doing for them. But if your work is focused in just one or two forms of media (video and disc-based, or web sites and print materials, for example) you can create just those folders.

Inside each folder you can then create a meaningful set of sub-folders based on the various types of files you are likely to accumulate throughout the project. The following illustration shows one possible set of sub-folders:

In this example for a disc-based multimedia project, the backup folder is used to store saved copies of files, the media folder is used to store media assets used in the authored title, the processing folder is used to place media for processing, and the source folder is used to store all important source files (media, documents, etc.) used during the project.

Depending on your work habits, you can go on to create another set of folders within these folders and so forth, but be careful not make the structure too "deep," which defeats the purpose by requiring you to navigate through too many complicated levels.

This approach is also based on the simple principle that it is easier to *delete* than it is to *create*: in other words, when you start a new project, simply delete all folders and files that have no relevance for the project, and you are ready to go.

After creating and saving these files to a central location, begin each new project as follows:

1. Copy the top-level folder "project" to a location for the new project.

If you work in a networked environment with a production team, you can set up your folders on a central server.

2. Rename the top-level folder with the name of your project.

3. Delete all folders and files that you know you will not use. (If you think you might use them in the future, it doesn't hurt to keep them around.)

4. (Option) If you are using the Advanced Project Templates for project development, move the Advanced Project Templates folder into the newly named project folder, and rename it "development."

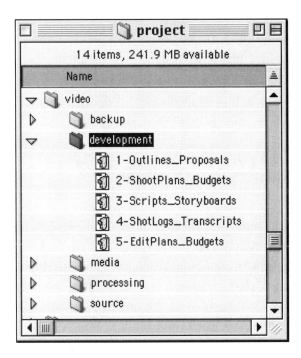

Now you have a complete set of folders and you are ready to go to work.

For networked environments, you can set up networked versions of Filemaker Pro for sharing the development files among production team members. For more information, consult the Filemaker Pro documentation.

The Starting Point: Outlines and Proposals

Many projects begin with a proposal and an outline (or some kind of design document). Outlines and proposals are probably the most difficult documents to "pin down" for the purposes of standardized project development because they can be so free form, while they can also be very specific depending on the demands of a particular "client" or production environment.

If you already work with a certain type of proposal or outline document, then we must leave you to your own devices. You can skip over the next section and continue with "Storyboarding" on page 48.

If you have some flexibility in this regard, or if you are looking for a new solution for this first phase of project development, then we offer you an opportunity to integrate your first concepts from the roughest beginnings directly into the flow of all subsequent development, as described in the following section.

Project Template Workshop: Preparing Proposals and Outlines

Our Advanced Project Templates offer you an entirely new way of developing your concepts and the logistical details required to bring them to fruition. We've designed a database structure that works more like the way you think as a producer, allowing you to develop concepts and build up project details gradually, while printing them out in appropriate formats at various stages with the click of a button.

Throughout the process we've attempted to eliminate all repetitive entry of information. In other words, if used properly you can enter any number of ideas and details only once, and never have to repeat them in another document or draft. For the first time perhaps you can do away completely with that old notion of the creative writer who yanks page after page out of the typewriter and throws it in the basket.

We've also attempted to make effective use of the computer's innate talent for doing the calculations for you. These templates are set up to help you automatically calculate budget items and time durations for such things as shoot days and scripts.

The Database Approach

These templates require a slightly different mindset in your approach to typing up information. In this database approach you work dynamically with "records" (versus the more linear approach of a word processor, for example, in which you type information down the length of a page). If you can learn the basic ground rules for working in a database, these templates can serve you effectively for years to come.

To put it simply, you must begin to think of each piece of the presentation (a paragraph in the script, for example, that describes a series of shots or lays out a piece of narration) as an individual "record" in the database. Once you enter these "records," you can then begin to attach additional details to these pieces of the puzzle as the project progresses. When you are ready to commit something to paper, your final output is based on what has traditionally been called a "report" in database terms. On the printed page, however, it looks like the same rough draft, or storyboard, or shot plan in its final form — you just arrive at it in a different way.

You can learn more about the database approach by reading the documentation that comes with Filemaker Pro. You can also learn how to adapt and customize these templates to suit your own purposes. For more information on the software requirements for using these templates, see "Requirements for Using the Advanced Project Templates" on page 26.

Building a Proposal

Let's start with the simplest form: the proposal. To begin, double-click the file labeled 1-Outlines_Proposals. The following screen appears.

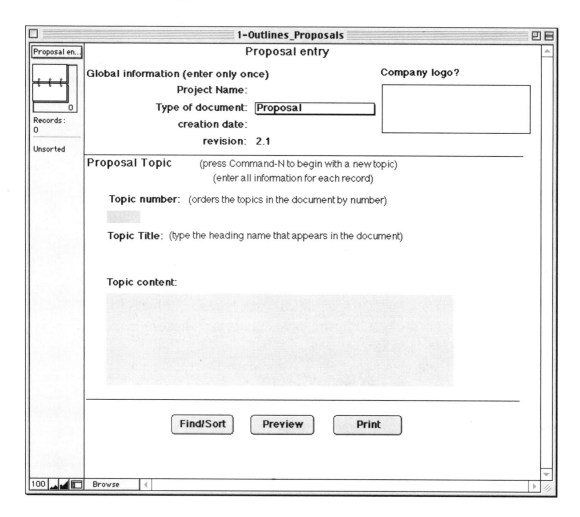

Create your proposal as follows:

1. Enter global information for the project in the top portion of the entry form.

Proposal entry

Global information (enter only once)   Company logo?

Project Name: Project name here

Type of document: Proposal

creation date (d/m/yr:

revision:

As the label implies, *global* information applies to the entire project — such as the project name — therefore you enter this information only once. These items will appear on all title pages and in headers and footers.

- Enter the project name, creation date, and revision by clicking in the text box for each and typing the information.

- Enter the type of document by choosing one from the pop-up menu.

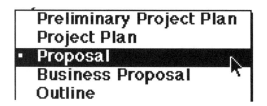

Preliminary Project Plan
Project Plan
Proposal
Business Proposal
Outline

- (Option) Add a company logo to appear in headers and title pages by importing a file into the container labeled Company logo. For more information on importing image files into a Filemaker database, see "Importing Images" on page 55.

2. Create individual records for each section or topic of the proposal by entering information into the individual record section of the entry form.

Proposal Topic   (press Command-N to begin with a new topic)
(enter all information for each record)

Topic number: (orders the topics in the document by number)

1

Topic Title: (type the heading name that appears in the document)

Purpose

Topic content:

Here's the purpose

Topic number:

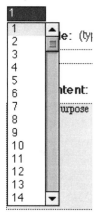

a. Choose a number from the Topic number pop-up list. You can also click in the text box and type a number.

The topic number determines the order in which each topic appears in the proposal when printed. For example, the topic with the number 1 appears first in the proposal when printed. This allows you to reorder the topics in a proposal at any time, in any way you like. Instead of copying and pasting topics around as you would in a word processor, simply renumber the topics.

b. Choose a name for the section or topic from the Topic Title pop-up list. You can also click in the text box and type a name.

Topic Title:

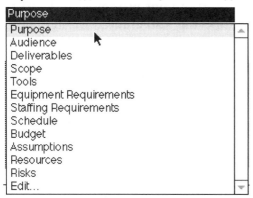

The topic title appears as the heading for the section when the proposal is printed.

The topics in the pop-up list are based on typical proposal forms used in the high-tech and media production industries. If you would like to change the contents of this list, you can choose Edit from the list and add, delete, or rename topics.

    c. Type the content of the topic into the Topic content text box. This content forms the paragraphs of description that appear under each heading when the proposal is printed.

3. After you finish entering an entire topic as a record, press Command–N to begin a new record or topic.

4. Repeat steps 2 and 3 for each additional section or topic in the proposal.

5. When you complete all sections of the proposal, use the buttons at the bottom of the entry form to finalize your work.

       Find/Sort   **Preview**   **Print**

- Click the Find/Sort button to find and sift out only those records that will be used in your proposal, and sort them according to the numbering you entered in Step 2a.

- Click the Preview button to preview how the document will look in its final printed form.

FORESIGHT**media**

	Proposal	6/29/99
	8.0 Upgrade CD-ROM	Revision 2.1

Purpose

To use the particular advantages of an interactive CD-ROM to communicate significant changes in the underlying platform for Release 8.0, to provide upgrade and installation instructions, and to present additional resources available to the field including the new Knowledge Base.

Audience

ACSRs working for Resellers and rental houses, as well as Avid Field Support, AEs and possibly phone support reps.

Deliverables

One CD-ROM gold master and backup on or before May 15, 1999.

Scope

The narrative or linear presentation thread of the title should run no more than 30 minutes, while the user has available at any time the ability to "go interactive" and navigate the title in a nonlinear fashion through a series of navigational screens. The title will include voice narration, video, graphics, and music. The main topics are as follows:
- Overview.
- Introduction to hardware changes
- Upgrade procedures
- Connecting storage
- Installing software and drivers
- Performing system tests
- Additional resources and support
For more information see the attached outline.

- Choose Print from the File menu to print the document.

- To return to form entry, Choose Browse from the Mode menu, then choose an entry form from the pop-up menu.

Building an Outline

The Advanced Project Templates provide great flexibility in creating outlines based on the specific needs of your project. In addition, you can build directly on the outline you create now when storyboarding and scripting later.

To begin, open the file labeled 1-Outlines_Proposals, then choose Outline Entry from the Layout pop-up menu.

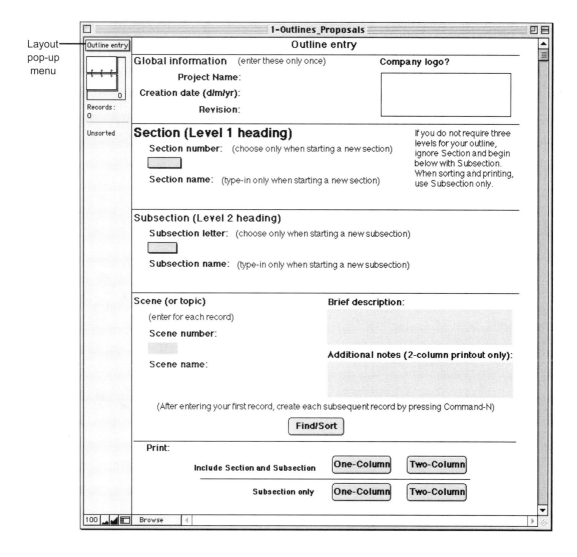

Layout pop-up menu

The outline format in the templates has three levels of headings, which is suitable for most purposes. If you only need two levels for your outline, ignore the Section (Level 1 heading) part of the form, and begin with Subsection entry (the Section heading will not appear in the printed outline if no section information is entered). Likewise, if you need to quickly add another heading level below a scene or third level heading, you can type and format bullets within the scene description text box.

You can also create additional levels, or remove levels, by customizing the layouts. For more information on customizing layouts, consult your Filemaker Pro documentation.

Create your outline as follows:

1. Enter global information for the project in the top portion of the entry form if you haven't already done so when creating a proposal. For more information, see "Building a Proposal" on page 36.

2. Enter information for the first section of the outline. A section is the same as a level 1 heading in the final document.

Section (Level 1 heading)

Section number: (choose only when starting a new section)

Section name: (type-in only when starting a new section)

If you do not require three levels for your outline, ignore Section and begin below with Subsection. When sorting and printing, use Subsection only.

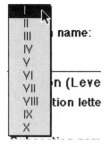

Section number:

name:

n (Leve

tion lette

a. Choose a roman numeral from the Section number pop-up menu.

The section number determines the order in which each section appears in the outline when printed.

b. Enter a name for the section in the Section name text box.

3. Enter information for the first subsection of the outline. A subsection is the same as a level 2 heading that falls under the section (or level 1 heading) in the final document.

Subsection (Level 2 heading)

    Subsection letter: (choose only when starting a new subsection)

    Subsection name: (type-in only when starting a new subsection)

a. Choose a letter from the Subsection letter pop-up menu.

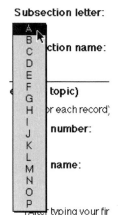

The subsection letter determines the order in which each subsection appears within a section in the outline when printed.

The form uses roman numerals, letters, and numbers for the three levels in order to differentiate them more effectively in the layout.

b. Enter a name for the subsection in the Subsection name text box.

As you add additional subsection entries in subsequent records, you can also click on the Subsection name text box to choose from a pop-up list of all subsection names as shown below.

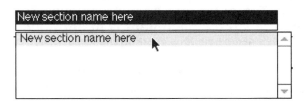

4. Enter information for the scene. A scene is the same as a level 3 heading in the final document. Each scene forms a separate record in the database.

The designation "scene" can denote a series of shots in a certain location in a video project, a single stand-up or paragraph of voice-narration, or a scene in a multimedia title. The designation is flexible; however, the more accurate you can be in breaking down "scenes" based on different parts of the presentation, the more effectively you can build detail into your outline later on.

Scene (or topic)   Brief description:

  (enter for each record)

  Scene number:

  Scene name: Additional notes (2-column printout only):

(After typing your first record, create each subsequent record by pressing Command-N)

> **Find/Sort**

  a. Type a scene number into the Scene number text box.

  The scene number determines the order in which each scene appears within the subsection in the printed outline.

  b. Enter a name for the scene in the Scene name text box.

  c. Type a description of the scene into the Brief description text box. This description appears next to the scene name in the printed outline.

You can copy and paste text from another document, such as a Microsoft Word document, directly into the Advanced Project Template text boxes. However, text formatting from the source document is maintained, so you might have to reformat the text after pasting.

  d. (Option) To use a two-column layout for the outline, you can type information into the Additional notes text box. This information will appear in the second column next to the description text.

Example: if your outline describes an interactive multimedia project you can display information about the linear, narrative presentation of the title in one column, with parallel information about nonlinear interactivity in the second column.

5. After you finish entering the scene information, press Command–N to begin a new record (scene).

Note that the Section and Subsection entries persist in each new record. Enter information for these only when you are finished adding scenes and are ready to begin a new subsection or section.

6. Repeat steps 2 through 5 for each new scene in the outline.

7. (Option) At any time during your typing you can click the Find/ Sort button to reorder the scenes (records) based on section, subsection, and scene number.

Because you can sort these records at any time, you can enter your scene information in any order, as long as Section and Subsection numbering and names are accurate. As soon as you click the Find/Sort button, the scenes are placed in the right order.

8. When you complete all entries for the outline, use the buttons at the bottom of the form to finalize your work. First, click the Find/ Sort button to find and sift out only those records that will be used in your outline, and sort them according to Section, Subsection, and scene.

9. Complete either a one-column or a two-column document as follows:

Print:

- Click one of the Two-Column buttons to find and sort all records and then display them in a preview of the final document. If you include section and subsection, the document has three heading levels. If you include subsections only, the document has two levels as shown.

| FORESIGHT**media** | 8.0 Upgrade CD-ROM | Created 6/29/99 |
| | Outline | Revision 2.1 |

A   Introduction

Notes:

- Welcome

  Narrator introduces the CD

  Images of system hardware dissolve on and off

- Purpose

  Narrator states the purpose

  Screen lists the various goals of the CD

- Using the CD

  Narrator describes procedures for using the CD

  Screen shows the available interactive controls

- Qualifications

  Narrator describes qualified personnel for performing the upgrade

  Screen lists the qualified personnel

- Courses

  Narrator mentions that courses are also available

  Screen shows the phone number for Educational Services

- Required Tools

  Narrator lists the tools necessary for installation

  Screen shows the tools, along with list

B   Hardware Overview

Notes:

- Intro to hardware

  Narrator introduces hardware section

  Base platforms are displayed on screen

- Intro new devices

  Narrator introduces Meridien hardware and audio I/O device

  Hardware displayed on screen

- Avid PCI Extender

  Narrator describes the purpose of the PCI extender

  Extender and systems shown on screen

- 9600 intro

  Narrator describes the 9600 platform

  Screen shows the system

- Meridien hardware

  Narrator describes the Meridien hardware

  Screen shows the hardware

- Click one of the One-Column buttons to find and sort all records and then display them in a preview of the final document. Choose Print from the File menu to print.

FORESIGHT**media**   **8.0 Upgrade CD-ROM**   Created 6/29/99
                              Outline   Revision 2.1

A   Introduction

- Welcome
  Narrator introduces the CD

- Purpose
  Narrator states the purpose

- Using the CD
  Narrator describes procedures for using the CD

- Qualifications
  Narrator describes qualified personnel for performing the upgrade

- Courses
  Narrator mentions that courses are also available

- Required Tools
  Narrator lists the tools necessary for installation

B   Hardware Overview

- Intro to hardware
  Narrator introduces hardware section

- Intro new devices
  Narrator introduces Meridien hardware and audio I/O device

- Avid PCI Extender
  Narrator describes the purpose of the PCI extender

- 9600 intro
  Narrator describes the 9600 platform

- Meridien hardware
  Narrator describes the Meridien hardware

- To return to form entry, Choose Browse from the Mode menu, then choose an entry form from the pop-up menu.

Once your outline is complete, you have the foundation for subsequent development of scripts and storyboards. When you are ready for the next stage, the Advanced Project Templates allow you to import the details of your outline and begin developing scripts and storyboards right away, without having to re-enter the flow of topics in your presentation, as described in the "Project Template Workshop: Preparing Storyboards" on page 51 and "Project Template Workshop: Preparing a Script" on page 66.

Storyboarding

Storyboarding creates a visual map of your program. A storyboard is a sequence of frames, each of which contains a visual representation of that moment in the program, and an accompanying caption of the spoken lines. You can use this tool to communicate to others (crew, clients, funders, executive producers) and gain final approval for the production. Also, the process of storyboarding enables you to test whether your ideas are too vague, intellectual, or impressionistic; or whether they have found the right concrete form. For example, if you write in the script, "montage of early morning city life," do you know the kinds of shots that will work together in the context of this program?

For some types of productions, including animations and commercials, storyboarding is mandatory. For others, such as corporate image pieces and dramatic works, you may or may not choose to create a storyboard. For still others, including documentaries, magazine-style programs, corporate training pieces, they may be rare. But even if you don't need to create a storyboard for your entire program, you might want to sketch out a particularly difficult scene to make sure it will work.

You may sketch a storyboard on paper, and your budget may not enable you to choose another option. However, keep in mind several problems:

• If you have limited drawing talent, the storyboard may have limited value. For example, are you capable of drawing elements such as relationship to the camera (both distance and angle)? If not, the drawings may not help your crew.

- Revising the content of a frame is time-consuming.

- Rearranging the frames is difficult, if not impossible.

You may hire a storyboard artist to eliminate the first problem.

You can also use a software program specifically designed for creating storyboards. You can use the storyboard template provided on the companion CD-ROM or an off-the-shelf product such as Story-Board Artist and StoryBoard Quick, both by PowerProduction Software™. The following section provides a description of Storyboard Quick.

Storyboard Quick

Storyboard Quick is an affordable previsualization tool that you can use to create storyboards. Some of its features are:

- A database of built-in characters, props, and locations that you can place in a frame by pointing and clicking.

- Ability to zoom in and out to resize characters, props, and locations, thus creating long shots, medium shots, close-ups, and over-the-shoulder shots.

- Character rotation, six angles available (front, back, two to the right, two to the left).

- Characters available in five actions: standing, sitting, running, jumping, and prone.

- Captioning, by typing comments into a caption window or importing scripts from any scripting program that supports FCF and TXT file format. When you import a FCF or TXT file, the frames are automatically created with the selected text elements in the caption windows.

- Rearrangement of frames (the captions follow).

- Storyboard formats in standard increments from one to sixteen frames per page, arranged vertically or horizontally.

- Ability to print the frames and captions together or separately. You can use the captions-only option to create a shot list.

- Frames come in four aspect ratios.

- Ability to import graphics from a Macintosh PICT or Windows Metafile or Bitmap drawing, painting, scanning, or video capture files. Import GIF images from the Internet. Layer these imported graphics into a frame with the built-in elements.

- Ability to bring frames into a graphics or paint application for modification.

Storyboard Artist

The makers of Storyboard Quick also provide Storyboard Artist, a more expensive and feature-packed previsualization tool. Pre-drawn props, characters, and locations are integrated into the application for quick visualization.

StoryBoard Artist offers all the features of StoryBoard Quick, plus:

- Use built-in artwork (characters, props and locations) or import graphics from other sources: digital photos, scans, paint or drawing programs, and drawing tools

- Use preset or custom aspect ratios

- Create your own libraries for easy access to custom and frequently used images: logos, locations, custom characters.

- Each object occupies its own layer for easy rearranging and composition

- Imports PICT or BMP, TIFF, QuickTime, JPEG, GIF, QTVR and AIFF or .WAV sound files

- Key color feature enables color transparencies for compositing images

- Alpha Channel support allows for 256 levels of transparencies between images

- Adobe Photoshop Plug-ins technology is enabled for using plug-ins to manipulate in-frame images.

- Each frame can have two captions: add script, dialog, shot info, camera notes, project breakdown info, etc. Import Text or FCF (File converter format) for preserving scriptwriting text categories Shuffle frames to edit project in Frame Overview

- Camera controls can zoom, pan, and tilt the entire frame image

- Timeline feature allows you to set variable frame durations with transitions

- Add sounds into two sound tracks for runtime playback

- Enhanced nonlinear storyboarding: create links between frames and view or print link overview. Creates a visual outline as well as prototype of your project using the linking feature and link over-view printout.

- Export your boards to HTML to show your boards using the Inter-net.

Project Template Workshop: Preparing Storyboards

Storyboarding with the Advanced Project Templates has
several advantages:

- You can import topics directly from the outline created earlier and continue developing them in the storyboard, as described in "Importing Scenes from the Outline" on page 54.

- You can preview and print out the storyboard in various layouts that are useful in different contexts, as described in "Customizing Layouts and Print Options" on page 65.

- You can import scene illustrations directly into the storyboard script, and then display the frames in various sizes, as described in "Importing Images" on page 55.

- You can develop a database of production details within the storyboard — such as animation, titles, sound effects, or still images — that you can sort, sift, and display in various list formats, as described in "Generating Lists" on page 64.

To begin, open the template file labeled 2-Scripts_Storyboards. The following window appears.

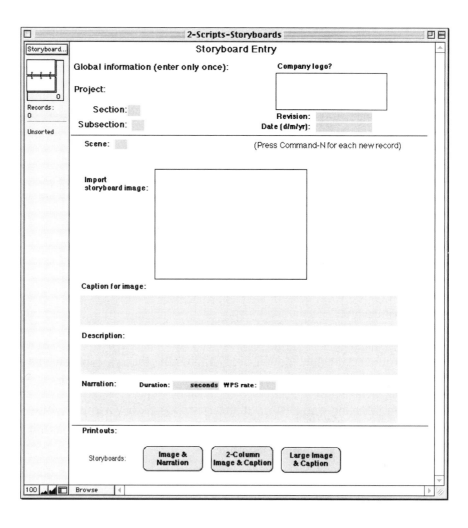

Entering Global Information

To begin a storyboard you should first enter global information for the project. As the label implies, *global* information applies to the entire project — such as the project name — therefore you enter this information only once. These items will appear on all title pages and in headers and footers.

For more information, see "Building a Proposal" on page 36.

Manually Adding Project Name, Section, and Subsection

If you already developed an outline in the Advanced Project Templates as described in "Project Template Workshop: Preparing Proposals and Outlines" on page 34, you can skip these steps and enter project name, section, and subsection information automatically for each record as described in "Importing Scenes from the Outline" on page 54.

If you are just beginning project development now at the storyboarding stage, enter the information as follows:

1. Enter the project name in the Project text box.

2. Choose a section number from the pop-up menu.

   The form uses roman numerals, letters, and numbers for the section, subsection, and scene in order to differentiate them more effectively in the layout and avoid confusion.

3. Enter a section name in the text box.

   If you only need two levels for your storyboard (subsection and scene), ignore these Section entries, and begin with Subsection entry.

4. Choose a subsection letter from the pop-up menu.

5. Enter a subsection name in the text box.

Importing Scenes from the Outline

If you already developed an outline in the Advanced Project Templates as described in "Project Template Workshop: Preparing Proposals and Outlines" on page 34, you can enter project name, section, and subsection information automatically for each record as a starting point. Once you import the outline records you can change them, delete them, or add additional records in the Script/Storyboard templates as needed.

If you are beginning your project development at the scripting/storyboarding stage, you should skip this section and begin with "Entering Global Information" on page 53.

To import a topic from your outline, simply click in the Scene text field and type the exact name of a scene from the outline.

It is helpful to have a list of the scenes from the outline available when importing the scenes so that you can type the correct names. Consider printing out your outline first from the Proposals_Outlines template to double-check the scene names.

Scene: 1 New scene name here   (Press Command-N for each new record)

Import
storyboard image:

Caption for image:

Type a caption that describes the image here.

Description:

Type description of the scene or shot sequence here.

As soon as you type in the scene name, the correct information appears for Section, Subsection, Project name, and description in the form. These now form your starting point for further development of the storyboard.

Importing Images

You can import graphics files directly into the image field in the storyboard template. Once imported, the images can be scaled and printed out with the storyboard in various sizes. You can update these graphics throughout the production process.

The template supports import of a variety of file types including PICT, EPS, BMP, TIF, and GIF files. Depending on the stage of development, you can acquire graphics for the storyboard in a number of ways:

- After sketching out the storyboard, you can scan the sketches and import the resulting graphics files.

- You can create graphics based on rough sketches in a third-party application such as Adobe Photoshop or Illustrator.

- As the assets are created and integrated into the project, you can make screen captures of the actual run-time scenes and include these in the storyboard.

To import an image:

1. Click in the center of the image container in the entry form.

2. Choose Import Picture from the Import/Export submenu of the File menu in Filemaker Pro.

   A Directory dialog box opens.

3. Navigate to the location of the image file, select the correct file, then click Open.

   The image appears within the storyboard frame.

Entering a Caption

To finish a storyboard record, type a brief caption into the Caption text box.

Captions are meant to be short, pithy descriptions of the visual content of the storyboard frame, and appear in the layouts in a small area just below each image.

Adding More Records

As you finish each storyboard record, press Command-N to create the next record and repeat the steps described in "Importing Scenes from the Outline" on page 54, "Importing Images" on page 55, and "Entering a Caption" on page 56.

Printing a Basic Storyboard

Three basic printout options appear at the bottom of the Storyboard Entry form:

Printouts:

Storyboards: [Image & Narration/ Description]   [2-Column Image & Caption]   [Large Image & Narration/ Description]

- Before previewing a storyboard, click the Find/Sort button to find all records for the storyboard and sort them according to Section, Subsection, and Scene.

- Click Image and Narration/Description to preview a storyboard that displays three records per page in a portrait orientation. Each record includes image, caption, description, and/or narration. Choose Print from the File menu to print.

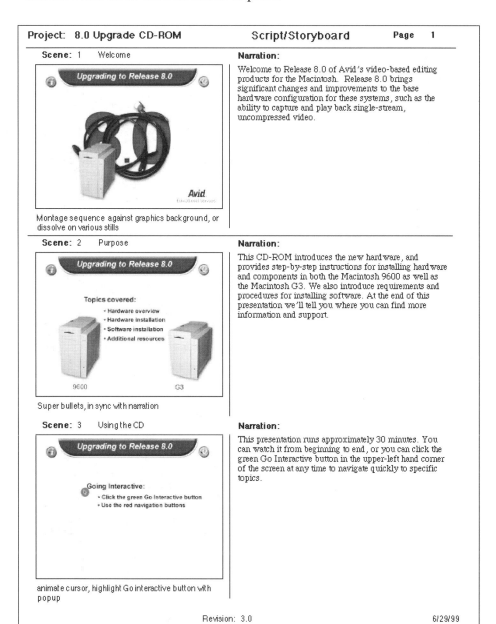

- Click 2-Column Image and Caption to preview a storyboard that displays four records per page in two-columns in landscape orientation. Each record includes image and caption only. Choose Print from the File menu to print the script.

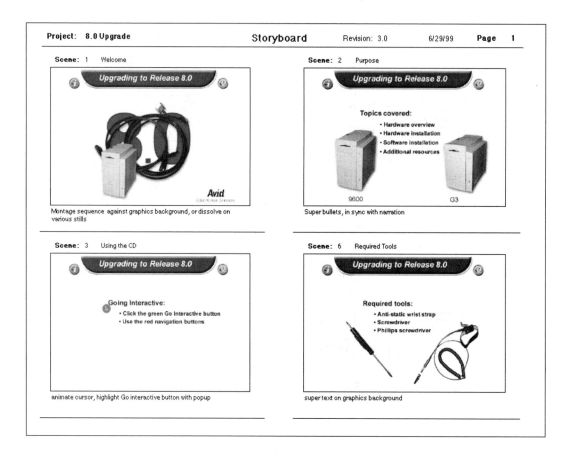

- Click Large Image and Narration/Description to preview a story-board that displays one large image frame, caption, description, and/or narration per page in portrait orientation. Choose Print from the File menu to print the script.

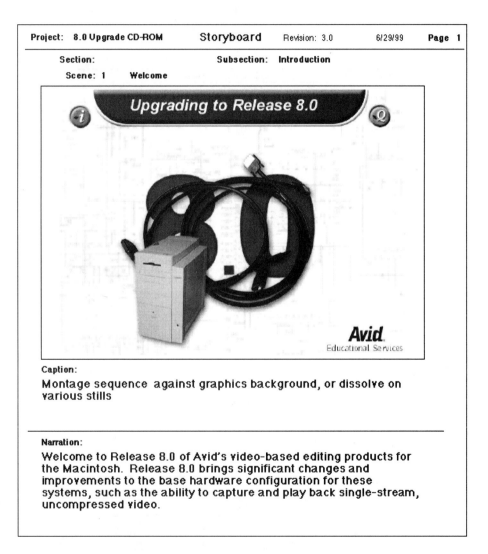

| Project: 8.0 Upgrade CD-ROM | Storyboard | Revision: 3.0 | 6/29/99 | Page 1 |

Section: Subsection: Introduction

Scene: 1   Welcome

Upgrading to Release 8.0

Avid
Educational Services

Caption:

Montage sequence against graphics background, or dissolve on various stills

Narration:

Welcome to Release 8.0 of Avid's video-based editing products for the Macintosh. Release 8.0 brings significant changes and improvements to the base hardware configuration for these systems, such as the ability to capture and play back single-stream, uncompressed video.

For more information on customizing layouts, see "Customizing Layouts and Print Options" on page 65.

Adding Information about Production Elements

As your project progresses, you can add more detail to your storyboard and scripts — such as required stills, graphics, music, titles, and animation — by using the Elements Entry form.

To begin, open the Scripts_Storyboards file if it is not already open, then choose Elements Entry from the Layout pop-up menu.

Layout pop-up menu

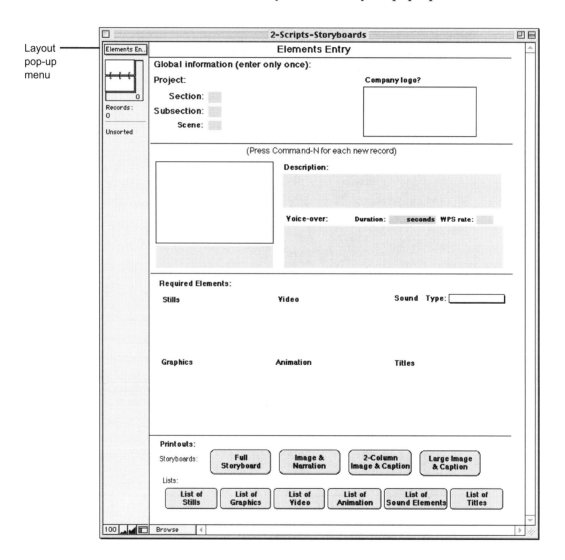

The top two sections of the entry form — global information and the section containing a frame, caption, and description — are there primarily for reference as you enter information about the production elements. You can, however, make changes to these details in the records displayed here.

To enter production details:

1. Beginning in the third section of the form, add narration to the storyboard by typing text into the Voice-over entry field.

2. Type information into each of the text boxes for the different element types displayed in the third section of the form.

Required Elements:

Stills	**Video**	**Sound Type:** SOUND EFFECT
Type list of stills required for the scene or shot sequence.	Type list of video footage required for the scene or shot sequence.	List sound effects or music elements here.

Graphics	**Animation**	**Titles**
Type list of graphic elements required for the scene or shot sequence.	Type list of 2D or 3D animation required for the scene or shot sequence.	Type list of titles required for the scene or shot sequence.

Items you enter under Video can be any number of things, from a list of camera setups for a dramatic scene to a list of shots to be captured in the field for a documentary project, to processed video clips for use in a multimedia project.

Items you enter under Animation can include 3D or 2D animation for the opening of a television program, animation sequences for a multimedia project, and so forth.

3. For sound elements, choose the type of sound element from the pop-up menu.

This menu includes sound effects and music. You can edit, add, or delete items from this menu by choosing Edit and then making changes in the dialog box that appears.

Printing a Detailed Storyboard

Four printout options appear at the bottom of the Elements Entry form for printing detailed storyboards that include some or all of the required production elements:

Full Storyboard	Image & Narration/ Description	2-Column Image & Caption	Large Image Narration/ Description

- Before previewing a storyboard, click the Find/Sort button to find all records for the storyboard and sort them according to Section, Subsection, and Scene.

- Click Full Storyboard to preview a storyboard that displays three records per page in a landscape orientation. Each record includes all details for that record as shown.

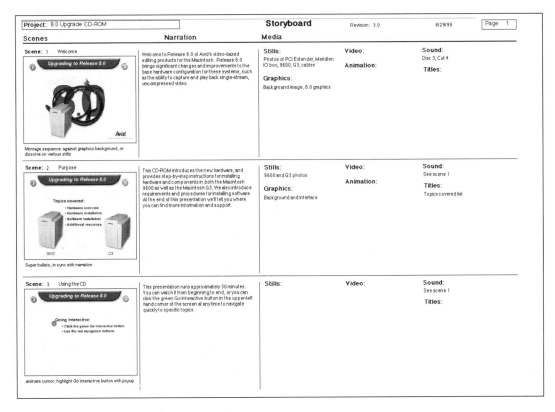

- Click Image and Narration/Description to preview a storyboard that displays roughly three records per page in two-columns in portrait orientation. Each record includes image and caption on the left and voice narration on the right.

- Click 2-Column Image and Caption to preview a storyboard that displays six records per page in two columns in portrait orientation. Each record includes image and caption only.

- Click Large Image and Narration/Description to preview a storyboard that displays one large image frame, caption, and description per page in portrait orientation.

For more information on customizing layouts, see "Customizing Layouts and Print Options" on page 65.

Generating Lists

Six printout options appear at the bottom of the Elements Entry form for printing lists of required production elements. For example, you can send a list of required graphics to the design department or give a list of required stills to an archivist or a photographer.

List of Stills	List of Graphics	List of Video	List of Animation	List of Sound Elements	List of Titles

- Before previewing a list, click the Find/Sort button to find all records for the storyboard and sort them according to Section, Subsection, and Scene.

- Click List of Stills to find, sort, and preview a list of still images organized by section, subsection, and scene. Choose Print from the File menu to print the script.

Project: 8.0 Upgrade CD-ROM   **List of Required Still Images**   **Page 1**

Introduction

Scene: 1   Welcome   **Stills:** Photos of
                                                    PCI Extender
                                                    Meridien IO box
                                                    9600
                                                    G3
                                                    cables

Scene: 2   Purpose   **Stills:** Photos of
                                                    9600
                                                    G3

Scene: 3   Using the CD   **Stills:**

Scene: 6   Required Tools   **Stills:** Photos of
                                                    screwdriver
                                                    wrist strap

Hardware Overview

Scene: 1   Intro to hardware   **Stills:** Photos of
                                                    9600
                                                    New G3
                                                    Original G3

Scene: 2   Intro new devices   **Stills:** Photos of
                                                    Meridien IO Box
                                                    8-channel audio device

Scene: 3   Avid PCI Extender   **Stills:** Image of
                                                    G3
                                                    PCI Extender

Scene: 4   9600 Intro   **Stills:** Image of
                                                    9600
                                                    PCI Extender

Scene: 5   Meridien Hardware   **Stills:**

- Click List of Graphics to find, sort, and preview a list of graphics required for the project, organized by section, subsection, and scene. Choose Print from the File menu to print the script.

- Click List of Video to find, sort, and preview a list of video elements required for the project, organized by section, subsection, and scene. Choose Print from the File menu to print the script.

- Click List of Animation to find, sort, and preview a complete list of animation sequences for the project, organized by section, subsection, and scene. Choose Print from the File menu to print the script.

- Click List of Sound Elements to find, sort, and preview a complete list of sound elements for the project, organized by section, subsection, and scene, and labeled according to the type of sound. Choose Print from the File menu to print the script.

- Click List of Titles to find, sort, and preview a complete list of titles for the project organized by section, subsection, and scene. Choose Print from the File menu to print the script.

Customizing Layouts and Print Options

You can vary any of the storyboard layouts included in the templates in a number of ways. For example, you can enter Layout mode, go to any of the layouts, and alter the layouts directly. Or you can go to a storyboard layout in Layout mode, choose Page Setup from the File menu, then enlarge or reduce the storyboard display or change the orientation between portrait and landscape.

For more information about customizing layouts see the Filemaker Pro documentation.

Here are some examples of alternative Page Setup settings and their results with different layouts:

- Full landscape: Choose landscape, 11 x 17 paper, at 100% or US Legal paper at 70% for larger printouts.

- Image and Description or Image and Narration: Choose portrait, and include more or fewer images per page by enlarging or reducing the size percentage.

- Two column frames: Choose landscape, 11 x 17 paper, at 100% or US Legal paper at 70% for larger images.

- Lists of elements: Choose portrait and reduce to 70% to show more information per page.

Scripting in Advance

Depending upon the type of production you are working on, you might want to begin scripting in advance. For some types of production — such as drama, commercial spots, or multimedia projects — the script is often completed before a single element is produced. For these types of production, storyboarding or using our storyboard templates might be the most appropriate path for pre-production development of content (see "Project Template Workshop: Preparing Storyboards" on page 51). You can also develop these scripts in advance using the Script Entry form of the project templates as described in the following section.

Because the documentary or news-magazine producer is capturing events and interview content in the field, the final script work often does not begin until after the footage is shot. The materials video producers prepare before the shoot might include some simple outlines on paper, storyboards, shoot plans, interview questions, or the occasional "standup" narration written ahead of time for the on-air talent. These specific needs are also addressed in the Script Entry form of the project templates, as described in "Project Template Workshop: Preparing Standups and Field Notes" on page 86.

Project Template Workshop: Preparing a Script

The Script Entry form of the Advanced Project Templates allows you to continue building on the outline or storyboard you started previously (see "Project Template Workshop: Preparing Proposals and

Outlines" on page 34 and "Project Template Workshop: Preparing Storyboards" on page 51). You can also begin your project at the scripting stage directly using the Script Entry form.

To begin, open the file labeled 2-Scripts_Storyboards. If the file is already open and you are working in another form layout, choose Script Entry from the Layout pop-up menu. The following window appears:

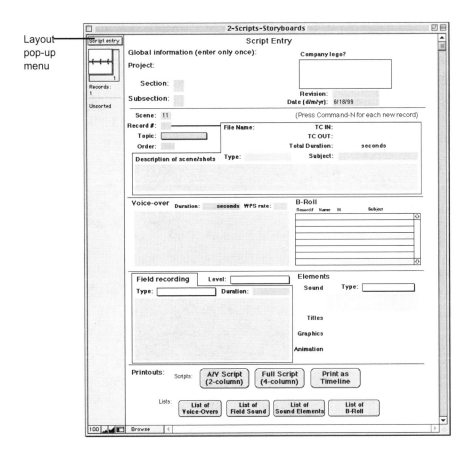

Entering Global Information in Script Entry

To begin a script you should first enter global information for the project. If you already entered global information previously, you can skip this section. If you are just beginning project development with script entry, you enter global information into the upper section of the form as described in "Entering Global Information" on page 53.

Importing Scenes from the Outline

If you already imported scenes when creating a storyboard in the templates, you can skip this section.

If you developed an outline in the Advanced Project Templates as described in "Project Template Workshop: Preparing Proposals and Outlines" on page 34, you can enter project name, section, and subsection information automatically for each record as a starting point. Once you import the outline records you can change them, delete them, or add additional records in the Script/Storyboard templates as needed.

For more information, see "Importing Scenes from the Outline" on page 54.

Building the Script

To build the script:

1. Enter voice-over text into the Voice-over text box.

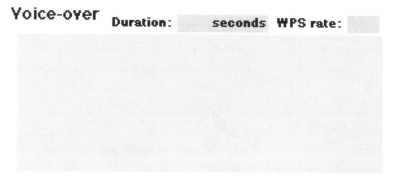

2. (Option) Enter an estimated words-per-second rate (WPS) for the voice-over. The duration is determined automatically based on the WPS and the content.

3. Enter any sound elements that you want to include in the script, such as music or sound effects. These only appear in the 4-column layout option when previewing and printing.

4. Choose the type of sound from the pop-up menu.

Previewing and Printing Scripts

The bottom section of the Script Entry form includes two options for printout of your script.

- Click Sort by: Scenes to sort the script entries by section, subsection, and scene.

- Click A/V Script (2-column) to preview a two-column script that contains visual description in one column and voice-over narration in the section column. Choose Print from the File menu to print the script.

  The A/V script is suitable for the traditional uses of the script for review of the narrative, or for pre-production stages of script development before footage has been shot and details have been added.

- Click Full Script (4-column) to find and sort all records according to section, subsection, and scene and then preview a four-column script that contains a column for video, a second column for field-recorded sound such as natural sound-on-tape and interviews, a third column for voice-over narration, and a fourth column for noting music and sound effects. Choose Print from the File menu to print the script.

For more information on optimizing a four-column script for the edit room, see "Project Template Workshop: Preparing Final Edit Scripts" on page 167.

Additional Pre-Production Tasks

For additional information on pre-production, also see the following:

- For information on preparing shoot plans, see "Shoot Plans That Work" on page 84.

- For information on preparing post-production plans and budgets, see "Making Digital Post Decisions" on page 179.

Producer's Checklist: Development Resources

Create Project Folders

- (First Time Only) Create a master set of folders and subfolders that you can reuse in other projects

- Customize your master set of folders for current project

Creating the Project Proposal

- Create the project proposal, optionally using the Advanced Project Template

- Review the proposal for accuracy, completeness, spelling and punctuation, and creativity

Creating an Outline

- (Option) Create the outline, optionally using the Advanced Project Template

- Plan how deep to nest the outline

Creating a Storyboard

- (Option) Create the storyboard, optionally using the Advanced Project Template or off-the-shelf software

- Import images or draw storyboard frames

- Make the captions concise and meaningful

- Customize the layout

- Locate a color printer, if you require a color printout

Writing the Script

- Write the script, optionally using the Advanced Project Template, off-the-shelf scripting software, or standard word-processing software

- (Option) Customize the script for different people's needs, including executive producer/client, actors, narrator, director, editor, teleprompter

- Print the script in the appropriate layout(s)

Preparing for the Shoot

- Generate the appropriate lists of production elements from the Elements Entry form (Advanced Project Template)

CHAPTER 4

Preparing to Shoot

Capturing source material in the digital age requires you to master not only the basics of the technology at work, but also a new set of concepts that affect everything from the cost of production to schedules to the all-important quality of the captured material. This chapter provides you with a foundation for planning a successful digital shoot.

Chapter Topics

- The New Age of Digital Capture

- Shoot Plans That Work

- Project Template Workshop: Preparing Standups and Field Notes

- Project Template Workshop: Preparing Shoot Plans and Schedules

The New Age of Digital Capture

Despite the title of this section, the truth is digital video has been around for much longer than you might think. During the heydays of Betacam SP back in the late 1980s, D1 and D2 digital video decks (digital recording and playback of component and composite video, respectively) started appearing in broadcast facilities around the same time that digital nonlinear editors started creating a stir at NAB conventions. QuickTime became a hit in the realm of multimedia soon afterward.

Digital field capture took longer to evolve. Facilities that could afford it might from time to time record to a D1 deck on location, but the weight and expense of D1 technology have always made it impractical for field production.

Betacam SP continues to hold its own in that context, but within the last few years digital field capture technologies have gained in popularity and sophistication. As a result, there are a slew of new low-cost capture formats that you can now bring into the mix when planning a shoot.

New Formats to Consider

As in all other areas of production, digital technology is creating many new and sometimes confusing options for capturing footage in the field, at the same time that it makes possible a cheaper and faster production process. This section provides guidance for making the right choices in the newly crowded field of professional formats for recording video.

DV, Digital–S, and Digital Betacam: New Life for Videotape

Creators of digital nonlinear editing systems have often expressed the long-term goal of supplanting all forms of videotape with the computer disk drive. In one case at least, they might be succeeding (see "Digital News Gathering: The Death of Videotape?" on page 83).

Ironically, a series of new digital formats have breathed new life into the plastic reels. Mostly as a result of the higher costs, greater weight, and other technical challenges of carrying computer drives into the field, videotape remains a viable technology for the foreseeable future when combined with the advantages of these digital newcomers.

Examples of these new formats are:

- **Digital Betacam:** As you might expect, the digital version of the venerated Betacam SP format.

- **Digital–S:** A high-quality digital format that uses the same size cassettes as S-VHS. You might think of it as the next generation of S-VHS.

- **DV formats (including DVCAM, DVCPro, and MiniDV):** A new format that has made a big splash in recent years, replacing analog formats in many news operations due to the ever popular combination of high quality with low cost.

- **Digital 8:** Another new format that is just recently coming into use. Like Digital–S, Digital 8 is the next generation of another popular "prosumer" format, Hi8.

Point of View

A lot of documentary now is being done in MiniDV. Editors have been telling me they've been running into it more and more. MiniDV tends to be shot by producers who are out shooting their own footage. There's the series called *Trauma* on the Learning Channel, which is shot in MiniDV. Also, MiniDV tends to be used for the "fly on the wall" type of stuff, because the cameras are smaller, and the producer can shoot with it by himself.

Larry Young — Avid editor, Cameraperson, Producer

DVCAM Versus MiniDV: What's the Difference?

DVCam and MiniDV are two different tape formats based on the DV standard. There is no real difference in image quality between the two: each uses the same DV specification for the video data stream. But there are some subtle differences that you need to consider when deciding which format to use for a shoot:

- Designed with consumer cameras in mind, MiniDV cassettes are smaller, lighter, and less robust than DVCAM tapes. They are also more subject to damage during heavy use, for example when editing from tape. If your project will involve heavy editing or multiple transfers from the source tapes during post, consider using the sturdier DVCAM format. However, if you plan to capture the footage and transfer it just once for disk-based editing, there is no disadvantage in terms of image quality to using the MiniDV format.

• One often overlooked fact is that with MiniDV tapes, audio tracks are not locked to video. DVCam has a higher tape speed, which allows audio to be locked to video and produces less dropout in the audio channels. With MiniDV you will experience more pops and mutes in the tracks. If first-rate audio is important to your shoot, choose DVCam.

The Digital Advantage

At the moment, digital formats that are recorded on tape provide no major advantages in terms of the time it takes to store and retrieve the footage. Like analog videotape, digital tape must be rewound or forwarded to cue up each recorded shot. Soon you will be able to copy data from tapes using the DV standard at four-times normal speed, which is a step in the right direction.

Most digital formats also involve some degree of compression of the video signal (see the sidebar "What is Compression?" on page 81), but don't be too concerned. For a variety of technical reasons, any loss of image quality that might occur due to compression is often imperceptible. But there are differences of quality between the various formats worth considering. For more information, see "The Right Image" on page 80.

The big gain with a digital format, if handled properly, is that you can do away with generation loss. Digital formats allow you to basically make pristine copies of the data from tape to disk drive and back to tape again with no loss of image quality.

In theory it works that way. In reality, there are some tricks to keeping your digital source clean. Here are a couple of things to keep in mind if you are considering one of these formats:

- **Check for postproduction compatibility:** Before choosing a digital format, make sure your posting facilities can handle the format in its native form. The worst case scenario might require you to convert your digital footage to analog form for input, and then back again, which defeats the whole purpose. The ideal environment includes nonlinear editors with Serial Digital Interface (SDI) input, or systems that can handle direct input of DV formats via an IEEE 1394 (also known as Firewire) capture card. For more information, see the sidebar "What is Firewire?" on page 78.

- **Consider your nonlinear editing requirements:** If you are working with one of the DV formats, consider that most DV-native editing systems are not as full-featured as high-end editing systems such as the Avid Media Composer, although new DV editing systems appearing Fall of 1999 from Avid and others aim to change that.

  For information on the latest systems from Avid, visit: avid.com.

  Also, some editors that can handle the DV format do not yet display the appropriate aspect ratio during editing. Like other professional formats such as Betacam SP, the DV format uses non-square pixels (versus the square pixels used in some computer-based editing systems). As a result, the DV image appears distorted during editing on systems that can't handle non-square pixel aspect ratios. If you require state-of-the-art in your nonlinear editing environment, a DV-native video path might not be appropriate for your project.

- **Consider your effects editing requirements:** The benefits of digital copies can also be undone by multiple passes that require encoding and re-encoding of signals when applying, rendering, and reapplying effects. If your production is effects heavy and requires many passes at rendering, you might experience some loss of quality when using DV-native editing systems in particular.

What is Firewire?

Firewire is the colorful trademark name Apple gave to the connection and transfer technology it pioneered in the mid-1980s which was adopted industry-wide in 1995 as the IEEE 1394 standard. A number of IEEE 1394 products are now available including digital camcorders with the IEEE 1394 link, IEEE 1394 digital video editing equipment, digital VCRs, digital cameras, digital audio players, 1394 ICs, and a wealth of other infrastructure products such as connectors, cables, test equipment, software toolkits, and emulation models.

The IEEE 1394 multimedia connection enables simple, low-cost, high-bandwidth isochronous (real-time) data interfacing between computers, peripherals, and consumer electronics products such as camcorders, VCRs, printers, PCs, TVs, and digital cameras. With IEEE 1394-compatible products and systems, users can transfer video or still images from a camera or camcorder to a printer, PC, or television, with no image degradation.

The strong multimedia orientation, self-configurability, peer-to-peer connectivity, and high performance of 1394 have encouraged rapid development. Native IEEE 1394 support has been added to Microsoft Windows operating systems, while other applications that benefit from IEEE 1394 include nonlinear (digital) video presentation and editing, desktop and commercial publishing, document imaging, home multimedia, and personal computing. The low overhead, high data rates of 1394, the ability to mix real-time and asynchronous data on a single connection, and the ability to mix low speed and high speed devices on the same network provides a truly universal connection for almost any consumer, computer, or peripheral application.

HDTV: Back to the Future

You might have noticed that we haven't spent a lot of time discussing HDTV (high definition television). HDTV is definitely on the horizon, and some of you might already be dabbling in HDTV projects. For most people HDTV isn't really an option just yet; first of all, production is expensive, and, secondly, the audience remains small due to the high cost of high definition television sets. But a few words about this promising format are certainly in order prior to making your shoot decisions. For a more complete description of the HDTV future, see Chapter 9.

While in many respects HDTV is a completely new animal, in other respects its development has a very long history going all the way back to the early days of cinema. In fact, more than any other video format to date, HDTV has a shared history with both television and film.

Consider that the HDTV aspect ratio of 16:9 (versus the 4:3 aspect ratio of standard television) has its genesis in film formats, such as Super 16mm, that have been around for years. Also consider that the high number of pixels in the image is meant to take us that much closer to the high quality images of film.

Also, HDTV takes advantage of the fact that most Hollywood and big network productions are shot on film before being transferred, edited, and duplicated on videotape. With HDTV, the path from original film footage to final broadcast becomes much less tortured (see "24P: The Next Big Thing" in Chapter 9).

Even if you are not willing to consider HDTV as a format for your project, perhaps the most important question you can ask yourself prior to shooting is: "Just what kind of life will my project have three or five years down the road?"

In other words, if your project is likely to be played just once or twice in the immediate future and that's the end of it, then don't bother. However, if there is a chance your project will be replayed sometime in the HDTV future, you might want to plan ahead now so that your footage can be revived or adapted to the wide screen down the road.

For smaller budgets, the costs of true HDTV field capture are prohibitive, but there are viable alternatives that will leave you some flexibility in the future. Here are two examples:

- Many of the digital cameras nowadays allow you to record your standard-resolution source footage in the 16:9 aspect ratio of HDTV. You don't capture all the pixels of a true HDTV signal, but you do have the option of "up-rezing" (as they say) to high definition for future broadcasts.

- A "halfway there" option that is slightly more expensive than video but not as expensive as HDTV is film. Yes indeed, it's back to the future with a format like Super16 that allows you to capture high-quality ("high-definition" by default) footage for a reasonable cost. Film is definitely back in style for all types of production.

Point of View

There is some program origination in 16:9, but not much, although the BBC has been shooting a lot in 16:9. Very few shows are actually shot in HD; these tend to be very high-bucks productions. If people want to have a show in 16:9, they shoot Digi-Beta in the 16:9 aspect ratio, and then uplink to HDTV. So all they're doing is a standard conversion. It's a cheaper way to do it, and you really can't tell. It's very, very acceptable.

In the early eighties, we used to do the same thing with 3/4" tape. We'd just shoot it and edit it on 3/4", and we'd bump it up to 1" for the master. We broadcast it on 1", and nobody could tell the difference.

Larry Young — Avid editor, cameraperson, producer

The Right Image

Of course we're not referring to the way a shiny new DV camera makes you look in the field. But now that we're on the subject, occasionally the size and appearance of a camera can be an important consideration. For example, in sensitive situations — when shooting for a documentary in a politically troubled region, or when recording a shy interview subject — a small and inobtrusive MiniDV camera might just do the trick. On the other hand, a larger DVC camera with professional features might allow you to produce on a smaller budget and still look professional next to the Digital Betacam shooters.

The image we really want to discuss in this section is the look of the footage. With all these new formats appearing on the market, how do you choose among them?

What is Compression?

You might have thought compression was something you only had to worry about in the post phase, when you must wrestle with the many flavors of nonlinear editing and the many varieties of digital video output. So why, you might ask, are we addressing this question in a chapter about the shoot?

The simple answer is, compression begins in the camera. Even with analog video capture, the simple RGB (red, green, and blue) signals that get received by the camera chips undergo a subtle mathematical transformation before being recorded on tape in order to make the signal more efficient: hence the Y (which stands for luminance), R–Y (Red minus luminance), and B–Y (Blue minus luminance) designations for the three signals carried in the component video standard. Not exactly compression as we know it today, but it's a start.

All digital component video systems perform another manipulation of the signal that is referred to as color sampling, and is represented in the familiar designation 4:2:2 — for every four samples of the Y (luminance) signal there are two samples of the B–Y and R–Y signals.

With digital capture, the real fun begins. A D1 deck applies no compression, storing and restoring the original signal on demand without any image loss. Most digital cameras apply compression to the video signal in order to lessen the bandwidth and storage demands on the system. In many cases compression is essential, since the hardware might not be capable of handling the heavy streams of data required for real-time playback and recording of uncompressed video.

Compression involves applying mathematical algorithms to reduce the size of digital data — by reducing or eliminating duplicate information, for example. There are many different formulae for performing this digital magic — Motion JPEG and MPEG are two common standards. The loss of quality can range from imperceptible to severe. Damage to the image results in so-called "artifacts" which look like tiny blocky areas where sharper detail once existed.

Here's the basic rundown of the types of compression you can expect with the major digital video formats described in this chapter.

Format	Color Sampling	Compression Ratio	Data Rate (mega-bits per second)
D1, D5	4:2:2	1:1 (none)	approx.160 mbps
Digital Betacam	4:2:2	1.6:1	approx.100 mbps
Digital–S	4:1:1	3.3:1	50 mbps
DV formats	4:1:1	5:1	25 mbps
Digital 8	4:1:1	5:1	25 mbps

To begin with, the DV formats are all Component 4:1:1 formats, while Digital-S, Digital Betacam, D-5, and D-1 are all 4:2:2 formats. In addition, the DV formats use a specific type of 5:1 compression, while Digital-S and Digital Betacam use slightly less compression. However, the type of compression used in the DV format is highly effective, and the difference in data loss is not very noticeable in the image.

News organizations around the world find the 4:1:1 formats suitable for broadcast, but how important is the extra information in 4:2:2 formats for your project?

The truth is there is no one answer. Here are a few scenarios:

- The types of images you expect to shoot can be a factor. Complex images, such as crowd scenes or natural environments with trees, are captured in greater detail in formats that use less compression, such as Digital Betacam. At the same time, less complex images, such as talking heads or motion images, are not as sensitive to compression.

- Images that will be compressed even further — for example when preparing a multimedia CD-ROM or DVD title — should be captured at the highest quality your budget can afford. Noise or pixellation in images that might not be noticeable in the source footage gets amplified when compressed in these circumstances. Not only does it look worse, but it can also raise the throughput requirements for smooth playback.

- There are other circumstances in which you want the highest-quality source video possible, for example when transferring video material back to film.

- If you plan on shooting chroma key footage, you might want to use a high-end format such as Digital Betacam in order to capture and manipulate the colors more accurately.

Also note that a new generation of DV formats is on the way which raises the color sampling rate to 4:2:2 (doubling the data rate of the video stream to 50 mbps in the process), bringing the DV format up to par with other high-end digital formats such as Digital Betacam.

As you might imagine, rental and purchase prices for the gear supporting these formats cover a wide range, but as a rule of thumb you could probably guess that less compression means more expense. Compared to traditional formats such as film and Betacam SP, however, several of these formats can literally cut your rental budget in half. For this reason alone they are worth a careful look.

Digital News Gathering: The Death of Videotape?

There is one more digital format that breaks the mold of videotape transports altogether. This is the first true disk-based field recorder called the CamCutter, pioneered by Avid Technology, Inc., and included in the Editcam field production unit produced by Ikegami. Unlike digital videotape formats, the Editcam brings the full suite of nonlinear digital advantages from the edit room out into the field, thereby opening up some really stunning and completely new possibilities such as the following:

- **Random access in the field:** The greatest advantage of the nonlinear disk is the ability to randomly access a desired scene, anytime, thus broadening the possibilities not found in videotape.

- **Deleting clips and saving storage:** Unwanted takes can be deleted during free time to open up additional storage space while in the field. This also means less footage to screen and log during post.

- **Editing in the field:** Though this is more important for timely newscasts, the Editcam allows you to begin editing a final sequence right in the camera, before you return to the studio, which can be an advantage for any type of production. For example, you can get the cameraperson's take on a shot sequence before they disappear into the next assignment. You can also save time and money from your post schedule by performing some partial editing beforehand during off-time in the field.

- **No need to transfer or digitize:** After you shoot, you can remove the drives from the camera, plug them into a compatible nonlinear editing system, and start preparing your final cut.

- **Environmental resistance:** Environmental performance problems often encountered by VTR are controlled by the disk's characteristics. Stable operation is ensured against dust, sand and salt, and humidity.

At the moment Editcam has been adopted by a number of news organizations where its unique features make for fast turnaround of news stories. However, considering the rate at which computer hard disk prices are dropping, as well as the advent of ever-smaller drives, it might not be too long before videotape really is a thing of the past. If you have the budget for it and a need for its unique talents, consider using one for your next project.

Shoot Plans That Work

Armed with knowledge of the digital arsenal, the next step is to plan a shoot that takes particular advantage of the new formats and cameras. With careful planning you'll find that these technologies can save you both time and money.

How Digital Changes Field Production

One of the most obvious differences in using these new formats boils down to appearance: this stuff is small! Depending on your choice of gear, you can find yourself capturing broadcast quality footage with hardware that feels like it was meant for your home videos. This can have a big effect on a number of areas of your shoot plan, particularly if you are on a short budget:

- Smaller means lighter: You can manage even a complicated shoot with fewer hands, which means less personnel and lower costs. Lighter equipment is also less tiring, and can allow for long periods of shooting with fewer shoot days.

- Smaller means tighter: You can bring your small camera into tighter spaces or capture from angles that would not be possible with a larger camera. You can also travel to shoot locations, perhaps for the first time, with little or no extra baggage. For quick turnaround, you can avoid baggage claim altogether by traveling light and sticking your little camera into the overhead compartment.

- Smaller means faster: Setup and breakdown times are usually shorter with the mid-range formats such as DV. Some cameras include a useful combination of professional features along with some of the time-saving features previously available only in consumer cameras, such as auto white balance and more intuitive menu controls.

- Smaller means cheaper (usually): In most cases, the smaller cameras and formats, such as the DVC formats or MiniDV, are less expensive to rent or buy. In fact, many smaller facilities or independent producers who once rented are finding affordable broadcast quality cameras for purchase, which changes the economics of production entirely. MiniDV and DVC tape stock is also less expensive. Postproduction budgets can be similarly scaled down when working with some of the mid-range digital formats.

There are some other ways in which digital formats can shorten production cycles in the field. For example, most DV cameras automatically record IN and OUT points for every start and stop, while some cameras let you designate each shot as OK or no good. One as-yet-unfulfilled promise is the ability to transfer this information directly into your editing system, saving you hours of logging time. Most editing systems do not yet support this capability.

Point of View

I may be going to Nigeria this summer, and it's a tense country, and now it's still not clear how open people are going to be, because what I want to do is moderately political. So I'm just going to take in a little digital camera and shoot, myself. I learned how to shoot film in film school, but I actually can't do it very effectively any more. However, with a little digital camera, I can. I will probably hire a sound person in Nigeria. I wouldn't just use the sound on the top of the camera; I would set up a separate sound connection.

— *Barbara Holecek, producer*

Point of View

I try and recommend to [producers] some new techniques that other people are using with small format cameras. There's a lot of people out there
who will have a Beta rig on their primary interview subject, and they'll take
their DV camera, reverse it on the interview subject. Since the interview
subject is going to get a couple of nodding smiles, why spend extra
money to have another whole rig there? In my color correction suite, I
can make them match pretty exactly, particularly if it's lit well.

Also, some people are stacking their DV camera as a wide shot and a
closeup. Another thing that people are doing (and this is one of my favorites): One of my producers just bought a Steadicam JR, the little junior
Steadicam, that he used with a little DV camera. And he got the most gorgeous, sexy stuff; it looked like he had a Luma Crane. He would do these
sweeping long shots through scenes — he'd follow people through hallways; he'd come swooping into their office. Just these little things added
this really nice flow to their production.

— Tim Mangini, production manager, FRONTLINE

Project Template Workshop: Preparing Standups and Field Notes

Prior to shooting, you can use the Advanced Project Templates to prepare stand-up text for the talent to read, and to prepare notes.

- To prepare notes, such as questions to ask interview subjects or an
  outline of subjects to shoot, use the Outline Entry form as
  described in "Project Template Workshop: Preparing Proposals
  and Outlines" on page 34.

- To prepare and print a list of locations and other shoot details, use
  the Shoot Plan Entry form as described in "Project Template
  Workshop: Preparing Shoot Plans and Schedules" on page 88.

To prepare a list of stand-ups for the talent to read on location, do the
following:

1. Open the file labeled 4-ShotLogs_Transcripts. If the file is already
   open and you are working in another form layout, choose Log/
   Transcript Entry from the Layout pop-up menu.

2. For field recorded sound that you script in advance, such as
   stand-ups with talent to be recorded on location, type that information into the Field Recording text box.

Type:

Transcript:

If you type stand-ups in advance, make note for future reference. This will save you a step later when logging and transcribing tapes containing the stand-ups within the project templates.

3. Choose the type of field recording from the pop-up menu.

This menu includes four choices. You can change, add, or delete items from this menu by choosing Edit and making your changes in the dialog box.

4. In the print options at the bottom of the form, click Transcript Only to printout a complete list of the stand-ups.

When you return to the shot log templates to log footage after the shoot, the stand-up text will already be entered. You can then add timecode information from the field tapes.

Project Template Workshop: Preparing Shoot Plans and Schedules

The Advanced Project Templates allow you to continue building on the outline or script you started previously (see Chapter 3, "Computer-Based Project Development"). You can also begin your project at the shoot plan stage directly.

To begin, open the file labeled 3-ShootPlans_EditPlans. If the file is already open and you are working in another form layout, choose Shoot Plan Entry from the Layout pop-up menu. The following window appears:

Layout pop-up menu —

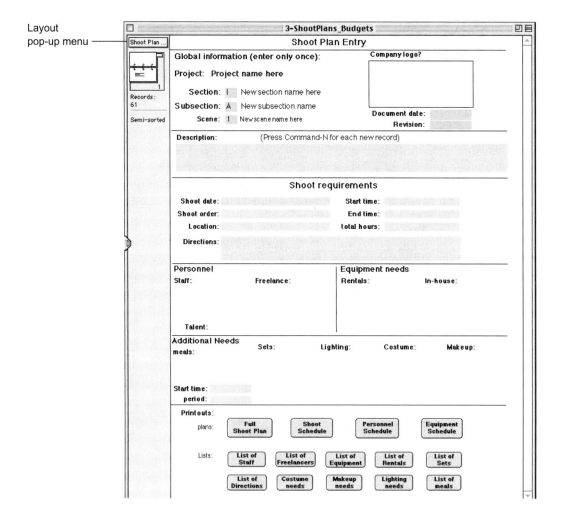

Entering Global Information in Shoot Plan Entry

To begin a shoot plan you should first enter global information for the project. If you are just beginning project development with shoot plan entry, you enter global information into the upper section of the form as described in "Entering Global Information" on page 53.

Note that with each new revision of your database you can enter a new revision number in the global information area that will appear in headers and footers for your printouts. However, to preserve earlier revisions of the database you should first make a duplicate of the database and save it in a backup folder before making changes.

Importing Scenes from the Outline

If you developed an outline, storyboard, or script as described in Chapter 3, you can enter project name, section, subsection, and description information automatically for each record as a starting point. The description field in the Shoot Plan Entry layout is there for reference only, and will not appear in any of the shoot plan printouts.

Once you import the records you can change them, delete them, or add additional records in the templates as needed.

For more information, see "Importing Scenes from the Outline" on page 54.

Breaking Down Scenes

To prepare a shoot plan or schedule effectively, you might find it necessary to break down your imported scenes even further into sub-scenes that reflect the details of the shoot.

For example, one scene in the script might require two or three different camera setups to acquire the footage. You might, in fact, need to shoot these setups out of order, or even on different days.

To reflect this in your plans, do the following:

1. In Browse mode in Filemaker Pro, duplicate the scene by choosing Duplicate Record from the Mode menu.

2. In the Global Information area of the Shoot Plan Entry form, change the scene number to reflect a subscene. For example, if the scene number is 1, change the duplicate scene's number to 1a. Change the numbers to 1b, 1c, and so on for additional duplicated records.

3. Enter the details for each subscene based on your shooting needs, as described in "Building the Shoot Plan" on page 90.

   These scenes will then sort appropriately and appear in the right order in your plans and schedules.

Building the Shoot Plan

To build the shoot plan:

1. In the top area of the Shoot Requirement section, enter general information for each scene or subscene, such as shoot date and location, into the text boxes. If you do not know the shoot date yet, you can enter this later.

Shoot requirements

Shoot date:	Start time:
Shoot order:	Duration:
Location:	End time:
Directions:	Total hours:

2. Enter a Start time for shooting the scene using a 24 hour format shown in this example:

   13:30:00 (i.e., 1:30 PM)

3. Enter a duration for the shoot in hours and minutes.

   End time and total hours for shooting the scene are calculated automatically.

4. (Option) If you have directions for getting to the location, you can enter those in the text box.

   If the information you enter extends beyond the size of the text box, a scroll bar appears allowing you to enter and view as much information as necessary.

5. In the Personnel area of the entry form, type information about staff personnel, freelance personnel, and talent that you would like to include in the shoot plans for that scene. For example, you can type names and phone numbers of personnel required to perform the shoot.

   Personnel
   Staff: Freelance:

   Talent:

6. In the Equipment needs area of the entry form, type information about rental or in-house equipment required for shooting the scene.

   Equipment needs
   Rentals: In-house:

7. In the Additional Needs area of the entry form, type information about meals, sets, lighting, costumes, makeup, or other requirements for the shoot.

   If you do not enter information into any of the text boxes for a category included in the entry form, that category will not appear in the final printout.

| Additional Needs meals: | Sets: | Lighting: | Costume: | Makeup: |

Start time:
period:

8. (Option) You can type a Start time and time period for meals into the text boxes. If you enter this information it is automatically included in the calculations for Start time, End time, and Total time for the shooting the scene, and will appear in printed schedules.

Printing Shoot Plans and Schedules

The bottom section of the Shoot Plan Entry form includes several options for printout:

- Click the Find/Sort button first to find and sort all shoot plan records according to date and start time.

- Click Full Shoot Plan to preview a document that contains all information for shooting each scene. The Full Shoot Plan requires that you change to landscape layout in the Page Setup dialog box.

- Click Shoot Schedule to preview a document that contains a summary timeline of production that includes basic information such as scene, location, start time, and end time.

- Click Personnel Schedule to preview a document that contains information on all staff, freelance, and talent required for shooting each scene.

- Click Equipment Schedule to preview a document that contains information on all rental or in-house equipment required for shooting each scene.

- After previewing a document, choose Print from the File menu to print the document.

In addition to the more comprehensive schedules and shoot plans just described, you can print out schedules of individual requirements for the shoots that you can then submit as request forms or for more detailed accounting. For example, you can print out a list of just rental equipment and fax this to the vendor; or you can print out a schedule of meals to send to a caterer.

To return to form entry, Choose Browse from the Mode menu, then choose an entry form from the pop-up menu.

Extending the Templates

You can simplify the task of building a budget and lower the margin of error even further by integrating the templates with a larger accounting system, making full use of Filemaker Pro's relational database capabilities.

For example, if you create a system of accounts for your company using Filemaker Pro, you can customize the shoot plan templates to reference another database of services used company-wide to generate budgets, invoices, and other financial documents.

To go one step further, for projects that are produced for a client you could customize the templates to generate both a budget and a series of invoices for services provided, based on a centralized accounting system.

For more information on customizing the templates, see your Filemaker Pro documentation.

CHAPTER 5

Going Digital in the Field

Going digital in the field involves more than just renting the latest digital camera. You must also think ahead to the nonlinear editing phase to make sure you are capturing your source material properly in order to save time and effort later. You also have new options available for capturing shot log information and tracking the production phase electronically while you shoot.

Chapter Topics

- Field Production Practices

- Logging in the Field

- Project Template Workshop: Logging in the Field

- Project Tracking in the Field

Field Production Practices

Point of View

Our programs are shot all over the place. They're almost never shot in a single city. So if you can't bring your crew everywhere, option number 1 is: Pick up a sound man and bring the shooter. Option number 2 is: Bring the camera, and hire the shooter. But failing that, if you're going to pick up crews and you're going to be using their rig, then you need to do the best you can to get those interviews to be shot uniformly. You have to impose yourself in the process. First, get your favorite shooter to shoot something for you, even if it's an interview of you. Then, if you can, get your shooter to diagram how they do it — what lights they use, where each instrument is, how much softness they use, what the average watt-age is of each lamp. Take the tape and diagram to every shooter and say, "This is what I want you to match." In the shoot, make sure you put that tape in the machine, and if necessary, say, "You know what? This is not the same." So first you have to educate yourself, and then you have to be prepared to be unpopular.

— *Tim Mangini, production manager, FRONTLINE*

I like producers who can really describe what it is they're doing, who have a good handle on their subject, who know what they're looking for, and who know what they've already shot (if I'm one of several cameramen on a project) and can explain it to me. Or if I'll be shooting the whole project, I like it if they can give me an idea of what they want their project to look like so I can design lighting and camera moves. I like it if we can figure out what's practical, and what's not practical; what will work, and what won't work. We need to know all these things, and you can't if there is no com-munication. The problem with television traditionally has been that it's a communication business where nobody communicates. The producer doesn't communicate with the director. The director doesn't communi-cate with the cameraman. And then finally it's all dumped on the editor, who has to make chicken salad.

— *Larry Young, Avid editor, cameraperson, producer*

There are a number of practices that you, as the producer, can imple-ment during the shoot which will help the editor later during post-pro-duction:

- Instruct the camera operator on the best camera settings for time-code:

  - REC RUN (record run)

  - DF (drop frame) or NDF (non-drop frame) for NTSC

    (Consult with your editor about the preferred setting. If you are unsure, use drop frame, especially for broadcast.)

- Use 5-second pre-roll and post-roll, if you're not using assemble edits.

- Clearly label or number each tape, and pick a clear consistent naming scheme.

  If you plan to use fewer than 24 tapes, you might want to match the HOURS timecode digits with the tape number.

Setting Field Timecode

Instruct the camera and/or deck operator to set the timecode generators according to the following guidelines.

Using RECORD RUN Versus FREE RUN

Timecode generators in the field provide two methods for handling continuity of timecode at a camera cut. When you edit on nonlinear editing systems, RECORD RUN (REC RUN) is the preferred type of timecode to record in the field for efficient digitizing in the edit suite.

- RECORD RUN records timecode only when the camera is running.

  RECORD RUN is the preferred timecode setting for nonlinear editing. In this mode, timecode runs only when the camera is recording. The tape records with almost no breaks in the timecode. When you digitize your footage, the nonlinear editing system can cue the tapes and input footage in a highly automated way, saving you time and money.

- FREE RUN timecode records time of day, with timecode continuing to run while the camera is turned off.

  Some news reporters like to use FREE RUN to take timecoded notes in the field by referring to their watches. However, every time you power down the camera there is a break in timecode equal to the elapsed clocktime. FREE RUN causes problems for computerized editing systems: At each of the breaks, the editor may have to intervene in the input process to manually cue the tape for the edit, taking more time.

Using Drop Frame Versus Non-Drop Frame

Most nonlinear editing systems work with field tapes recorded with drop frame (DF) or non-drop frame (NDF) timecode when working in NTSC (this issue does not apply to PAL projects). A sequence can be created as a DF or NDF sequence. In fact, you can shift between these modes at any time.

When timecode counts 30 frames, we call it one second. Actually, 30 frames of video play slightly (.1 percent) longer than a second. We call 108,000 frames one hour, but we have an extra 3.6 seconds of information compared to the timecode reading. To match timecode and clocktime, you have to drop this extra 3.6 seconds every hour. Drop frame timecode performs this operation.

- **DF**: 1 hour of TC = 1 hour of playtime

- **NDF**: 1 hour of TC = 1 hour and 3.6 seconds of playtime

The preferred setting for video shoots varies according to the application.

- DF timecode is used most often for broadcast video, where it's crucial for the tape's playtime (measured in timecode) to correspond exactly with clocktime.

- NDF timecode may be preferred for animation and film projects (where frame count must be precise), non-broadcast programs (where exact correlation between playtime and clocktime is not crucial), and short programs (such as 30-second commercials).

Because the choice of DF or NDF timecode depends on numerous variables, check with your editor for his or her preference for camera setting.

Recording Pre-roll and Post-roll

For safety, remember to record pre-roll and post-roll during your shoot. You will need them for inputting footage into a nonlinear editing system, particularly footage with timecode breaks. Remember, even with REC RUN you will have breaks in the tape when the field camera is powered down.

If you do use free run timecode, make sure you provide at least 5 seconds of pre-roll when you start recording, and wait another 5 seconds before you stop recording at the end of the shot. Newer decks, including most Betacam SP decks, require less pre-roll, but record the full amount just to be safe.

Naming Tapes

Your tape naming scheme should be consistent from the shoot through the edit. When you are in the middle of the edit and need to digitize a single B-roll shot on one of a hundred tapes, you want to make sure you have a 1:1 correspondence between tape names logged in the computer and tape names written on the tape box.

During the shoot, give each tape a unique name, and write it clearly on the tape cassette and box. Duplicate tape names can confuse the nonlinear editing system. The simplest and most reliable method is to number your tapes consecutively. In most cases, start with 01 or 001 (if you expect to have 100 or more tapes for the project) and increment from there. You can also add to the number a unique description for the project, such as "001BD," using initials or the first few letters of the project name. You might also write the date of the shoot on the tape cassette and box.

Shooting B-Roll Footage

In the linear editing environment, some producers shoot alternate visuals on separate physical tapes for dissolves and other effects to avoid dubbing images that are on the same reel. Nonlinear editing makes this procedure unnecessary.

Logging in the Field

One of the last great holdouts of pen and paper, the field location has never lent itself easily to the charms of the word processor. Not even the electric typewriter has found a place here. Out in the field, production personnel must be light and quick and unburdened.

From field production through post, logging has traditionally been one of the most time-consuming tasks that the producer or production assistant undertakes. Though we take it for granted as an unfortunate necessity, if you think about it logging is also one of the biggest wastes of time and money, considering that in logging you are basically transposing information that has been recorded once already by the camera gear.

With a little time and effort, the true digital producer can always find a way to cover more ground with better technology. A slew of new logging tools in recent years is finally breaking the barriers, and logging in the field for the electronically inclined is now both practical and economical.

Here are just three of the many logging tools that are best suited for work in the field. We also discuss additional logging products that are more suited to the post-production phase in Chapter 6, "Preparing for Digital Post." If used properly these tools can literally save you hundreds of dollars and many hours of effort.

Following this section, we also describe how to use the Advanced Project Templates (provided on the companion CD-ROM) for logging in the field.

Production Magic's Shot Logger™

When it comes to field production, good things invariably come in small packages. Production Magic keeps it small by combining effectively designed software with an Apple Newton, the palm-sized portable computer device. Shot Logger uses wireless technology to do away with cable links to the camera for recording start and stop time-codes automatically. Any camera, video cassette recorder, professional camcorder, Nagra, or device supplying a pulse timecode signal can be used by Shot Logger. Having a cable can seriously limit camera movement and creativity, while using a Notebook computer forces you to always be sitting. For this reason Shot Logger is one of the best options for logging in the field.

Additional capabilities of this tiny tool are impressive:

For more information on Shot Logger, visit productionmagic. com.

- You can instantly label shot as NG (no good), good, better, or best with the tap of a pen.

Shot Logger interface

- You can quickly input repetitive data such as notes or clip descriptions from customizable pop-up windows.

- You can use a built-in stopwatch (accurate to the second, but good enough for many producer uses).

- You also have the option of using handwriting recognition/translation capabilities or you can access an optional portable keyboard or a virtual keyboard.

- You can set it up so that the takes are defined by the camera start/stop trigger, and if you touch the face of the MessagePad, it increments the scene number as well.

- At any time you can sort and sift the list, and output only one category of takes. You can also check off only those takes that you want included when digitizing.

- You can reload the project with character names, scenes, take definitions (CU, zoom out, XCU, WS, etc.), and reel names so that the amount of data entry is minimized.

- You can upload your logs and further manipulate the information on either a Mac or PC.

- You can prepare and import your logs to many popular nonlinear editing systems such as Media Composer, Avid Xpress, Adobe Premiere for Windows, and Media 100.

If you are producing alone or with a cameraperson in the field — handling all the details of production between you — you might find any logging tool distracting. However, for productions that include at least one assistant, you can easily capture log information once and remove the logging process during post-production altogether. Shot Logger is the least obstrusive (and lightest) tool available for accomplishing this on location. For some productions this means saving days and even weeks of logging time during post, not to mention renting or tying up a VCR for playback during the process.

e-trim™ from Eidria, Inc.

For more information on e-trim, visit eidria.com.

e-trim is a videotape logging and machine control package for the 3Com Palm Computing platform, including licensees such as Symbol and the IBM WorkPad.

e-trim™ creates log files by capturing timecode values from the source via an LTC/RS-422/LANC connection. When you synchronize your PalmPilot/PalmIII with your Macintosh or Windows computer, the log is uploaded. The log file can then be converted easily into various popular log file and EDL formats.

LogWriter is the software portion of the e-trim package that runs on your Macintosh or Windows computer.

e-trim's Tag feature allows the simultaneous marking of in and out points of a clip. The user specifies whether the in or the out point should be captured at the current location, and then the other data point is back-timed or front-timed from that point.

Machine control is a big plus of e-trim, allowing you to connect to a deck or camera and remotely control the tape transport functions of the device as well as capturing frame accurate time code values from the tape, making e-trim the only handheld solution to provide machine control and timecode capture. You can also hook e-trim directly to a VHS deck with an LTC stream recorded on one of the audio channels, or to an LTC tap on a camera for field logging without any additional hardware, cabling, or adapters.

The Executive Producer™ from Imagine Products

The Executive Producer for Macintosh (MacTEP) or PC (WinTEP) is a more in-depth software application for use on desktop computers or laptops. For field logging, a laptop is the only practical option.

For more information on TEP, visit imagineproducts. com.

With a laptop you forego the portability of a tool like Shot Logger, and therefore an Executive Producer is more suited to a larger production including a dedicated production assistant or logger for performing this task. If your budget allows it, an assistant can use Executive Producer to create comprehensive and easy-to-use logs and output batch digitizing lists for all popular nonlinear editors. In addition, Executive Producer adds storyboarding features unavailable in Shot Logger which can be useful for previsualizing scenes or for presentation during post-production.

Unlike Shot Logger, Executive Producer and other tools like it provide deck control, which means you can control a camera or VTR from within the software while you are logging. This is not so helpful during field production, but comes in handy during the post phase when you need to revise or add to your shot logs.

Executive Producer allows you to:

- Play running video in a window

- Grab thumbnail images of the footage for storyboarding purposes

- Manually or automatically mark timecode IN and OUT

- Select print fonts and timecode capture

- Control a camera or tape deck with Play, Rewind, Fast Forward, Pause, Shuttle, Jog, and Single Frame Advance/Reverse

- Cue to TC IN and pause or play footage

- Copy and paste pictures into storyboards

- Select, sort, and arrange clips

- Print B&W or color storyboards

- Output EDLs to auto assemble in a videotape suite

- Output batch digitizing files for all popular nonlinear editing systems

AutoLog™ from Pipeline Digital

For more information on AutoLog, visit www.pipelinedigital.com.

Like Executive Producer, AutoLog from Pipeline Digital works on a desktop computer or a laptop, and allows you to control a tape deck through a serial digital cable and automatically log IN and OUT marks while adding additional shot log information. What sets AutoLog apart, however, is the ability to control this application from within a Filemaker Pro database. As a result we've designed the Advanced Project Templates to interface directly with AutoLog, thereby allowing you to add serial deck control to your logging functions in the templates provided on the companion CD-ROM.

Like Executive Producer, AutoLog also allows you to capture thumbnail images through a capture card, if your computer has one, which you can use to create storyboards. Other features of AutoLog include the following:

- You can automatically stamp reel, scene, and take numbers into your log.

- When linked up with Filemaker Pro, you can automatically grab pictures right into the database.

- You can import or export shot logs for use in many popular non-linear editors including Avid systems, Adobe Premiere, Scitex, Media 100, D/Vision, and Radius Edit.

- You can customize logging of timecode formats to specify drop or non-drop frame timecode, for example.

AutoLog does not support EDL export, however, so if you plan on working with your source tapes in an online suite, you should consider another logging tool. For nonlinear editing, and for working with our Advanced Project Templates, AutoLog can extend the templates to shorten your production cycles even further.

Project Template Workshop: Logging in the Field

The Advanced Project Templates allow you to start your logging on location, if equipped with a laptop. In addition, unlike other logging applications, you can begin to transcribe the content of interviews or other sound-on-tape right away, without waiting for the post-production phase.

If you purchase the AutoLog application, you can interface directly with the camera via serial digital cable to capture timecodes or thumbnail image files directly into your database. For more information, see "AutoLog™ from Pipeline Digital" on page 104.

To begin, open the file labeled 4-ShotLogs_Transcripts. If the file is already open and you are working in another form layout, choose one of the following from the Layout pop-up menu:

- Choose Shot Log Entry. This layout is appropriate for logging in the field during a shoot.

Layout pop-up menu

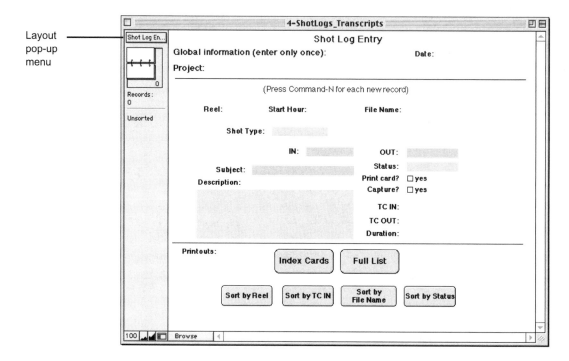

Entering Global Information

To begin a log you should first enter global information for the project. If you are just beginning project development with Shot Log entry, enter global information into the upper section of the form as described in "Entering Global Information" on page 53.

Note that with each new revision of your database you can enter a new revision number in the global information area that will appear in headers and footers for your printouts. However, to preserve earlier revisions of the database you should first make a duplicate of the database and save it in a backup folder before making changes.

Importing Scenes from the Outline

If you developed an outline, storyboard, or script as described in Chapter 3, you can enter project name, section, subsection, and description information automatically for each record as a starting point. Once you import the records you can change them, delete them, or add additional records in the templates as needed. For more information, see "Importing Scenes from the Outline" on page 54.

Starting a Record

Press Command-N (Macintosh) to create the first record.

Note that a record number (number 1 in this case) automatically appears in the Record# field. This number is automatically generated for each new record in the database, and makes it easy to identify each record as the database develops. You also use the record number to call up shot log records during scripting.

The Record# field is yellow. All yellow fields contain information that is generated automatically. These include:

- Date: Updates automatically each time you alter any of the records in the database

- File Name: Created from the first three letters of the project name, the reel number, and the record number. File names become the names of the clips digitized from the shot log

- TC IN: SMPTE timecode format based on the number in the Start Hour box and the time you enter for the IN point. Two zeroes are added for frames, rounding off time to the second.

- TC OUT: SMPTE timecode format based on the Start Hour and time you enter for the OUT point. Two zeroes are added for frames, rounding off time to the second.

- Duration: Calculated from the TC IN and TC OUT

Customizing the Entry Form for Faster Logging

The top region of the Shot Log Entry Form contains several pop-up menus that you can customize to suite the particular needs of your project and speed the logging process. This is especially useful in the field where time is short between takes. You can do this during off-hours or in advance of the shoot so that you are ready when the camera rolls.

To customize the entry form:

1. Click the Shot Type menu and choose Edit.

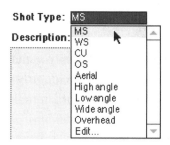

2. Review the list of shot types to make sure you have all the types you need to describe your shots. Revise as necessary.

3. Choose Edit from the Status menu.

4. Review and revise the types of status listed here.

The Advanced Project Templates use non-drop-frame timecode format by default. You can change it to the drop-frame timecode format as follows:

1. Choose Fields from the Define submenu of the File menu.

2. In the Define Fields dialog box, click New IN and click Options.

3. In the formula for New IN, change the colons to semicolons. Do the same for the New OUT field, then click Done.

   All logs and scripts will now contain drop-frame timecode.

Using the Tab Key

The Tab key on the keyboard can be your most valuable ally when entering information into a database form. If you can train yourself to use it consistently, it will save you a lot of time and effort.

In the Advanced Project Templates, pressing the Tab key moves you consecutively through all the boxes that allow you to enter information. When you tab to a pop-up list, the list automatically opens, allowing you to make a choice.

The Tab key takes you through the Shot Log Entry form in order of the topics that follow.

Entering the Project Name

Type a project name into the Global Information area at the top of the form. The name is global because it remains the same for all records in the database, therefore you only enter this information once.

Note that the date is automatically entered.

Entering Reel and Start Hour Information

Enter reel and start hour information at the top of the entry form as follows:

Reel: Start Hour:

- Enter a reel number or name into the box. If you have more than 100 tapes, a common convention is to use a three-digit number, typically starting with 001. If you have less than 100 tapes, a common convention is to use a two-digit number, starting with 01.

- Choose a Start Hour from the pop-up list, based on the hour of the starting timecode on the source tape. This number is used in generating the SMPTE timecode entries for the log.

  Reel name and start hour are persistent: they remain the same for each new record you create until you change them again.

Building the Shot Log

To build the shot log:

1. (Option) Enter the name of the subject of the shot into the Subject text box. For example, you can enter the name of an interview subject,or a specific location. This helps with sorting and printing later.

2. Choose a Shot Type for the current shot from the pop-up menu. This is not a repeating field and should be chosen for each shot. The shot type appears in the logs and in scripts.

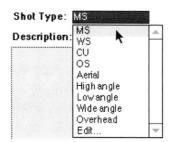

3. Enter an IN point for the shot in minutes and seconds using the format shown in this example:

   05:25 (non-drop frame) or 05;25 (drop frame)

4. Type a description. This should be a brief visual notation, appropriate for the Video column of a typical A/V script.

   If the information you enter extends beyond the size of the text box, a scroll bar appears allowing you to enter and view as much information as necessary.

5. Enter an OUT point for the shot in minutes and seconds using the following format:

   05:25 (non-drop frame) or 05;25 (drop frame)

   Note that TC IN, TC OUT, and Duration are automatically calculated based on your entries for IN and OUT.

6. (Option) Enter miscellaneous notes about the shot into the Comments text box.

7. Choose a status for the shot (such as Good, No Good, or Use) from the pop-up menu. This information helps with sorting and capturing the appropriate clips. You can enter this information later, after you print out and organize the shots.

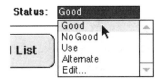

8. (Option) If you know that you want to print out the shot you just logged when printing cards or lists, click the Print Card checkbox. You can also do this later, after you log and review all the shots.

9. Press Command-N for each new shot, and repeat steps 1 through 8 for each additional shot.

For information on printing the logs, see Chapter 6.

Project Tracking in the Field

Because schedules and logistics can change drastically from shoot day to shoot day — or even minute to minute — tracking the progress of your production and making adjustments and calculations along the way is an essential part of any successful shoot. Bringing a laptop into the field can be extremely useful for this purpose, and if you are travelling to a distant location with no chance of racing back to the office, a laptop can be indispensable.

Depending on how deeply you go into the digital production workflow, you might find yourself with any number of computer-based tools and documents you can use to frequently update and recalculate the details of your shoot plans. Here are a few tips for working successfully.

Laptop Survival Tips

When carrying a laptop, before all else you should equip yourself for survival in the field. Particularly if you are traveling long distances, there are a number of things you should look into ahead of time. For example:

- **Get your numbers straight:** If you plan to use email or surf the web on location, make sure you bring the right access phone numbers for the location you are shooting at to save money and stay connected. You should also bring an extra phone cable for hooking up.

- **Don't black out:** Bring extra batteries and an AC battery charger for your laptop if available. Also, review power-saving tips for preserving battery charge, which you can probably find in your laptop's documentation or Help system. You don't want to "black out" during an important shoot.

- **Adapt and survive:** When traveling overseas, bring along the appropriate adapters for the power sources used at the location. If you're not sure which adapters will work, bring along a full set of adapters to make sure you can plug in when you get there.

- **Don't forget your contacts:** Not your lenses (you don't want to forget those either) but your phone numbers. Whether you use an address book, a portable assistant, or a program on your computer, don't forget to pack it or you'll end up wasting a lot of money dialing information.

You can also visit www. 555-1212.com to look up listed phone numbers.

- **Pack a Yellow Pages:** Sure, the book is heavy, but you can also find comprehensive phone listings in CD-ROM form or even through the Web. If you think you might need quick access to resources during production in faraway states, it's worth looking into.

- **Getting it in print:** When you revise shoot plans in the field, you'll probably want to print them out. You can try to bring along a small portable printer, but most hotels now have computer centers where guests can hook up and print. You might want to call ahead to see what facilities they have and what kind of printers, in case you need a specific driver.

If you don't have access to a printer and your modem supports faxing, you can send the document as a fax to the front desk of the hotel or to a local print shop to create an instant "copy."

- **Using the templates:** If you used the Advanced Project Templates to develop your shoot plans, you can load the database into your laptop and bring it with you on location to make quick changes. You can use the automatic calculation capabilities of the templates to quickly update schedules or test out different scenarios. For more information, see "Project Template Workshop: Preparing Shoot Plans and Schedules" on page 88.

CHAPTER 6

Preparing for Digital Post

Preparing for posting starts well before the editor makes the first "splice." During pre-production or early in post-production you must choose your facilities and workflow in order to calculate the time and money required for the edit. After the shoot, the more thoroughly you prepare before entering the edit room, the more successful — and economical — your final cut will be.

Chapter Topics

- Logging and Transcribing

- Project Template Workshop: Logging and Transcribing

- Scripting Tips and Tricks

- Project Template Workshop: Preparing Final Edit Scripts

- Making Digital Post Decisions

- Project Template Workshop: Generating Edit Plans and Facilities Requests

- Producer's Checklist: Preparing for Post

Logging and Transcribing

The first step in preparing to edit your program is to log and transcribe the footage. Digital methods afford you the opportunity to improve many aspects of what has traditionally been the most tedious and time-consuming task for the producer.

Advantages of Logging Digitally

Well-prepared digital logs enable the editor to expedite digitizing and to access shots quickly while editing. The editor can spend more time editing and less time searching for the right footage. For example, if the editor wants to find just the right close-up of a truck or the best line read, it should take little time to find the shot. This applies to projects with 1 or 100 hours of footage.

Digital logs also allow you to pass information more easily between applications. For example, you can use your logs to build a script, or in most cases you can input your logs directly into a nonlinear editing system.

There are many advantages to automating the logging process, among them:

- Reducing the chance of error during logging because you do not have to manually enter timecode and other numerical data

- Taking advantage of computer-based calculations for such things as time durations

- Better sharing of information with the editor because information can be imported directly into the nonlinear system

- Faster digitizing and better use of disk storage because you will make decisions about what to digitize while you log

- More efficient preparation of scripts and shoot plans, for example by automating the exchange of information between logs, transcripts, scripts, and shoot plans, as described in "Project Template Workshop: Preparing Final Edit Scripts" on page 167.

Digital logging programs automate the logging process. When you enter information about your shots into the program, you gain speed and flexibility in the edit suite. Searching capabilities enable you to instantaneously find a particular shot, replacing the laborious searches through paper logs. Sorting capabilities enable you to organize shots, so you can obtain a list of all wide shots, all shots taken at a particular location, and so on. With paper logs, you have to create new lists manually; the more footage you sift through, the more likely you are to make mistakes.

Digital logs don't necessarily make paper logs obsolete. Paper logs are still useful for jotting notes about your takes. However, even if you use paper logs, you may still log (at least) your selected takes digitally and put them on disk. The editor can enter the disk in the NLE system, and use the information on it to reduce digitizing time.

The producer needs to be more organized than ever. You may spend more time screening tapes, logging and selecting clips than when you worked on a linear system. But in the long run, the work you do saves time and disk space during the crucial editing phase.

Point of View

Logging with the [Avid] MediaLog system is fabulous for me; it was actually a huge breakthrough. When I was working in film or linear editing, a production assistant used to do the logging; now I do it myself. This is how the process works: a production assistant or I takes minimal logs while we're shooting. After the shoot, I rent a 3/4-inch deck or a VHS editing deck and sit and look at every frame. It may take me two weeks or more to log the footage in MediaLog if I've shot around 30 hours of footage. But by the end, I have a fairly good idea of what the rough assembly is going to be. So by the time I get into the edit room, I really remember almost every single shot, the way an editor would. This has cut down enormously the amount of time I spend preplanning or driving an editor crazy by not knowing what I'm going to do.

— Barbara Holecek, producer

Logging on Paper Versus Digitally

There are many ways to create a log; you will want to develop the system that works best for you, your editor, and your project.

The following list of methods gives you an idea of the range of possibilities, ranging from least to most reliance on digital logs.

- Use paper logs only

  You create paper logs during or after the shoot, and then the editor and/or you look through the footage to make your selects before digitizing.

  This method takes time, but does not require any special software or computer skills.

- Log only your selects digitally

  You look through your logs and/or footage, make your selects, and digitally log your selects.

  This method saves logging time, but limits your editor's options.

- Log all footage digitally

  You look through your paper logs from the field and review your footage as you log your shots (or groups of shots), recording useful information for your editor.

  This method provides the editor with the best access to footage during the edit.

Planning to Log

Before you begin to log, you should think about how the footage you shot will be organized to represent the concept and structure of your video. The better you plan for the edit by knowing your footage and your concept, the more smoothly the edit will progress. This planning will be reflected in how well your logs are organized. The amount of planning you do can make the difference between an efficient or a time-consuming edit.

Approaches to Logging Footage

This section covers two topics: what footage you will log, and whether you will log shots individually or in groups.

Logging All or Selected Shots

In the world of handwritten logs, you generally sit down at a tape deck, watch the footage, and take notes on each shot. You describe each shot, note whether it's a good or bad take, and so on. You log everything because the written log serves as a key tool in the edit, and it's easy enough just to keep writing.

During the edit, if the editor asks if you have, say, a "French toast" shot to use as a transition, and you remember the perfect shot, you can look through your paper logs and locate it.

However, when you work with digital logs, you might be tempted to be more selective, and log only the shots you intend to use in your video. Then, if the editor asks for the French toast shot, you may or may not have a log entry for that shot.

In the long run, it is less aggravating and less time-consuming to log all the footage and indicate to the editor the shots to be digitized.

Logging Individual or Groups of Shots

Do you log each shot individually, or log groups of shots together? Here are three options with an evaluation of each:

Option 1: Log each shot.

Each shot is logged into a separate clip.

- Advantage: Log is the most accurate representation of the shoot.

- Advantage: Best method for sorting and sifting clips in bins, so you can later find shots.

- Disadvantage: Digitizing is slow because of separate tape preroll for each clip.

- Disadvantage: May input extra material because overlap may be logged for each clip.

Option 2: Log groups of shots.

This option logs groups of shots into a clip. It is useful for logging multiple takes of a scene, multiple shots in a sequence, or shots of short duration.

- Advantage: Digitizing is faster because you reduce preroll and record overlap.

- Disadvantage: Log is not as detailed as Option 1.

Later, when you organize your bins, you can always subclip the group shots into the smaller individual shots.

Option 3: Log each shot and groups.

Log each shot, as in Option 1. When you discover a group of consecutive shots that you would like to input into the nonlinear editing system, create separate clips for this series of consecutive shots. Make a note in the log to digitize the group shot instead of each individual shot.

- Advantage: The group of shots will be digitized, but the individual clips are still available for sorting and sifting.

- Advantage: You conserve an accurate log, while reducing the digitizing time.

- Disadvantage: It takes longer to log.

Point of View

For the piece I'm working on now, I just spent the last two hours logging about five tapes, all B-roll. I logged everything. I just shuttled through the shots; if I didn't like one, I still logged it, added it to my bin, gave it a name, and then moved on to the next one. I can shuttle through a 40-second shot in about ten seconds. Now that I've logged the shots, I'll batch digitize only the shots I need into the Avid.

— *Arnie Harchik, Avid editor*

We always set up our bins by tape number because we have found it to be the fastest, most efficient way to digitize. Once we have everything loaded in this giant footage bin and broken it down by tape number, then we can start pulling things into work bins. That's how I do it. I actually disapprove of doing complicated logging where clips from the same tape are in separate bins because it is a digitizer's nightmare.

— *Vanessa Boris, Avid editor*

Log loose. Don't over-select. Don't do the editor's job before the editor does it. Keep big elbow room. Because you never know. Those shots that you say, "I'd never use that in a million years," always turn out to be the shots that save the show.

— *Tom Hayes, Avid editor*

Logging with LogExpress® from Alba Editorial

In the previous chapter we described tools ideally suited for logging in the field (see "Logging in the Field" on page 99). In the following sections we describe three more tools that provide excellent features for logging after the shoot, prior to entering the edit room.

For more information on LogExpress, visit albaedit.com

LogExpress from Alba Editorial focuses on logging your media as digitized clips referenced by a user-designated thumbnail. LogExpress allows for seven different methods of logging, and also interacts with key areas of production and post-production, including digitizing of clips. With this application you can:

- Digitize media clips to QuickTime or AVI format

- Add user-definable key words and descriptions

- Conduct Boolean searches on database contents

- Reference clips with multiple thumbnails

- Perform unattended logging via Parallel and RS422 VTR control ports

- Capture timecode via LTC (with most sound cards) or via OCR (from burn in window)

- Import EDLs

- Import scripts in text format

- Associate lines of script with thumbnails

Logging with Scene Stealer™ from Dubner International

Scene Stealer offers a low-cost solution for logging clips and managing a video library. Scene Stealer features include:

For more information on Scene Stealer, visit dubner.com

- Color and monochrome video capture plus phrase cutpoint technology for closed captioning and subtitling operations

- Automatic location and logging of video cut points

- Preparation of EDLs

- Insertion of phrase cutpoints on-the-fly or during playback for closed captioning and subtitling operations

- Printing of catalog pages and storyboards

Logging with Avid MediaLog™

For more information on Media-Log, visit Avid.com

Avid MediaLog is a logging program that is essentially a subset of Avid Media Composer. MediaLog has the same functionality as Avid Media Composer's Logging tool, and creates bins that are compatible with most Avid video-based editing systems. If you expect to edit on Avid systems, MediaLog is a good choice. This software, or another Avid-compatible logging program, should provide considerable cost savings in preparing and digitizing footage on an Avid system.

Logging with MediaLog provides several features that save time and reduce error:

- You can create the logs on a separate computer, instead of monopolizing an expensive Media Composer system.

- In most cases the bins you create can be opened instantly in Media Composer (in some cases, compatibility requirements might involve a brief translation of the bins to a newer version; consult with your editor).

- Timecode reading is automated, reducing chance of error. For example, the timecode is "marked" directly when you click the IN (START) frame button.

- You can create the logs on a Macintosh, Windows 98, or Windows NT system, whether the computer is connected to a tape deck or you type in the timecode from paper logs.

- You can print reports and lists of shots that meet specific criteria.

Connecting a Deck

To control the deck from within MediaLog, connect the deck to the computer using a serial cable, and set the Remote/Local switch on the deck to Remote.

If you are running MediaLog on a Windows 98 or Windows NT operating system, the direct serial video deck connection requires an RS-232 to RS-422 serial adapter and two serial cables with male 9-pin connectors at both ends. See the MediaLog documentation or Help system for further instructions on setting up the hardware.

Preparing to Log Material

To prepare to log your footage, you must:

1. Create a new project and new user, or select existing ones.

   The project folder contains the bins and clips, along with other information about your project. Plan to give the project folder the same name in MediaLog and Media Composer.

   Only one project can be open at a time. To open another project, close the one you are in.

2. Create a bin where you want to store your clips.

   You may create more than one bin if your project size or organization requires it.

   Bins should contain no more than 100 clips for efficient handling.

3. With that bin highlighted, choose Go To Logging Mode from the Bin menu or press Command-B (Macintosh) or Ctrl-B (Windows).

   The screen displays the Logging tool.

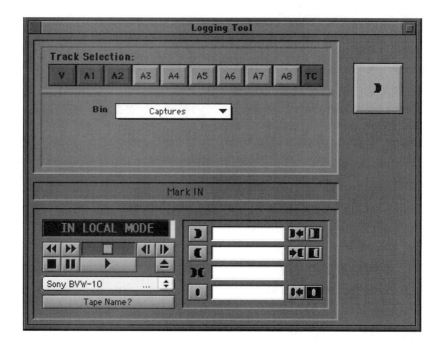

Configuring the Deck

With your deck properly connected, you can instruct MediaLog to automatically configure the deck. Choose Autoconfigure from the logging tool, and MediaLog will search the system ports and configure the attached deck.

If this doesn't work, you will need to manually configure the deck, using the Deck Configuration and Deck Preferences settings. See the MediaLog documentation or Help system.

Selecting the Source

In some cases, your source material may not reside on a video tape deck. You can also select other source devices, such as a Digital Audio Tape (DAT).

To identify the source where the material is found:

1. Use the deck pop-up menu to display a menu of available online sources.

Identifying the Source Tape

To specify the source tape's name:

1. With the deck set to Remote, insert a tape into the play deck.

   The Tape Name dialog box opens.

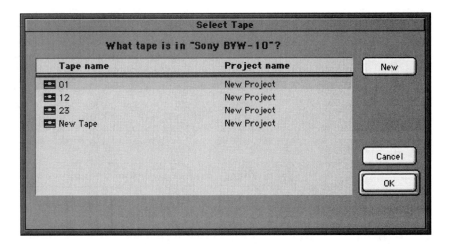

2. Play a few seconds of video so the timecode reader can identify the type of timecode on the tape.

3. Double-click the name of a tape already listed in the dialog box or click New if the name of the tape isn't shown in the list.

   A new tape name line appears.

4. Type the tape name and press Return.

   Remember to use a unique name for each new tape. The best naming schemes are incremental numberings such as 001, 002, and so on, or "001BD" (project initials). The flexibility of the Media Composer editing system relies in part on the system's ability to correctly associate clips with the correct physical tapes. The system cannot distinguish between two tapes with the same name or number. Once you have named a tape source in Media Composer, any change to that tape name automatically changes the tape's name everywhere it occurs; avoid changing the tape name.

Tape names must consist of only alphanumeric characters (A-Z, 0-9), with no spaces and no punctuation. The system distinguishes between upper and lower case. Although MediaLog allows tape names of up to 31 characters, most online houses accept names of no more than 6 characters. If you use a long tape name, Media Composer truncates it when creating the EDL for the online facility.

Point of View

The numbers that you enter into the nonlinear editing system should exactly match the numbers you wrote on the tape boxes during the shoot. You should always use the following system: The first tape is numbered 01. The 500th tape is numbered 500. Every tape has an individual number, period. I know somebody who's cutting a 5-hour series on women in rock and roll. They have 900 tapes. The first tape number is 01 and the last tape number is 900. The only exception is a multi-camera shoot. So if I have four cameras, I'll have tape 01A, 01B, 01C, and 01D. And that's the way all the editors I know work.

— *Larry Young, Avid editor, cameraperson, producer*

Selecting Tracks

Select the video and audio tracks for each shot that you would like the editor to digitize.

Selecting the Target Bin

To select a target bin:

- Use the bin pop-up menu to choose the target bin in which you want to log your captured material.

  The pop-up menu lists all available open bins. If the menu does not list the target bin you want, make sure the bin is open.

- Choose a previously created bin by choosing Open Bin from the File menu, or by pressing Command-O (Macintosh) or Ctrl-O (Windows).

- Create a new bin, by choosing New Bin from the File menu, or by pressing Command-N (Macintosh) or Ctrl-N (Windows).

Organizing the Bins

There are several ways to organize your bins. Here are a few of the most common.

Method 1: If you are working with a lot of source material, you can create your bins before logging, naming each according to the type of shots it will contain.

Method 2: You might prefer to log each tape into its own bin, identified by Tape ID, for a couple of reasons:

- It is easier and more efficient to digitize all material from the same tape at the same time.

- It is more difficult to log portions of a tape into separate bins.

- Your editor might prefer you to allow him or her to organize bins.

- Later, you can easily duplicate clips and move them to different bins, according to content-based criteria.

Method 3: You might want to create one or more Selects Bins, containing the clips you have selected to digitize.

You should evaluate these options with the editor before proceeding.

Selecting Video Compression and Audio Rate

You can select the compression settings that affect video and audio quality using the Compression tool (select it from the Logging tool window or from the Tools menu). The editor can also set or change these settings for you while digitizing.

Capture rates that are not available on your system are dimmed in the pop-up menu.

Logging Procedure

Once you have created the project and bin, selected the compression settings (optional, for now), and chosen your logging approach, you can use the Logging tool to begin to log.

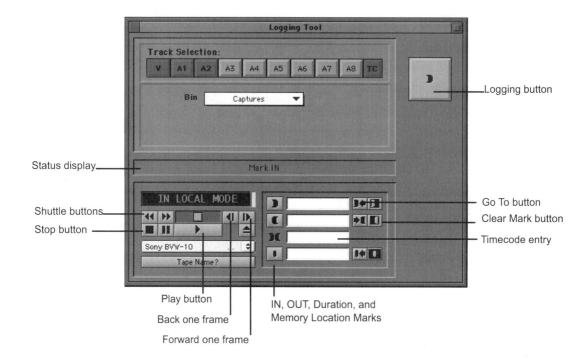

Logging button

Status display

Shuttle buttons

Stop button

Go To button

Clear Mark button

Timecode entry

Play button

Back one frame

Forward one frame

IN, OUT, Duration, and
Memory Location Marks

Method 1: Logging Timecode Manually

You can use the MediaLog's Logging tool to enter clip data manually into a bin. You might choose this method while travelling, or any time you don't have access to a deck. You can also use it to type in numbers read from a VHS dub with burn-in or from a field log.

For NTSC tapes, you should first select drop frame or non-drop frame timecode in the Deck Preferences window. (To access this window, click Settings in the Project window and then double-click Deck Preferences.)

To log manually, you set up the Logging tool as described in the previous section. Even though you have no physical tape, you must still assign one to the clips you create. So, click on the tape name display and select an existing name or name a new tape in the dialog box.

Instead of shuttling to the IN and OUT points on the tape, you manually type in two of the three following timecodes for each clip you want to log: IN point, OUT point, and duration. The procedure is:

1. Select the tracks you want to log.

2. Type the IN timecode and press Return.

3. Type the OUT timecode (or Duration) and press Return.

4. Click the Pencil icon in the large Logging button.

5. Rename the clip.

Here's a sanity check for typing errors: After you type a pair of IN and OUT timecodes, quickly look at the duration to see if it makes sense.

Don't forget to save as you log, by pressing Command-S (Macintosh) or Ctrl-S (Windows).

Method 2: Logging from a Source Tape

You can use the Logging tool to log from a tape to a bin. This tool enables you to control a source deck, select shots (clips) from your source tapes, and record clip data directly into a bin.

Marking the IN and OUT Points

To log clips directly from a source tape to a bin:

1. Load your tape in the deck.

   A message in the Status Display indicates that the system is waiting for you to mark an IN point. The Logging button displays an IN mark.

2. Using the motion control buttons in the Logging tool, play or shuttle to the point where you want to mark an IN for the start of the clip.

3. Mark an IN by doing one of the following:

   • Click the large Logging button that now reads IN.

   • Click the IN mark to the right of the motion control panel.

   The timecode for the IN point is displayed, the icon in the Logging button changes to an OUT mark and a pencil, and the Logging Messages bar displays a message that the system is waiting for an OUT point to be established.

At this time, you may type the name of the clip. The name will not appear until you enter an OUT mark in the log.

4. Mark an OUT by doing one of the following:

- Shuttle or play to the place where you want to mark the OUT point of the clip. Click the large Logging button that now has an OUT mark and the pencil icon.

- Click the small OUT mark button, then click the pencil icon in the Logging button.

The clip is logged into the bin.

The tape pauses for a few seconds, then continues to play. The clip name is the name you typed earlier or a default name (the bin name plus a number).

5. Use this pause to type in a name for the logged clip, if you have not done so already.

To log a clip, you must enter two of the following three timecodes, in any order: IN point, OUT point, and Duration. The system fills in the remaining timecode.

6. Repeat these steps until you have logged all your clips.

Don't forget to save frequently as you log, by pressing Command-S (Macintosh) or Ctrl-S (Windows).

It is important for you to log *all* footage. Even if you know a take is not good, log it. Later, the editor can select what to digitize based on your notes. The editor may be able to use a small segment of the shot. For example, the editor might find a good reading of a particular sentence in a take that is otherwise flawed.

Log "loose"; do not mark tight IN and OUT points. For interview clips, you might want to log very loose to allow extra footage for split edits. Resist the temptation to perform the editor's job while you log.

Give your clips meaningful names. Think of them as keys (or combinations of keys) that you can use to search through a database (see Sorting and Sifting sections later in this module). For example, if you name a clip, CU John Cooking, you can sort by shot size, name, or action.

See Steve Stone's interview in the appendix for a system of logging specifically devised for sorting and sifting.

Using Motion Controls

You can use keyboard motion controls to speed up the logging process. The following table lists keyboard shortcuts.

Table 6-1: Keyboard Shortcuts

Command	Keys
10 Frames Back	1
10 Frames Forward	2
1 Frame Back	3
1 Frame Forward	4
Mark IN	E or I
Mark OUT	R or O
Mark OUT and LOG	L
Go to Mark IN	Q
Go to Mark OUT	W
Pause	S
Play	F or D
Stop	A or Spacebar
Clear Mark IN	Z
Clear Mark OUT	X
Rewind	C
Fast Forward	V

Organizing Your Clips

When you log your footage, you provide MediaLog with all the information about your shot that the editor needs to input your footage into the system. This information resides in columns that may be displayed in a number of standard views. Along with the Avid-supplied Statistical columns, you may create your own columns, called Custom columns.

When you create Custom columns, you are, in effect, creating a database of useful data about your footage and setting up the search criteria. These columns enable you and the editor to search the log for subsets of information.

Statistical Columns

MediaLog shows a standard and predefined set of Statistical columns for all of your clips. Your only role in creating these columns is to input a unique name for each clip. The system automatically creates information for statistical columns for the clip.

Statistical information about your clips is available in Text view. Statistical information created by MediaLog includes:

- Project information

  - Frames per second (FPS)

  - Audio resolution (sample rate)

- Shot (clip) information

  - Clip name

    You must provide a unique, useful name for each clip. Note that the name is not automatically created by the system.

  - START and END frames

    The head frame and tail frame of each clip

- IN and OUT frames, if any

  The frames for a marked segment, if created

- Tape

  The source tape

- Tracks

  All video and audio tracks used by the clip

- Video

  The video resolution

Modifying the Bin View

You can modify your view of statistical columns by hiding or revealing particular columns. You are not actually adding or deleting information, simply changing your view of the information.

To add headings to your current view:

1. Choose Headings from the Bin menu.

   A window appears displaying all of the available headings, with the ones already displayed in your bin highlighted in black.

2. Click on the heading in the list to select it.

To remove (hide) a heading:

1. Click on the highlighted heading in the list to deselect it.
2. Click OK.

To hide a column directly from the bin:

1. Click on its heading.
2. Press delete.

   This hides the statistical column, but does not delete it.

Creating Custom Columns

Creating custom columns is one of your most important logging tasks. Think of your log as a database of information about your shots. Like any database, you enter data in columns that you can then search and sort.

For example, a company's Customer database might include column headings such as name, street, city, state, zip code, social security number, and so on. The database is created and updated by inserting information about each customer.

The database is as useful as its data columns. You can search this database for names in alphabetical order, by zip code, or by state. Or you might want more specific information, such as all customers, arranged in alphabetical order, living in a particular state. However, if you want a list of customers sorted by area code, you're out of luck if you have not created a column for that data.

MediaLog's custom columns let you create additional search criteria for your log database, enabling you to search the log for subsets of information. For example, you might want to search the log for all scenes with a particular character, or search for all shots in scene 5.

The usefulness of your shot log depends on the search categories, or columns. You cannot print a report of all close-ups unless you have a column recording that information.

When you enter information in the custom column, you must be consistent. For example, always refer to a close-up as CU, instead of mixing CU and C/U. If you do not, Media Composer will consider CU as one type of shot, and C/U as another type.

Here are some custom columns you might like to consider:

- Character

  List the character(s) in each shot.

- Shot size (CU, MS, LS)

- Shot type

  List Interview, Cutaway, Master, POV, and so on.

- Location

- Quality

  Keepers, NG (No Good), and so on.

  Alternately, use asterisks (* for the worst takes, **** for the best), to describe the relative quality of takes.

- Digitize

  If you create a thorough log, you can use this column to indicate the selects for the session. Type a D in this column to tell the editor which clips to digitize.

- Cost

  Useful for stock footage, music copyright fees, and so on.

- Resource

  Useful for keeping track of stock footage houses.

Point of View

I'm still a little bit used to a film system, so I have in my own mind shot 1, 2, 3, 4, 5, to 1,000, and the roll number. I also describe the shot: long shot, pan, holding shot, whether there's something the matter with it, along with a description of the content of the shot. And then I give the shot a priority number... I mean priority in terms of what gets digitized. There's going to be way too much material, so I'll either digitize just all the #1 shots, or all the #1 and #2 shots. Or, if a shot is not good but I know I need it, I may call it a #3 shot but I'll add a little star, and say this has to be digitized anyway. So that's what I take in to the editor, along with the treatment. So before they even get into digitizing, they at least know what the film is about, and have some detail about the film.

— Barbara Holecek, producer

For scenario-based shows, I log using three columns, Name, Scene, and Comments. I log the scene number as the clip's Name because on our Avid the clip's Name is what shows up on the timeline, and it helps when you're trying to do a fast search for a particular scene. Under the Scene column I log what kind of shot it is, such as: master, reversal, narrator, or B-roll. And under the Comment column I usually log which take it was, or any kind of description that will help me later. Logging doesn't take long because the project book enables me to skip over any of the unusable footage.

— Steve Stone, producer

Adding Custom Columns to a Bin

To add a new, custom column:

1. Click T in the View Selector panel to put the bin in Text view.

2. Click an empty area to the right of the current headings.

3. Type the column heading you want. Column headings must contain fewer than 30 characters, including spaces. Press Return.

   This puts the pointer in the data box, beside the first clip in the bin.

4. Type the information and press Return to move to the next line.

5. Create any additional columns and enter information.

6. You can move any column to the right or left by using the mouse to "drag and drop" it.

7. Use the Tidy Up command after you have entered the new column heading.

   The following table provides information on modifying your view of custom columns and short cuts for entering data.

Table 6-2: Modifying Custom Columns

To	Do This
Repeat information from another cell in the same column (this modification applies only to custom columns)	Hold down the Option key (Macintosh) or Alt key (Windows) and press on the cell in which you want the text to appear. A pop-up menu of the items already entered in that column appears. Select the correct text from the menu.
Change a column heading after pressing Return (this modification applies only to custom columns)	Hold down the Option key (Macintosh) or Alt key (Windows) and click the heading. The heading text is highlighted. Type the new text for the heading.
Delete a column	Click the column heading and choose Clear from the Edit menu, or press the Delete key. Note that you can delete only Custom text columns. You cannot delete Statistical text columns (but you can hide them).

Table 6-2: Modifying Custom Columns (Continued)

To	Do This
Hide a column	Click the column heading and choose Hide Column from the Bin menu.
Show a previously hidden column	Choose Headings from the Bin menu, and select the previously hidden column.

Sorting and Sifting Clips

After you create custom columns, you can use them (and statistical columns) to sort and sift your material. Sorting and Sifting enable you to search logged footage for a specific clip, or to search for clips that meet specified criteria, creating different views of your data.

*   *Sorting* clips: Arranges all the clips, in alphanumerical order, based on the content of one or more columns.

    For example, sort the Scene column, in ascending order, and you will create a report of all clips of Scene 1, followed by all clips of Scene 2, and so on. You might sort by Timecode to obtain the order in which the clips appeared in your field tapes.

    You can also sort multiple columns at once. For example, you can sort all takes, in ascending order, within all scenes.

*   *Sifting* clips: Shows only the clips that meet specific search criteria. Sifts can also be based on more than one column. Two examples of sifting are:

    *   Sift the Name column for John. Your report gives you all shots of John, even if "John" is not the first word of the clip name.

    *   Sift the Quality column for ***.

Point of View

When I started using the Avid, I realized that if you log properly by making shots sortable and by using scene numbers, the scenario-based show is basically cut for you. And the documentary style show is a lot easier to cut when all your material is organized in bins, and all your clips are sortable by category and/or content. I know using the Avid has greatly improved all of our shows here at Creative Video, as well as my own productivity.

— Steve Stone, producer

Sorting Clips

You can sort clips to find a specific clip, or to find clips that meet specific criteria. You can sort clips in ascending order or descending order, or perform multilevel sorts on two or more columns.

For example, you might perform a multilevel sort on our Customer database. Let's say you need a report of all names for each zip code in alphabetical order. You sort by all customer names in ascending order *within* zip codes in ascending order.

Sorting Clips in Ascending Order

To sort clips in ascending order:

1. In Text view, click the heading of the column that you want to use as the criterion.

   The column is highlighted.

   Choose Sort from the Bin menu, or press Command-E (Macintosh) or Ctrl-E (Windows). (If the Sort option is grayed out in the Bin menu, make sure the column is highlighted.)

   The objects in the bin are sorted.

Sorting Clips in Descending Order

To sort clips in descending order:

1. Click the heading of the column that you want to use as the criterion.

   The column is highlighted.

2. Hold down the Option key (Macintosh) or Alt key (Windows) while you choose Sort Reversed from the Bin menu, or while you press Command-E (Macintosh) or Ctrl-E (Windows).

Option- (Macintosh) or Alt- (Windows) Sort displays the column in descending order.

Performing Multilevel Sorting

Multilevel sorts enable you to sort one criterion within another. For example, let's say you created a custom column called "Character," that lists the names of all characters in your show. You can sort by Character, and within that all of the Tape names. The result is a list of John's clips, first on Tape 001, then Tape 002, and so on. Then you see a list of Mary's clips, first on Tape 001, then 002, and so on. If you add a third criterion, START time, the shots of each character in Tape 001 are listed by increasing Start timecode, and so on.

Print out the list for a good reference of where you can find shots of all your characters.

To set up a multilevel sort, you select multiple columns in a bin by Shift-clicking their headings (in Text view). The left-most selected column becomes the primary criterion for the sorting operation. You can rearrange the columns in the bin in order to establish which column is primary.

You can perform a multilevel sort in ascending or descending order, as described in the previous section.

Sifting Clips

Sifting clips allows you to show only those clips that meet certain criteria. For example, you might want to sift the clips in your bin to show only the clips that contain "CU" in the Name column.

You can use the sift function to display two sets of clips, each of which can meet up to three sets of criteria. For example, you might want to find all shots of John in tape 1 and all shots of Dede in tape 4. (Each sifting set can have up to three criteria.) Media Composer shows the clips that meet the specifications in the first set of criteria, as well as all clips that meet the second set of criteria. This is how you set up the Custom Sift dialog box to search the criteria in our example:

```
┌─────────────────────────────────────────────────────────────────┐
│                    SuperDialog.00A0                               │
├─────────────────────────────────────────────────────────────────┤
│                                                                   │
│  Show clips that:                                                 │
│                                                                   │
│  [ contain   ▲▼] [ John          ]  in the  [ Descript    ▲▼] column, │
│  [ contain   ▲▼] [ 01            ]  in the  [ Tape        ▲▼] column, │
│  [ contain   ▲▼] [              ]  in the  [            ▲▼] column.  │
│                                                                   │
│  Also show clips that:                                            │
│                                                                   │
│  [ contain   ▲▼] [ Dede          ]  in the  [ Descript    ▲▼] column, │
│  [ contain   ▲▼] [ 04            ]  in the  [ Tape        ▲▼] column, │
│  [ contain   ▲▼] [              ]  in the  [            ▲▼] column.  │
│                                                                   │
│                  [  Clear  ]   [  OK  ]   [  Cancel  ]             │
│                                                                   │
└─────────────────────────────────────────────────────────────────┘
```

The resulting bin display includes only those clips that meet these criteria.

To sift clips:

1. Choose Custom Sift from the Bin menu.

    The Sift dialog box opens.

2. Press the top-left shadow box.

    A menu gives you a choice of:

    - Contain

    - Begin with

    - Match exactly

    Suppose you have a Quality column rating the quality of clips by asterisks (* to ****). To show clips equal to or better than ***, select "Contain." To show just the clips rated ***, select "Match exactly."

3. Choose the operation that you want to use.

4. Click the Sift Criteria box, and enter the text that you want the system to find.

5. Press the shadow box before the word "column."

 A menu lists the heading in the current bin view. You can also select Any to search all the columns.

6. Select the column in which the system should search.

7. Enter additional sift criteria, if necessary.

8. Click OK.

 The clips that meet your criteria appear in the bin, with the word "Partial" added to the bin name.

Showing Sifted and Unsifted Views of the Bin

After you have sifted the clips in a bin, you can display the bin in a sifted state or in an unsifted state.

 To view the entire bin:

• Choose Show Unsifted from the Bin menu.

 To view the sifted bin:

• Choose Show Sifted from the Bin menu.

 When you display sorted and sifted bins, here are some things to notice:

• The checkmark in the submenu indicates the current state of the bin.

• Unsifted and sifted are dimmed in the submenu if there is no Sift setup.

• The bin name says "Partial" when the sifted view is displayed.

Further Managing Bins and Clips

If you decide to log each tape into a bin and let the editor organize bins in a useful way before editing, you still might want to manage bins and clips for your own purposes. (Even if you organize the bins yourself, be prepared for your editor to rearrange them according to his or her preferences.)

For example, you may want to create a single bin to hold all interviews, all visuals from a particular location, or all selects, regardless of the tape ID. You can then print the contents of this bin for your own reference.

You can organize bins by moving or copying clips from one bin to another (see "Organizing Shots After Digitizing" on page 216). Remember that clips are simply pointers to the media, not the media itself. Therefore, you can store a clip in multiple bins, without consuming much additional disk space. For example, you can store a clip of Dede in a Dede bin and an At the Register bin.

To give just a few examples, you might want to arrange bins by:

• Scene number

• Character

• Location

• Subject matter

• Shot size

MediaLog allows you to create an unlimited number of bins.

The key to a successful nonlinear edit is organization, especially since storage is an issue. When you organize bins and clips, it's important to come up with good descriptions of your clips, create good "siftable" criteria, and organize the clips in bins to facilitate editing.

Printing Logs

After you reorganize the bins, you can print the entire log or sifted views of your logs. When you print, the bin printouts match your column selection and order in your bin.

Project Template Workshop: Logging and Transcribing

By using the Advanced Project Templates to log and transcribe, you can begin to bridge the major gaps that exist in the video producer's workflow. The Advanced Project Templates take into account the specific ways in which the producer of a documentary, news-magazine segment, or A/V project works, as opposed to the developer of a feature film or drama. In some respects the workflow is reversed. For example, a dramatic script may be written and rewritten a hundred times before a single frame of footage is shot. The final documentary script is prepared as the last step before editing, after all of the source material has been captured and painstakingly evaluated.

Advanced Template Workflow

The Advanced Project Templates attempt to apply some oil to the gears in this final grind. For example, some logging applications do not take into account the producer's need to transcribe interview content while noting timecodes and B-roll shots. Other logging applications require you to export or copy and paste data into a script during the final stages. The Advanced Project Templates allow you to log, transcribe, and begin shaping the final organization of the material simultaneously. You can print the material at any time in a variety of formats. You can access records from various files directly inside the scripting template without having to retype transcripts and shot log information.

To take full advantage of the Advanced Project Templates in preparation for the edit, we recommend the following workflow:

1. Log and transcribe the source footage, as described in "Logging and Transcribing with the Templates" on page 144.

2. Print out the logged elements onto index cards, as described in "Sorting and Printing Logs and Transcripts" on page 151. (This is one instance where paper still beats out the computer for convenience.) You can also print and review transcripts on letter-size paper, but index cards provide more flexibility. Use the index cards in a process of elimination to begin organizing topic areas while roughing out the order of elements in the final script.

   Keep extra index cards on hand to add notes and text for voice-overs while organizing.

3. Return to the logs/transcripts and add notes you made during the organizing phase regarding which shots to capture in post. You can print out final logs or export files for import into a nonlinear editing system at any time.

4. Go to the script templates, and use the organization of the index cards to automatically call up and organize those clips and sound bites required for the edit. Add voice over, titles, and other elements, then continue to shape the final structure of the script, as described in "Project Template Workshop: Preparing Final Edit Scripts" on page 167.

Logging and Transcribing with the Templates

If you purchase the AutoLog application, you can interface directly with a deck via serial digital cable to capture time-codes or thumbnail image files directly into your database. For more information, see "AutoLog™ from Pipeline Digital" on page 104.

To begin, open the file labeled 4-ShotLogs_Transcripts. If the file is already open and you are working in another form layout, choose one of the following from the Layout pop-up menu:

• Choose Shot Log Entry if you want to log just the basic shot information, such as IN and OUT marks and notes, without transcribing interview content, for example. This layout is appropriate for logging in the field during a shoot.

• Choose Log/Transcript Entry if you want to log all shot information with the option to transcribe interview content and add comments as well. This layout is appropriate for logging after a shoot, in preparation for building an edit script.

Layout pop-up menu

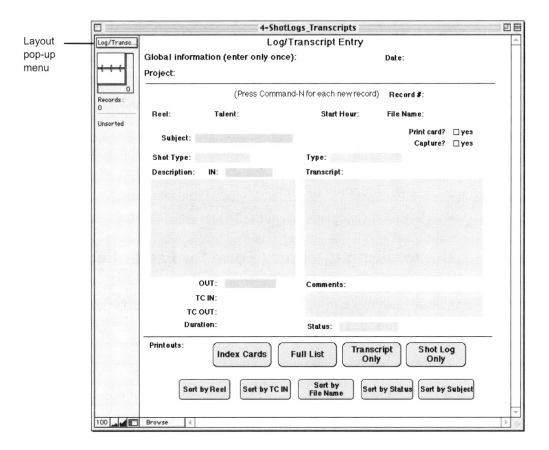

Starting a Record

Press Command-N (Macintosh) to create the first record.

Note that a record number (number 1 in this case) automatically appears in the Record# field. This number is automatically generated for each new record in the database, and makes it easy to identify each record as the database develops. You also use the record number to call up shot log records during scripting.

The Record# field is yellow. All yellow fields contain information that is generated automatically. These include:

- Date: Updates automatically each time you alter any of the records in the database

- File Name: Created from the first three letters of the project name, the reel number, and the record number. File names become the names of the clips digitized from the shot log.

- TC IN: SMPTE timecode format based on the number in the Start Hour box and the time you enter for the IN point. Two zeroes are added for frames, rounding off time to the second.

- TC OUT: SMPTE timecode format based on the Start Hour and time you enter for the OUT point. Two zeroes are added for frames, rounding off time to the second.

- Duration: Calculated from the TC IN and TC OUT

Customizing the Entry Form for Faster Logging

The top region of the Shot Log Entry Form contains several pop-up menus that you can customize to suit the particular needs of your project and speed the logging process.

To customize the entry form:

1. In the top area of the entry form, click the Talent pop-up list and choose Edit.

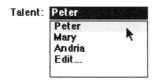

2. In the dialog box, enter the names of talent that you work with frequently. You won't have to retype these names in the future.

3. Click the Shot Type menu and choose Edit.

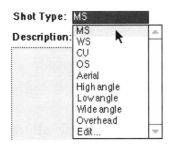

4. Review the list of shot types to make sure you have all the types you need to describe your shots. Revise as necessary.

5. Click the Type menu above the Transcript entry box and choose Edit.

6. Review the list of field-recorded sound types to make sure you have all the types you will need for your shoot. Revise as necessary.

7. Click the Status menu below the Transcript entry box and choose Edit.

8. Review the types of status listed here for the shots. Revise as necessary.

The Advanced Project Templates use non-drop-frame timecode format by default. You can change it to the drop frame timecode format as follows:

1. Choose Fields from the Define submenu of the File menu.

2. In the Define Fields dialog box, click New IN and click Options.

3. In the formula for New IN, change the colons to semicolons. Do the same for the New OUT field, then click Done.

All logs and scripts will now contain drop-frame timecode.

Using the Tab Key

The Tab key on the keyboard can be your most valuable ally when entering information into a database form. If you can train yourself to use it consistently, it will save you a lot of time and effort.

In the Advanced Project Templates, pressing the Tab key moves you consecutively through all the boxes that allow you to enter information. When you tab to a pop-up list, the list automatically opens, allowing you to make a choice.

The Tab key takes you through the Log/Transcript Entry form in order of the topics that follow.

Entering the Project Name

Type a project name into the Global Information area at the top of the form. The name is global because it remains the same for all records in the database, therefore you only enter this information once.

Note that the date is automatically entered.

Entering Reel, Start Hour, and Talent Information

Filmmakers call them reels; video people call them tapes, or sometimes reels. If you are recording onto disk, it's a misnomer altogether, but let's not go there. For now, it's "reel."

Enter reel, start hour, and talent information at the top of the entry form as follows:

Reel: Talent: Start Hour:

• Enter a reel number or name into the box. If you have more than 100 tapes, a common convention is to use a three-digit number, typically starting with 001. If you have less than 100 tapes, a common convention is to use a two-digit number, starting with 01.

- Choose a Start Hour from the pop-up list, based on the hour of the starting timecode on the source tape. This number is used in generating the SMPTE timecode entries for the log.

- Choose the name of the talent for the project.

Reel name, talent, and start hour are persistent: they remain the same for each new record you create until you change them again.

Building the Shot Log

To build the shot log:

1. (Option) Enter the name of the subject of the shot into the Subject text box. For example, you can enter the name of an interview subject, or a specific location. This helps with sorting and printing later.

2. Choose a Shot Type for the current shot from the pop-up menu. This is not a repeating field, and should be chosen for each shot. The shot type appears in the logs and in scripts.

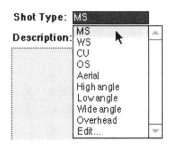

3. Enter an IN point for the shot in minutes and seconds using the format shown in this example:

   05:25 (non-drop frame) or 05;25 (drop frame)

4. Type a description of the shot. This should be a brief visual description, appropriate for the Video column of a typical A/V script.

   If the information you enter extends beyond the size of the text box, a scroll bar appears allowing you to enter and view as much information as necessary.

5. (Option) If you are transcribing as you log in the Log/Transcript Entry form, choose the type of field-recording from the Type pop-up list. This information appears in the logs and in scripts.

6. (Option) If you are transcribing as you log in the Log/Transcript Entry form, you can type the content of the interview into the Transcript text box.

If the information you enter extends beyond the size of the text box, a scroll bar appears allowing you to enter and view as much information as necessary.

7. Enter an OUT point for the shot in minutes and seconds using the following format:

05:25 (non-drop frame) or 05;25 (drop frame)

Note that TC IN, TC OUT, and Duration are automatically calculated based on your entries for IN and OUT.

8. (Option) Enter miscellaneous notes about the shot into the Comments text box.

9. Choose a status for the shot (such as Good, No Good, or Use) from the pop-up menu. This information helps with sorting and capturing the appropriate clips. You can enter this information later, after you print out and organize the shots.

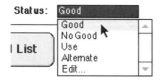

10. (Option) If you know that you want to print out the shot you just logged when printing cards or lists, click the Print Card checkbox. You can also do this later, after you log and review all the shots.

11. Press Command-N for each new shot, and repeat steps 1 through 10 for each additional shot.

Sorting and Printing Logs and Transcripts

The bottom section of the Shot Log Entry or Log/Transcript Entry form includes options for sorting and printing the logs in various ways.

Printouts:

In most cases you should click a sort option to put the records into the order that you want before previewing and printing. In Shot Log Entry, you can sort by reel, timecode IN, file name, or status (good, no good, etc.). In Log/Transcript Entry you can also sort by subject.

You can also use the find/sort capabilities of Filemaker to reorganize the records in many other ways. For more information, see your Filemaker Pro documentation.

After sorting, click a printout option:

• Click Index cards to find all records with the Print Card checkbox selected, and then preview a layout designed for A6 size index cards. After checking the layout preview, choose Print from the File menu to print the cards.

- Click Full List to preview a layout containing all shot log data, designed for letter-size paper. Information is ordered according to any sort you performed previously. After checking, choose Print from the File menu to print the list.

Full List layout

Project:	**Religion in America**					6/29/99
Reel	**Record #**	**File Name**	**Subject**	**Status**	**Content**	
01	15	Rel01-15	dorchester service	Good	**Description:** CU woman with drum	
TC IN: 01:50:13:00	**TC OUT:** 01:50:19:00					
Duration: 00:06					**Transcript:** Natural SOT	
					Comments:	
01	16	Rel01-16	dorchester service	Good	**Description:** CU black man singing	
TC IN: 01:50:20:00	**TC OUT:** 01:50:28:00					
Duration: 00:08					**Transcript:** Natural SOT	
					Comments:	
01	17	Rel01-17	dorchester service		**Description:** WS group, singing	
TC IN: 01:50:30:00	**TC OUT:** 01:50:45:00					
Duration: 00:15					**Transcript:** Natural SOT	
					Comments:	
22	19	Rel22-19	Rev. Wall and McMullen	Good	**Description:** CU Rev. Wall and McMullen	
TC IN: 02:37:40:00	**TC OUT:** 02:37:51:00					
Duration: 00:11					**Transcript:** INTERVIEW I'd say it's changed from a church that may have been focusing in on one ethnic group to try and be more inclusive.	
					Comments:	

• Click Transcript Only to preview a layout containing basic shot log data plus the transcript of field-recorded sound. Information is ordered according to any sorting you performed previously. After checking the preview, choose Print from the File menu to print the list.

Transcript layout

Transcript					6/29/99
Project: Religion in America				**Talent: Peter**	

Reel	Record #	File Name	Subject	Status	Transcript:
22	19	Rel22-19	Rev. Wall and McMullen	Alternate	INTERVIEW I'd say it's changed from a church that may have been focusing in on one ethnic group to try and be more inclusive.
TC IN: 02:37:40:00 **TC OUT:** 02:37:51:00					
Duration: 00:11					
22	20	Rel22-20	Rev. Wall and McMullen	Good	INTERVIEW Too many churches would say we're gonna stay with our own kind, we're gonna stay with the fold with the founders of the church, and we're not gonna branch out too much. But if you do not minister to the neighborhood you will begin to die. So that's one of the main challenges this church has undergone in the last decade.
TC IN: 02:38:05:00 **TC OUT:** 02:38:24:00					
Duration: 00:19					
22	27	Rel22-27	Rev. Wall and McMullen	Good	INTERVIEW We have Asian Americans, we have people from the South Shore, North Shore..we're developing a large college community that has come as a result of the after school programs we have here. College kids come to minister to young people and then say let's actually be a part of the church.
TC IN: 02:38:28:00 **TC OUT:** 02:38:50:00					
Duration: 00:22					
22	28	Rel22-28	Rev. Wall and McMullen	Use	INTERVIEW We see so many white and black families coming and wanting to be a part and it's not more white or more black, it's just an even flow of people coming in...
TC IN: 02:38:53:00 **TC OUT:** 02:39:18:00					
Duration: 00:25					

- Click Shot Log Only to preview a layout containing all shot log data without a transcript of field-recorded sound. Information is ordered according to any sorting you performed previously. After checking the preview, choose Print from the File menu to print the list.

Shot Log layout

Shot Log								6/29/99
Project: Religion in America						**Talent:**		
Reel	**Record #**	**File Name**	**TC IN:**	**TC OUT:**	**Duration:**	**Subject**		**Status**
01	9	Rel01-9	01:49:14:00	01:49:20:00	00:06	Dorchester service		Good
01	10	Rel01-10	01:49:26:00	01:49:30:00	00:04	dorchester service		Alternate
01	11	Rel01-11	01:49:43:00	01:49:53:00	00:10	dorchester service		Use
01	12	Rel01-12	01:49:43:00	01:49:49:00	00:06	dorchester service		Good
01	13	Rel01-13	01:49:55:00	01:50:04:00	00:09	dorchester service		Good
01	14	Rel01-14	01:50:05:00	01:50:11:00	00:06	dorchester service		Good
01	15	Rel01-15	01:50:13:00	01:50:19:00	00:06	dorchester service		No Good
01	16	Rel01-16	01:50:20:00	01:50:28:00	00:08	dorchester service		Good
01	17	Rel01-17	01:50:30:00	01:50:45:00	00:15	dorchester service		Use
22	19	Rel22-19	02:37:40:00	02:37:51:00	00:11	Rev. Wall and McMullen		Alternate
22	20	Rel22-20	02:38:05:00	02:38:24:00	00:19	Rev. Wall and McMullen		Good
23	22	Rel23-22	03:56:20:00	03:56:40:00	00:20	kids choir		Good
23	23	Rel23-23	03:56:42:00	03:56:50:00	00:08	kids choir		Use
23	24	Rel23-24	03:56:59:00	03:57:02:00	00:03	kids choir		Good
23	25	Rel23-25	03:57:08:00	03:57:18:00	00:10	kids choir		Alternate
23	26	Rel23-26	03:58:01:00	03:58:14:00	00:13	kids choir		Use

Exporting to a Nonlinear Editor

After entering shot log information into the Advanced Project Templates you can easily export your logs for use in popular nonlinear editing systems.

Two layouts are provided to meet the specifications of the Avid Log Exchange format for import into Avid products, as well as a text file format for import into Adobe Premiere's batch capture window.

To customize the export for use in other nonlinear systems, see your Filemaker Pro documentation.

Exporting to an Avid System

To export to an Avid system:

1. In Shot Log Entry or Log/Transcript Entry, click the Prepare Export button to find only those clips that were selected for capture, and sort them according to Reel and Timecode. This sort order is optimal for batch capture in Premiere.

2. Choose Avid Log Export from the Layout pop-up menu.

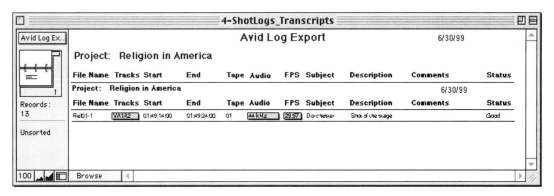

The Avid Log Export form displays your records roughly in a format in which they will appear when imported into a bin in the Avid system.

3. Three entries appear in blue for each record: tracks, audio format, and FPS (frames-per-second). These entries were added automatically when you logged your clips. You can override the defaults for these entries by choosing another option from each of these pop-up menus.

   For example, you can choose to capture only video for a particular clip by choosing V from the Tracks popup menu.

   FPS is a global entry, and will change for all clips when you choose an option. Choices are 29.97 fps for NTSC, or 25 fps for PAL.

3. Go to Preview mode to preview the log and make sure all the correct information appears.

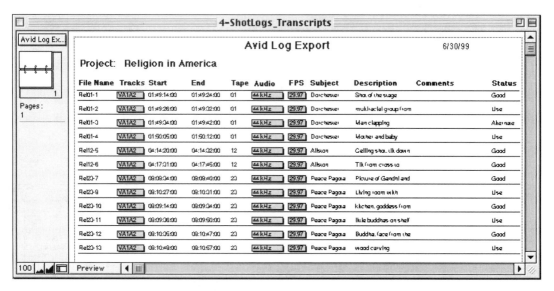

4. Choose Export Records from the Import/Export submenu of the File menu.

5. Name the file and choose Tab-Separated Text as the type, then click Save. The Export Field Order dialog box appears.

6. In the Export Field Order dialog box, move the appropriate headings into the right column as shown. The specific headings must be in this order for the export to work.

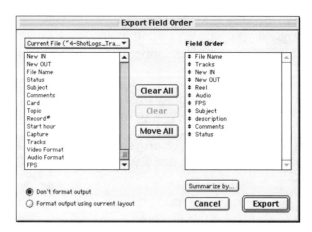

7. Click Export to complete the export.

8. Open the newly exported file containing your shot log entries. Select and copy all of the entries.

9. On the desktop, open the text file labeled AvidLogTemplate located in the folder containing the Advanced Project Templates. This file contains additional formatting required for Avid Log Exchange compatibility.

10. (Option) If you are working in a PAL project, replace the global entry for VIDEO-FORMAT from NTSC to PAL (located under Headings in the upper portion of the file contents).

11. Click and drag to select the entire paragraph located below the word Data.

12. Paste the text you copied from the exported file into the selected area of the AvidLog template.

    Alternatively, working in SimpleText on the Macintosh you can delete the paragraph of text below Data in the AvidLog template, and then drag and drop the contents of the exported shot log file directly into the template as shown below.

    Drag-and-drop method
    Drag the contents of the exported file into the AvidLogTemplate file.

13. From the File menu in the revised AvidLogTemplate file, choose Save As, type a new name for the file (add the extension .ALE so that the Avid system can recognize the file), and click Save.

The file is ready for import into an Avid system.

After you import the shot log into the Avid system, make sure you save the custom bin view created to include your custom headings such as Status and Subject.

Exporting to Adobe Premiere

To export to Premiere:

1. In Shot Log Entry or Log/Transcript Entry, click the Prepare Export button to find only those clips that were selected for capture, and sort them according to Reel and Timecode. This sort order is optimal for batch capture in Premiere.

2. Choose Premiere Export from the Layout pop-up menu.

The Premiere Export form displays your records roughly in a format in which they will appear when imported into the Batch Capture window in Premiere.

3. Go to Preview mode to preview the log and make sure all the correct information appears.

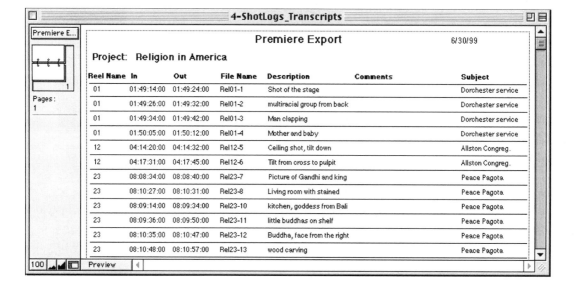

4. Choose Export Records from the Import/Export submenu of the File menu.

5. Name the file and choose Tab-Separated Text as the type, then click Save (add the extension .TXT so that the file can be recognized on a Windows system).

   The Export Field Order dialog box appears.

6. In the Export Field Order dialog box, move the appropriate headings into the right column as shown.

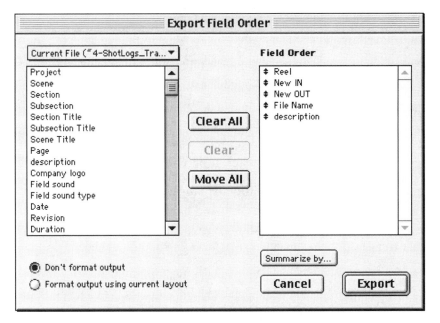

The first four headings must be in this order for the export to work with Premiere's default layout for the Batch Capture window. However, the fifth entry becomes a simple text entry in the Comments column in Premiere, and thus can be any item you want to include, such as Comments, Description, Status, etc.

7. Click Export to complete the export.

   The file is ready for import into Premiere.

Scripting Tips and Tricks

Through the Advanced Project Templates we attempt to show that the database model provides the greatest flexibility and versatility for logging and building scripts. However, if you are most comfortable working with a word processing application like Microsoft Word, there are other ways to take advantage of a desktop computer or laptop when building your scripts. Using the following tips and techniques with a word processing application, you can begin to cut down on the repetitive tasks and duplication of effort that occur during this crucial stage.

Here are some suggestions:

- Build a template or series of template files for your scripts in formats that you frequently use. For example, create a two-column table with appropriate text formatting for a typical A/V script. You can automate such things as entries for revision and date, and add a company logo if appropriate. Use these templates rather than rebuilding a new script each time you start a new project.

- Using the drag-and-drop capabilities of an application like Microsoft Word, you can log and transcribe in the application, and then literally select blocks of text in the logs and drag them into cells in the script table to place them in your script. Note that formatting of the text in the log file gets carried over into the script file; therefore, make sure you format the log text as you want it to appear in the final script to save time.

- With some careful study of the database conventions used in your favorite nonlinear editor, you can easily generate logs directly from a word processing application that can be imported into the system.

- When in the edit room, bring a laptop containing all your source logs and scripts with you. Working electronically, you can quickly find material, or make quick adjustments on the spur of the moment. The Find capability of your application will become your best friend, as you enter that one obscure phrase you remember from the interview into the Find dialog and then watch it appear instantly on your screen.

Script Integration: Discovering Avid's Hidden Jewel

If you frequently edit material in video-based editing systems from Avid Technology, you can take advantage of an excellent tool that is overlooked by most video producers, Script Integration.

The technology used in Script Integration has a long history going back to the Ediflex systems of the early 1980s. The basic concept is easy to understand by any hard-pressed producer: what if you could place your script directly in front of the editor, with all the source clips and editing information tied directly to their locations in the script? Sounds too good to be true, but this capability already exists in most Avid systems.

Unfortunately for the video producer, Avid's implementation of Script Integration is geared more toward digital filmmaking, which is one reason why video editors rarely use it. Based on the conventions of the lined script — which evolved during decades of trial and error in Hollywood — Script Integration is known well and used frequently on the west coast to provide editors with the coverage they need to edit scenes in a film or television show. It's time the rest of the production community made this important discovery.

Script Integration goes beyond the lined script to provide plenty of visual clues and interactive advantages for the editor. For example, "slates" appear for shots that are associated with the script, providing a preview of each shot. Script Integration also uses "script marks" to indicate points where lines in the script are linked directly to cue points in a clip. Double-clicking a script mark automatically loads and cues the footage to the appropriate frame. Color coding is also available to flag various types of shots and takes. If well prepared, a Script bin in an Avid system is like the ultimate storyboard, one that wires the editor to all source material directly from a fully interactive visual map.

It's important to note that Script Integration is available as an option on offline Avid systems as well as in Avid Xpress. For video producers, taking the time to learn more about Script Integration can be a big time-saver, especially on complex projects. In general, preparing a Script bin for an editor requires extra time prior to editing, but if you make the effort it can save you a significant amount of time where it really counts, in an expensive edit suite. And with a fully prepared Script bin, most experienced editors would find it possible to edit an entire program entirely on their own.

In larger production environments such as news-magazine shows for example, Script Integration can be used to literally revolutionize the logistics and finances of the production process. Here's a scenario.

Building the Virtual Rough Cut

A truly effective scripting solution should allow the producer to create a blueprint of the sequence that the editor can start out with the minute the edit session begins.

If producers were given access to an offline system from Avid that includes Script Integration, the scripting process could be taken one step further, allowing the producer, production assistant, or assistant editor to create a "virtual rough cut" on the offline system, based upon logged information and scripts. The assistant producer, assistant editor, or producer could import the final script into a Script bin in an Avid system, digitize the shot logs, then link up clips directly to locations in the script. Music and sound effects could also be dropped onto appropriate locations in the script.

The following is an example of an audio/visual script for a news-magazine piece, imported into the script window with most of the features of Script Integration applied.

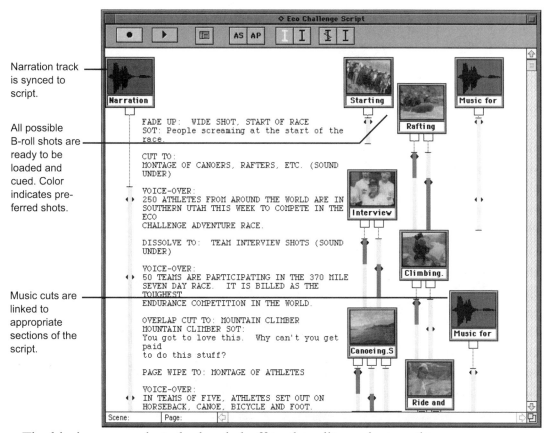

Narration track is synced to script.

All possible B-roll shots are ready to be loaded and cued. Color indicates preferred shots.

Music cuts are linked to appropriate sections of the script.

The bin is now ready to be handed off to the editor, who can then open the bin and instantly begin to assemble shot after shot. Quickly building a rough cut, the editor has more time to fine-tune the transitions and timing between shots, create overlap edits, clean up the audio, add layers and effects, and try out alternative shots.

Working with the script and all alternative shots right in front of him or her, the editor no longer needs the producer around to "translate" the script. This in itself would be a mini-revolution, eliminating the duplication of responsibilities in the edit room. This process can eliminate at last the need for producers to sit in the edit room throughout an edit session. In fact, it would be quite possible for the producer to simply review the sequence at various stages, make comments, and go away again. For independent producers working with a production house, this means that they could conceivably arrive at the facility toward the end, after the editor has already created a couple of alternative sequences.

Completing the Paradigm

To complete the new paradigm, Script Integration can be integrated into the team production environment. In many news-magazine environments, for example, teams of editors and producers work side by side to complete segments.

With three segments in one half-hour show, the daily post-production load of a news-magazine show — using analog scripting and editing methods — might require three fully equipped Betacam edit bays, with a producer and an editor working a full day on each segment, as shown:

By contrast a digital, networked environment could conceivably accomplish the same work with the following scenario:

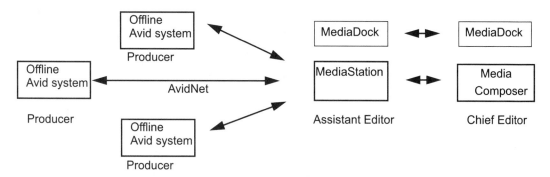

The workflow suggested in this diagram would go as follows:

1. Each producer transfers his or her logs to an assistant editor when finished logging. (In this scenario, the assistant editor acts as the media manager and liason throughout post-production between the producers and the chief editor.)

2. The assistant editor, using MediaStation, receives the files, digitizes the clips at a low resolution, and sends the media back to the producer.

3. The producer, equipped with an offline system with Script Integration, imports their script into a Script bin and links up the source clips based on notes. The producer returns these to the assistant editor when finished.

4. The assistant editor then passes the bins and media to the chief editor's online system. The chief editor then constructs the rough cut, and refines the sequence.

5. When finished, the chief editor sends a consolidated sequence back to the assistant editor for distribution and review by the director, show producer, and managing editors.

6. Any changes to the sequences can be quickly implemented in the nonlinear environment.

7. After all changes are complete, the chief editor hands off the bins to the assistant editor, who then redigitizes the sequence at a broadcast-quality resolution in preparation for sending it to air.

To summarize, a day of editing for a magazine show in the digital environment compares to the analog environment as follows:

Table 6-3: News Magazine Resources (1 half-hour show)

Production Requirement	Analog Environment	Digital Environment
Edit script preparation	3 desktop systems with word processors	3 offline systems with Script Integration
Editing supervision	3 producers	0 producers
Editing	3 editors	1 editor
Assistant editing	0 assistant editors	1 assistant editor
Edit facilities	3 Betacam suites	1 Media Composer suite
Digitizing	Not applicable	1 MediaStation Assistant
Networking	Not applicable	AvidNet Peer-to-Peer
Media storage/ transfer	(Betacam decks and tapes)	2 MediaDocks

For independent producers, a carefully prepared script bin can be taken directly into the online suite, bypassing the offline phase altogether in many cases. Without an EDL the online phase might take a little longer, but this would be offset by the overall savings in terms of time and money.

Table 6-4: Independent Project Resources (half-hour documentary)

Production Phase	Analog Environment	Digital Environment
Scripting	4 days (desktop system with word processor)	4 days (desktop system with word processor)

Production Phase	Analog Environment	Digital Environment
Edit script preparation	1 day (desktop system with word processor)	1 day (offline system with Script Integration)
Offline Edit	5 days (offline system)	None
Online edit	2 days (attended)	2 days (mostly unattended)
TOTALS	**12 days**	**7 days**

In addition to saving resources, the nonlinear digital environment also makes the editor's job more creative, with more room for experimentation and revision. In the analog environment, segments are usually put together one brick at a time throughout the day, with no time left for changes.

There are a few special requirements, however, to making this all work:

- Avid systems must be available with Script Integration. Most Media Composer systems since the mid-90's include the option. Also, editors must know how to use it, or be willing to learn it.

- Producers should have some degree of access to offline systems equipped with Script Integration. You can also buy the option for Avid systems that don't come equipped with it, such as Avid Xpress or Media Composer Offline.

Project Template Workshop: Preparing Final Edit Scripts

At the scripting phase you can reap the full benefits of the Advanced Project Templates. Script development in the templates resolves one of the fundamental weaknesses of the digital producer's workflow by seamlessly integrating the content of the shot logs with the script content.

The Script Entry form also allows you to continue building on an outline or storyboard you started previously (see "Project Template Workshop: Preparing Proposals and Outlines" on page 34 and "Project Template Workshop: Preparing Storyboards" on page 51). You can also begin your work in the templates at the scripting stage directly.

Before You Prepare a Final Script

If you prepared logs using the Advanced Project Templates, the following steps are recommended before starting your work in the Script Entry form:

1. Print out the logged elements from the file 4-ShotLogs_Transcripts onto index cards, as described in "Sorting and Printing Logs and Transcripts" on page 151. Use the checkboxes on the cards in a process of elimination to begin roughing out the order of elements in the final script.

2. Return to the logs/transcripts template and add notes you made regarding which shots to capture. Print out final logs or export files for import into a nonlinear editing system.

3. In the Script Entry form, use the notes on the index cards to automatically call up and organize the clips and sound bites you want, as described in the following sections.

If you prepared logs with another logging application, you can also import those logs into the Advanced Project Templates file named 4-ShotLogs_Transcripts for use in preparing a script. For more information on importing files, see your Filemaker Pro documentation.

Using the Script Entry Form

Open the file labeled 2-Scripts_Storyboards. Choose Script Entry from the pop-up menu. The following window appears:

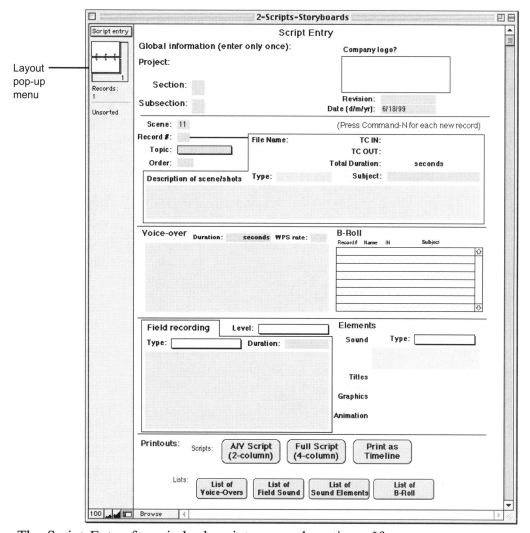

The Script Entry form is broken into several sections. If you are working with logs/transcripts that you developed in the templates, the areas outlined in gray include information that you can automatically import from the shot logs. If you did not create shot logs in the templates, you can also enter this information manually.

If you already created logs and transcripts in the templates, your work at the scripting stage is basically cut in half. In this case you work primarily in the areas of the Script Entry form that are not gray, by adding voice-overs and information about B-roll, sound, and graphics elements as you go along.

In most cases you should keep voice-overs that you write and transcript items from the shot logs (sound bites, for example) as separate records; if you add a transcript record, for example, and then enter voice-over text into the same record, the two items will appear to occur at the same time in the script or timeline printout.

Entering Global Information in Script Entry

To begin a script you should first enter global information for the project. If you already entered global information previously, you can skip this section. If you are just beginning project development with script entry, you enter global information into the upper section of the form as described in "Entering Global Information" on page 53.

Importing Scenes from the Outline

If you already imported scenes when creating a storyboard in the templates, you can skip this section.

If you developed an outline in the Advanced Project Templates as described in "Project Template Workshop: Preparing Proposals and Outlines" on page 34, you can enter project name, section, and sub-section information automatically for each record as a starting point. Once you import the outline records you can change them, delete them, or add additional records in the Script/Storyboard templates as needed.

For more information, see "Importing Scenes from the Outline" on page 54.

Preparing the Topic Sequence

If you prepared shot logs and transcript items using the index card printouts from the 5-ShotLogs_Transcripts file, you began to organize the records by topic areas and their order within the topic areas. You use these same topic areas to determine the flow of your final script.

To prepare the Script Entry form with topics, click the Topics pop-up list and choose Edit.

1. Type a list of topics that will be covered in the script, as noted on the index cards or in your outlines. These can be specific topics, or generic headings like Segment One, Segment Two, etc. Add numbers to the beginning of each name to determine their order of appearance in the script, otherwise they will sort alphabetically.

   These topic names do not appear in the final scripts. They are used behind the scenes to find and sort records when generating the scripts.

   You can reorder the topics at any time by repeating this procedure and renumbering the topics in the dialog box.

Adding Records from the Shot Logs

If you prepared logs and transcripts in the file named 5-ShotLogs_Transcripts, you can add the shot log records that you want to the script as follows:

1. Using the Index card printouts from the 5-ShotLogs_Transcripts file, type the record number for each shot into the Record # box.

   Items in the gray areas of the form automatically fill in with any information that exists in the shot log record.

2. Choose the topic area for each record from the Topic pop-up list, based on the notes you added to the index card printouts from the 5-ShotLogs_Transcripts file.

3. Enter the numerical order of the record within the topic area in the Order box, based on the notes you added to the index card printouts from the 5-ShotLogs_Transcripts file.

   You can reorder the topics at any time by changing the numbers in the Order box.

Adding Voice-Overs

When you enter voice-over text in the Advanced Project Templates, you can automatically calculate the duration of the voice-over by entering a word-per-second rate.

In most cases you should make a new record for all voice-over entries, rather than typing voice-overs into existing records containing transcript content from the field. This allows you to keep them separate in the final script.

To add voice-overs to the script:

1. (Recommended) Create a new record.

2. Choose a word-per-second rate for the voice-over from the WPS rate pop-up list.

   The WPS rate entry is persistent: it will remain the same for all new records until you change it.

3. Enter voice-over text into the Voice-over text box.

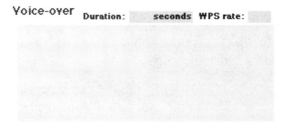

The approximate duration of the voice-over is calculated automatically.

If the information you enter extends beyond the size of the text box, a scroll bar appears allowing you to enter and view as much information as necessary.

4. Determine the placement of the voice-over in the flow of the script by choosing a topic area from the Topic pop-up list, and entering an ordering number into the Order box.

Adding Transcript Information

If you did not create shot logs in the file named 5-ShotLogs_Transcripts, you can create new records and enter the information manually in the Field Recording area of the Script Entry form.

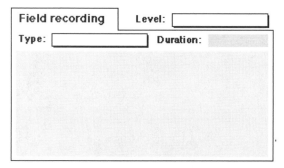

If you imported records from the shot logs/transcripts, you can add a basic note to your scripts regarding volume level for the sound by choosing UNDER (sound under) or FULL (sound full) from the Level pop-up list.

Adding B-Roll to Accompany Voice-Over

If you created shot logs in the file named 5-ShotLogs_Transcripts, you can quickly add a series of alternative B-roll shots that will appear next to voice-over on the script.

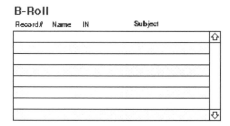

To add B-roll shots from the shot logs, click in the Record # column and type a record number for a shot.

The name, timecode INpoint, and subject of the shot appear automatically. This information also appears in the final script.

Adding Sound and Visual Effects to the Script

The Elements area of the Script Entry form allows you to add sound and visual effects information to the script. These elements will appear in the script along with any voice-over or transcript information that exists in the same record:

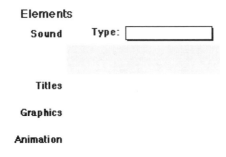

- For sound elements (music cuts, sound FX, etc.) choose the type of sound from the pop-up menu, then type the name, source information, or description in the text box.

- For titles, type the text content of the title into the text box.

- For graphics elements, type the name, source information, or description in the text box.

Previewing and Printing Scripts

The bottom section of the Script Entry form includes several options for sorting and printing out your script.

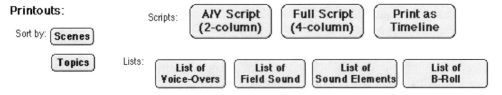

Before printing, find and sort the topics according to the type of script you are preparing:

- Click Sort by: Scenes to find and sort all records according to section, subsection, and scene. This method of sorting is useful when scripting in advance (prior to shooting), for development of a multimedia or corporate video project, for example.

- Click Sort by: Topics to find and sort all records according to entries for Topic and Order. This method of sorting is useful when scripting after a shoot, for a documentary, or news-magazine project, for example.

  Do one of the following to preview and print a script:

- Click A/V Script (2-column) to preview a two-column script that contains visual description in one column and voice-over or sound-on-tape transcript in the second column.

  The A/V script is suitable for the traditional uses of the script for review of the narrative, or for the early stages of script development.

Project: **Religion in America**	**Script**	**Date:** 6/29/99
		Revision: 2.1

Talent: Mary

Video	*Audio*
inside temple, buddhist sister	Natural SOT SOUND FULL
	buddhist sister chanting and beating drum
	Rel22-20 02:38:05:00 Duration: 19 seconds
DISSOLVE TO	THERE IS A SEARCH GOING ON. IN INNER CITY NEIGHBORHOODS AND AFFLUENT SUBURBS. A SEARCH THAT BEGINS WITH A QUESTION AS OLD AS TIME.
2 Rel01-2 01:49:26:00 Dorchester service	
7 Rel23-7 08:08:34:00 Peace Pagota	5
6 Rel12-6 04:17:31:00 Allston Congreg.	
	Duration: seconds
CUT TO	INTERVIEW SOUND FULL
Rev. Peterson on camera	People are beginning to ask once again, what is the role of religion, what is the ultimate meaing in my life?
	Rel22-27 02:38:28:00 Duration: 10 seconds
CUT TO	SOME FIND THAT MEANING IN THE ANCIENT TEACHINGS OF THE EAST. OTHERS IN THE TRADITIONS OF THE WEST. MEANING THAT UPWARD MOBILITY OFTEN DOESN'T PROVIDE.
1 Rel01-1 01:49:14:00 Dorchester service	
5 Rel12-5 04:14:20:00 Allston Congreg.	MUSIC
3 Rel01-3 01:49:34:00 Dorchester service	Disc 5, cut 7
	Duration: 5 seconds
CUT TO	INTERVIEW SOUND FULL
Rev. Wall on camera	We've tried moving to suburbia. You know, let's get out of the city, let's go to suburbia. And people are still hurting.
	Rel22-28 02:38:53:00 Duration: 25 seconds
DISSOLVE TO	STAND-UP SOUND FULL
Mary on Camera	CHURCH SHOPPING IS NOT A NEW CONCEPT. HISTORIANS SAY IT GOES BACK TO THE EARLY 19TH CENTURY. WHAT IS NEW IS WHAT PEOPLE ARE SHOPPING FOR. AS BABY BOOMERS REACH MIDDLE AGE AND TRY TO RAISE SPIRITUAL CHILDREN, THEY'RE OPTING FOR MORE INDEPENDENT, LESS STRUCTURED SETTINGS THAN SEEKERS OF THE PAST.
3 Rel01-3 01:49:34:00 Dorchester service	
7 Rel23-7 08:08:34:00 Peace Pagota	
5 Rel12-5 04:14:20:00 Allston Congreg.	
	Duration: 0 seconds

- Click Full Script (4-column) to preview a four-column script that adds two more columns to the A/V script: a third column for music and sound effects and a fourth column for visual effects such as titles, graphics, and animation.

Project: Religion in America	Script	Date: 6/29/99
Talent: Mary		Revision: 2.1

Video	*Audio*	*Music/SFX*	*Titles/Graphics*
inside temple, buddhist sister	Natural SOT SOUND FULL buddhist sister chanting and beating drum Rel22-20 02:38:05:00 19 seconds		
DISSOLVE TO			
(video clip entries)	THERE IS A SEARCH GOING ON. IN INNER CITY NEIGHBORHOODS AND AFFLUENT SUBURBS. A SEARCH THAT BEGINS WITH A QUESTION AS OLD AS TIME. 5 seconds		Graphic overlay: map
CUT TO			
Rev. Peterson on camera	INTERVIEW SOUND FULL People are beginning to ask once again, what is the role of religion, what is the ultimate meaing in my life? Rel22-27 02:38:28:00 10 seconds		Rev. Rodney Peterson
CUT TO			
(video clip entries)	SOME FIND THAT MEANING IN THE ANCIENT TEACHINGS OF THE EAST. OTHERS IN THE TRADITIONS OF THE WEST. MEANING THAT UPWARD MOBILITY OFTEN DOESN'T PROVIDE. 5 seconds	MUSIC Disc 5, cut 7	Matte key effect
CUT TO			
Rev. Wall on camera	INTERVIEW SOUND FULL We've tried moving to suburbia. You know, let's get out of the city, let's go to suburbia. And people are still hurting. Rel22-28 02:38:53:00 25 seconds		Rev. Bruce Wall

- Click Print Timeline to preview a unique five-column script that is specifically designed for the needs of the "digital producer" at the post-production stage. Turned on its side, the columns of this script make a rough correspondence with the five basic tracks of video and audio that might appear in the timeline of a nonlinear editing system: V2 for titles and visual effects, V1 for video, A1 for corresponding sound-on-tape, A2 for voice-over, and A3 for music and sound effects.

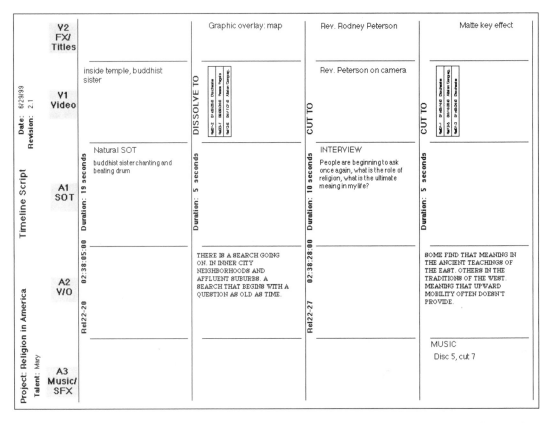

Use this script in the edit room and give a copy to the editor, who will easily understand the layout and could easily work alone on the program for long periods with this script.

Making Digital Post Decisions

Time and money — the producer's twin burden — are two sides of the same coin. How accurately you schedule the post-production process will definitely affect your bottom line.

During preparation for a nonlinear editing project, you need to rethink the time it takes to do certain tasks (such as logging and online editing) and build into the schedule certain tasks unique to nonlinear editing (such as digitizing footage).

Scheduling

How much time does it take to post on a nonlinear editing system compared to the linear model?

- **Less time**, if you plan well and don't expect to do much experimentation.

  The same set of instructions will take less time on a nonlinear editing system than on a linear system. If you have limited time and/or money and if you plan well, editing on the nonlinear system can take significantly less time than on a linear system.

- **Same amount of time**, but you can create a better program.

  In the time you used to assemble a sequential rough cut, you can experiment, revise, and refine.

- **More time**, if you do no planning, provide no guidance, demand an extreme level of refinement, or get lost in endless revisions.

It's easy to become seduced by the power and flexibility of the nonlinear editing system, so it's particularly crucial to plan the scope of your edit before it begins. As producer, avoid too little involvement in or too much micro-management of the edit.

If you do a nonlinear offline, you should save a lot of time at the online, whether you use a linear or nonlinear online system. That's because you have made more decisions in the nonlinear offline than you would have on a linear offline system.

Point of View

Nonlinear's great selling point is that it allows people to tinker with the show whenever they want. The drawback is they're allowed to tinker with the show whenever they want. You used to have to spend more time talking them out of last minute changes because if the change involved taking five seconds out of the middle of the show, you just shuddered as an editor.

But the real answer to [how long it takes to bring a project to a close] is the same for linear or nonlinear. Deadlines and budget decide this. I'll keep tweaking the program for as long as the producer likes, but at some point he has to let go. Either the show has to air, or he's run out of money. Next week I'm making changes to a show that I thought I finished three months ago. Those shows with no deadlines are the most "dangerous."

— Arnie Harchik, Avid editor

Determining Your Offline/Online Strategy

In the traditional linear model of post-production, you would choose to do the offline edit to work out all your editing decisions before going into the more costly linear online suite. Or if your program were simple or short enough, you could go right to the online, bypassing the offline phase.

When you edit using the nonlinear model, you have similar choices, though the specific methods differ somewhat. Here, for example, you can choose to work out all your editing decisions on a nonlinear offline system, and then conform your work in either a linear online suite or on a nonlinear online suite.

For many years they typical model was to offline on a nonlinear system and online in a tape-based linear online suite, mostly because the image quality of the compressed media could not match the quality of the final master produced on tape, even with some generation loss.

In recent years this situation has changed dramatically. Uncompressed, D1 quality video is quickly becoming standard on many nonlinear editing systems. Combining uncompressed media with increasingly sophisticated effects and corrective capabilities, a new crop of computer-based systems is destined to gradually replace the tape-based online suites over the course of the next ten years. As a result, your choices when planning an edit have grown more complex.

Offline and online nonlinear editing systems differ by image quality, number of video and audio tracks, and effects and titling capabilities, among other features. When you choose the offline and online systems, you want to match the system with the needs of your project.

Onlining on a Nonlinear Editing System

Until recently, it was assumed that you would need to use a linear online suite, either to build your video from scratch or to conform the offline edit. Many producers now finish their projects on the nonlinear system and output the master directly to videotape.

You might ask yourself the following questions when evaluating whether to use an online nonlinear editing system to finish your video and/or audio:

- Is there any noticeable difference between the image quality of the source footage and the digitized footage at 2:1 compression or 1:1 (uncompressed)?

- Can you create all video effects and titles?

- Does your program include nested effects (effects layered inside of other effects)? If so, how many layers are nested?

- Can you input all effects created on third-party software?

- Can you mix some or all of your audio in the system?

- Do you want the consistency of using the same editor for the offline and online edit?

  In many cases the same editor who does the offline edit also does the online on the nonlinear system.

If you have an offline nonlinear system, you can save money by doing the offline edit on that system, and then renting an online nonlinear editing system to finish your program.

Point of View

[The number one advantage of nonlinear online] is just having everything in one digital nonlinear format, coming from a variety of different places into one packaging suite. The elements of every FRONTLINE include the documentary itself, which is onlined nonlinearly; the packaging elements such as the FRONTLINE logo and lower third IDs; and any opening and closing PBS elements that have to be added. Having all of the elements in one digital nonlinear format allows us to work with them in a more seamless way, making it easier to package the program.

Another advantage is that it is much easier getting the show to time. All of our hour-long shows have to be exactly 56 minutes and 46 seconds. When you're in a linear online, you get to the end and find out you're 15 frames long or 20 seconds short. You have to figure out where to make the edits, and you make compromises, because you don't want to re-lay the whole show. So a great advantage is that it allows you to move things around easily.

— *Tim Mangini, production manager, FRONTLINE*

Planning for Audio

Audio is often the most overlooked piece of the post-production puzzle. But be forewarned: you neglect the requirements of audio at your own peril. Poor planning for your audio needs can end up costing you unexpected delays and expenses.

You can decide independently how to finish your audio — on the nonlinear editing system or at an audio post facility, depending on the type of project.

For example, when editing a documentary with a simple set of audio tracks including narration, sound-on-tape, and music, you can save a big chunk of time and expense by handling the audio carefully at full audio quality during nonlinear offline editing, and then transfer the tracks directly at the online phase and conform the video only.

Audio media consumes much less disk storage than video media, and the difference between the storage needs of 44.1 kHz and 48 kHz audio rates is negligible. Therefore, you needn't be as concerned with the audio rate as the video compression ratio, or with digitizing one versus two tracks of audio.

For more complex projects requiring careful mixing of multiple tracks, you have a similar choice between taking your audio to the traditional analog mixing suite, or finding a facility that uses a digital audio workstation (DAW) such as Digidesign ProTools or Audio-Vision to keep your mix in the digital realm. As in the video world, sound designers are increasingly turning to the nonlinear benefits of a new breed of computer-based tools.

Point of View

One thing to consider when you are digitizing, even for the rough cut, is that the audio going into the system may be your final audio. So when you are working in low-res [low resolution] video you are actually working with online audio. For a lot of my projects, we take the audio we originally digitized for the rough cut and use that audio in the mix.

To get good quality audio when you digitize, you need to get a clean signal from the deck to the Avid. I try to monitor the levels while I am digitizing which means I don't leave a digitize unattended. As long as the levels in your final rough cut sequence are clean and consistent, that audio should be fine for ultimately outputting to the mix. When you're ready to finish the program, such as an hour-long documentary, you only need to redigitize the video at a higher online resolution. This can save you hours of online time.

— Arnie Harchik, Avid editor

If you do choose to go completely digital with audio, take full advantage of this path by checking for compatibility between systems and making sure that you or your editor uses the proper procedures for exporting and reimporting the tracks between workstations to avoid any unexpected complications or degradation of the material.

Calculating Media Storage Requirements

Another one of the producer's often overlooked considerations during post-production is storage. In traditional tape-based editing, the only storage the producer needed to worry about was which box (or boxes) would be sufficient for carrying the tapes around. Along with its many advantages, nonlinear editing does require some added effort in calculating the needs of disk-based storage for your digitized media.

When you digitize a clip, the nonlinear editing system creates a separate media file for each track of video and audio data. Media files require a substantial amount of storage space, and thus are stored in most cases on separate, external hard drives. Because storage is a limited resource and your editor might charge drive storage fees, you need to do some careful planning before the editing process begins. Once your media is digitized, the drives containing the digitized footage are also the first resource you have for moving your media from one location to another. Another option is to transfer your media over a high-speed network when available, a method that is becoming increasingly common as production facilities and their networks continue to improve.

Selecting the Video Resolution

In addition to the physical resources required for storing digital media, the producer must also consider the various ways in which the media can be compressed.

Your choice of image resolution (compression ratio) affects the size of the media files. You should choose the resolution that gives you the best combination of file size and image quality needed for the job.

The number of resolutions available on your nonlinear editing system depends on the type of system and the available options. The types of resolutions include: single-field resolutions, two-field resolutions, and uncompressed media.

On Avid systems you can choose a single-field resolution, so that the system digitizes only one field for each frame of video (each frame of recorded video contains two interlaced fields). Digitizing one field can save considerable storage space. Most systems also enable you to compress the media during digitizing. When the system compresses media, it removes some of the information about the image, resulting in lower quality but also reduced storage demands.

If you do not require high-quality output, select the a resolution that will comfortably fit in your disk drive(s), making sure to calculate additional storage requirements for effects, imported elements, and so on.

One common strategy for conserving disk space is to use a low resolution for the media during offline editing, and then redigitize the final sequence at the finishing stage at the high resolution for output.

(For more information, see "Determining Your Offline/Online Strategy" on page 180.)

Two common ways of referring to compression are to state a ratio or to state the number of kilobytes (KB) of information that are stored for each frame. For example, the ratio 1:1 indicates that the video is uncompressed, whereas a ratio of 15:1 indicates a significant amount of compression. Or, in terms of kilobytes, two-field video captured at 200 KB per frame is roughly broadcast quality, while the same video captured at 33 KB per frame is offline quality. These figures depend on the specific capabilities of different nonlinear editing systems.

For a general introduction to compression, see the sidebar "What is Compression?" on page 81. The most common compression algorithm used in today's nonlinear editing systems is Motion-JPEG, a variation of the venerated compression scheme used for still photographs, developed by the Joint Photographic Experts Group (hence JPEG). However, a number of additional compression schemes are now entering the mix, as described in "Compression Revisited" on page 260.

The following table lists some basic Motion-JPEG compression ratios, KB-per-frame rates for the digitized media, and their typical uses.

Table 6-5: Basic Video Compression Levels

Compression Ratio	Approximate KB per frame	Uses
30:1	15	For maximum storage efficiency, or for playback from older or slower media drives.
14:1	30	For clear offline images with acceptable storage requirements.
6:1	50	For good quality (VHS-quality) offline images.
3:1	100	For acceptable broadcast-quality images. High but reasonable storage requirements.

Table 6-5: Basic Video Compression Levels (Continued)

Compression Ratio	Approximate KB per frame	Uses
2:1	200	For true broadcast-quality images with minimal artifacts. High requirements for storage and drive performance.
1:1	350 or higher	Full, uncompressed, broadcast-quality images. Maximum requirements for drive storage and performance.

When you deal with your post facility, they may offer you a specific nonlinear editing system model (with its selection of resolutions) with a specific number of disk drives. Or, the facility may give you a choice. In either case, you may want to do some calculations to determine the appropriate disk storage requirements for the amount of footage you want to digitize and the resolution at which you want to digitize.

Planning for Effects

Deciding how to handle effects in post can be a chicken and egg proposition: do you shape your effects based on the capabilities of the edit suite, or do you determine effects needs based on the requirements of the script and then make sure you have the right equipment?

• If money is no object, you can storyboard away and then pay for what you need to get it done in post.

• If money matters, as it usually does, you might want to begin by learning what your post facility can provide, and reshape the effects content of your script as necessary.

As with everything else, the more complete your planning the easier and more efficient the process. For example, if you take the time to sketch out the specific effects you are after, you can simply bring the drawings, storyboard, or script with you when you visit the facility, and the editor or in-house designer can help you decide the best way to get it done.

The complexity of effects can range from a simple dissolve all the way up to a multilayered composite of 2D and 3D artwork. There is also a broad range of effects capabilities built into the various types of systems you will encounter. After choosing the path that works best for you, you must further investigate the pricing and availability of the various systems available within your price range.

The process of creating effects is often a collaborative one. Depending on how complex the effect is, it may require the participation of a graphics designer, a photographer, an effects compositing expert, and the editor, altogether or in any combination. Simple effects, such as dissolve or wipe transitions, can be handled easily by any nonlinear editor. Many of these systems can also handle a certain degree of simple layering and compositing. With an application like Adobe AfterEffects, a single artist can handle complex compositing that rivals high-end systems from the likes of Discreet Logic and Quantel — but it takes time. Those high-end systems can produce the most stunning effects in a blazingly short time — but it'll cost you.

Advanced planning is essential: you might have to get some of the graphics elements prepared well in advance, and then bring them with you into the edit room or compositing suite. In some of today's collaborative environments, the various elements can be created at various workstations and brought together and composited in a nearly seamless process in something close to real time. Without planning, however, you can get caught short and find that you have to wait hours or even days to get a missing element produced.

Planning with the Editor

Don't organize your project in a vaccuum. Your editor may have certain preferences, and you should include those in your plans. Have a meeting with the editor to:

* Review your concept of the project

* Give the editor a copy of the marked-up script

* Review any significant events of the shoot

- Agree on a logging approach (See "Approaches to Logging Footage" on page 118)

- Determine clip and bin organization, and logging categories

- Determine effects and graphics requirements

Discuss how much you will do before the edit. At the very least, you should pick your clips and have a story structure, even if only a rudimentary one, before the edit. You should have screened the tapes and made story decisions. The earlier decisions are made — and the more that are made — the less footage you will need to digitize.

Discuss media storage requirements with the editor to determine compatibility requirements and to calculate the number of disk drives to use.

How much storage you require depends on the following factors:

- Maximum amount of footage to be stored

    If you anticipate having more footage than storage space, ask yourself if you can edit the program sequence by sequence. If so, you can digitize the footage needed for one sequence, build that sequence, delete the unused media files from the disk, and repeat this procedure for the rest of the program.

- Image quality, dependent on the degree of compression the image undergoes during digitizing

    The lower the compression ratio, the better the resolution, and the more disk space occupied.

- Number of audio channels being digitized

    You only need to digitize one audio channel if you recorded "dual mono."

Project Template Workshop: Generating Edit Plans and Facilities Requests

The Advanced Project Templates allow you to import records directly from your shoot script to build an edit plan. You can also begin working at the edit plan stage directly.

To begin, open the file labeled 3-ShootPlans_EditPlans. If the file is already open and you are working in another form layout, choose Edit Plan Entry from the Layout pop-up menu. The following window appears.

Layout
pop-up
menu

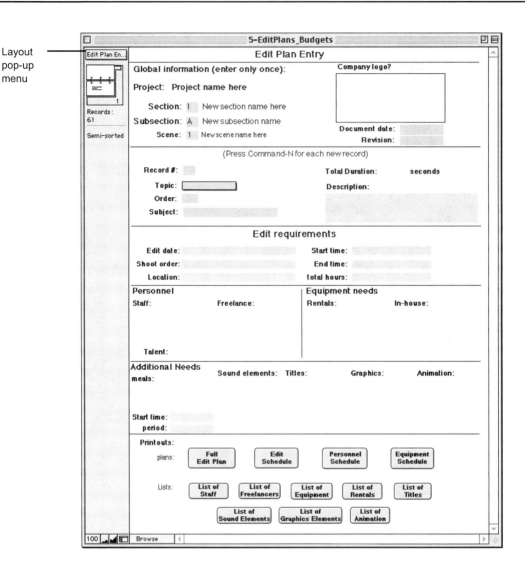

Entering Global Information in Edit Plan Entry

To begin an Edit plan you should first enter global information for the project. You enter global information into the upper section of the form as described in "Entering Global Information" on page 53.

Importing Scenes from the Outline

If you developed an outline, storyboard, or script as described in Chapter 3, you can enter project name, section, subsection, and description information automatically for each record as a starting point. The description field in the Shoot Plan Entry layout is there for reference only, and will not appear in any of the shoot plan printouts.

Once you import the records you can change them, delete them, or add additional records in the templates as needed.

For more information, see "Importing Scenes from the Outline" on page 54. To import all records at once from the script templates, see your Filemaker Pro documentation.

Building the Edit Plan

To build the edit plan:

1. In the top area of the Edit Requirement section, enter general information, such as Edit date and location, into the text boxes. If you do not know the shoot date yet, you can enter this later.

<table>
<tr><td></td><td colspan="2">**Edit requirements**</td><td>**Total hours:**</td></tr>
<tr><td align="right">Edit date:</td><td></td><td>Start time:</td><td></td></tr>
<tr><td align="right">Edit order:</td><td></td><td>Duration:</td><td></td></tr>
<tr><td align="right">Location:</td><td></td><td>End time:</td><td></td></tr>
</table>

2. Enter a Start time for editing the scene using a 24 hour format shown in this example:

   13:30:00 (i.e., 1:30 PM)

3. Enter a duration for the edit in hours and minutes.

   End time and total hours for editing the scene are calculated automatically.

4. In the Personnel area of the entry form, type information about staff personnel, freelance personnel, and talent that you would like to include in the edit plans for that scene. For example, you can type names and phone numbers of personnel required to perform the edit.

Personnel

Staff: Freelance:

Talent:

5. In the Equipment needs area of the entry form, type information about rental or in-house equipment required for editing the scene.

Equipment needs

Rentals: In-house:

6. In the Additional Needs area of the entry form, type information about meals, sound elements, titles, graphics, animation, or other requirements for the edit.

If you do not enter information into any of the text boxes for a category included in the entry form, that category will not appear in the final printout.

Additional Needs
meals:

Sound elements: Titles: Graphics: Animation:

Start time:
period:

7. (Option) You can type a Start time and time period for meals into the text boxes. If you enter this information it is automatically included in the calculations for Start time, End time, and Total time for the shooting the scene, and will appear in printed schedules.

Printing Edit Plans and Schedules

The bottom section of the Edit Plan Entry form includes several options for printout:

- Click the Find/Sort button first to find and sort all edit plan records according to date and start time.

- Click Full Edit Plan to preview a document that contains all information for shooting each scene. The Full Shoot Plan requires that you change to landscape layout in the Page Setup dialog box.

- Click Edit Schedule to preview a document that contains a summary timeline of production that includes basic information such as scene, location, start time, and end time.

- Click Personnel Schedule to preview a document that contains information on all staff, freelance, and talent required for shooting each scene.

- Click Equipment Schedule to preview a document that contains information on all rental or in-house equipment required for shooting each scene.

- After previewing a document, choose Print from the File menu to print the document.

In addition to the more comprehensive schedules and edit plans just described, you can print out schedules of individual requirements for the shoots that you can then submit as request forms or for more detailed accounting. For example, you can print out a list of just rental equipment and fax this to the vendor; or you can print out a schedule of meals to send to a caterer.

To return to form entry, Choose Browse from the Mode menu, then choose an entry form from the pop-up menu.

Extending the Templates

You can simplify the task of building a budget and lower the margin of error even further by integrating the templates with a larger accounting system, making full use of Filemaker Pro's relational database capabilities.

For example, if you create a system of accounts for your company using Filemaker Pro, you can customize the shoot plan templates to reference another database of services used company-wide to generate budgets, invoices, and other financial documents.

To go one step further, for projects that are produced for a client you could customize the templates to generate both a budget and a series of invoices for services provided, based on a centralized accounting system.

For more information on customizing the templates, see your Filemaker Pro documentation.

Producer's Checklist: Preparing for Post

During/After the Shoot

- Select a digital logging program.
- Select the logging method.

Meet with the Editor to:

- Review the concept.
- Review the shoot.
- Discuss the bin organization and custom columns.
- Give the editor a marked-up copy of the script.
- Decide whether to log each shot, groups, or both.

Prepare to Log

- Acquire a source deck, if needed.
- Log all footage.
- Log footage "loose."

Logging Checklist

When you log, think about:

- What custom columns should I create in the log?
- What entries will I enter in the columns so the columns can be sorted and sifted?

  For example, if you have a column, called Shot Size, will you list close-ups as CU, cu, or C-U? Be sure you are consistent or you will not be able to effectively sort and sift the items in that column.

When you log each clip, think about:

- Which bin will hold the clip?

- What information do I need to know about the clip?

Do Yourself or Hand Off to the Editor

- Sort and sift clips.
- Print reports of sorted and sifted clips.
- Reorganize bins.

Use Script Integration to Prepare for the Edit

- Build a virtual rough cut to hand off to the editor.

Plan for a Smooth Edit

- Budget all post-production expenses.
- Schedule dates for the edit as far ahead as possible, building in time for reviews and revisions.
- Plan your offline/online strategy.
- Plan your strategy for finishing audio.
- Plan your strategy for designing and creating graphics and effects.
- Calculate your media storage requirements, and discuss them with the editor/editing facility.

CHAPTER 7

The Edit Room

This chapter covers the dramatic opportunities nonlinear editing offers producers: to create better programs, to develop a more productive relationship with the editor, and to organize the edit in a more efficient and intuitive way.

Understanding the process of nonlinear editing will help demystify the editor's work and increase your participation in the edit session. If you have only worked with linear editing systems, this chapter might encourage you to think differently about the editing process.

Chapter Topics

- Editing in the Nonlinear Universe

- Digitizing Video Footage

- Creating a Rough Cut

- Working on Program Structure

- Optimizing the Effects Session

- Output

- Ending the Edit Session

- Producer's Checklist: Nonlinear Post-production

Editing in the Nonlinear Universe

The basic nonlinear work model is very simple — there are several steps from raw footage to finished product.

In this chapter, we define a particular division of labor between producer and editor (or their assistants). We realize you may prefer a different model.

In this chapter, we present terminology, features, and screens from both Avid Media Composer 8.0 and Adobe Premiere Release 5.1 to help explain the nonlinear editing process. If you are using a different system, details may differ, but the main principles should be the same.

The steps in the procedure are as follows:

1. *Input (log and digitize)* the source footage, copying it from tape to storage disk.

   The producer logs the footage in consultation with the editor.

2. *Organize* the footage.

   The editor organizes the footage in bins.

3. *Edit* the sequence.

   The editor edits the sequence; the producer attends all or part of the edit.

4. *Output* your material.

   The producer determines the needed output products.

5. *Clean up* the project's computer files.

   The producer consults with the editor on the backup strategy and takes away the Project folder on a disk.

Nonlinear Editing System's User Interface

The editing system's user interface consists of two high-level components, which may exist on a single or two separate monitors:

- Organizing Interface: the area where you organize your work

On a Media Composer system, this area is also called the Bin monitor. The Bin monitor displays the menu bar and disk icons. The Project window and any bins that you open are usually displayed on this monitor. The Bin monitor displays footage in pictorial or text form. If you created logs using Avid MediaLog, you are already familiar with the Organizing Interface.

In Adobe Premiere you use project windows and bins to capture and organize your clips.

- Editing Interface: the area where you edit

On Media Composer this area is also called the Edit monitor. The Edit monitor resembles the linear editing configuration. It displays two screens, one for source footage, the other for the edited sequence.

Adobe Premiere now includes a two-monitor interface (source and sequence preview). Older versions of Premiere, and some other editing systems, display source clips individually in their own windows and the sequence in a separate window.

Premiere, Media Composer, and most nonlinear editing systems also include a Timeline, which is a graphical representation of the edited sequence.

Understanding File Hierarchy

Before we explain each stage of the editing process, you should understand how the nonlinear system organizes footage in the Organizing area of the interface. The system represents footage as *clips*, stored in *bins*, residing in the *project*. (The following graphic shows a visual representation of this hierarchy.)

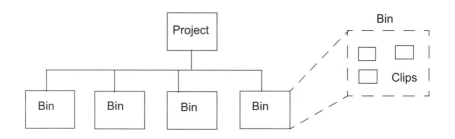

Project

The Project Folder contains all files of your project. The Project Window is the place where your work is organized. It contains all the information about your current job, including a listing of all the bins and folders in the current project.

Avid Media Composer Project   Adobe Premiere Project

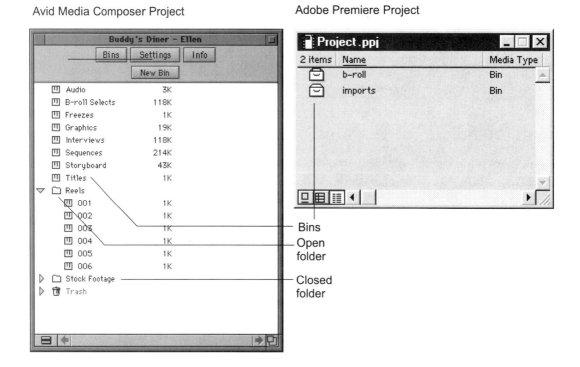

Bin

The bin is a "storage container" for the clips and sequences (edited programs) in your project. Depending on your system, you might also be able to store bins within folders, for one extra level of organization. It is the digital equivalent of the physical bin in which film is stored for retrieval during editing. Shots are logged and digitized into a bin, and stored there for use by the editor.

Media Composer Bin

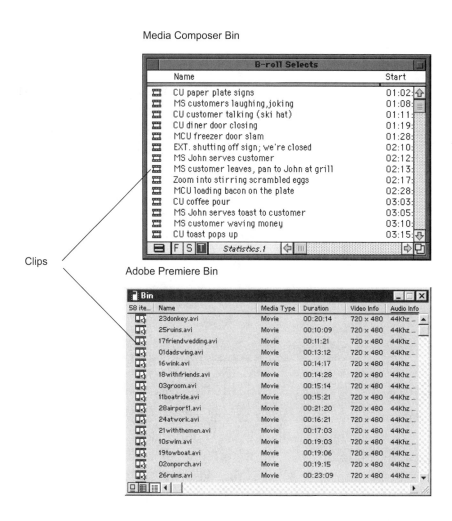

Adobe Premiere Bin

Clips

Clip

A clip is a pointer (reference) to actual video and/or audio media. It does not contain the actual picture and sound data, just references to it. Think of the media file as your actual footage, and the clip as an electronic pointer to the media. When you play a clip, the system looks for media files that contain the video and audio. Media files are "real"; clips are "virtual."

You create the clip when you log. Each clip contains information about the source footage — tape name, start and end timecodes — and about the way you want it to be captured.

Sequence

The sequence is your edited program, or "master tape." It is a "virtual master," easily created and modified. You create a sequence by editing clips together and storing them in a bin. When you play the sequence, the editing system accesses the clips.

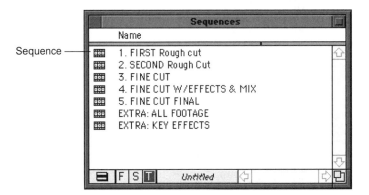

Sequence

Comparing Linear and Nonlinear Processes

Some of you are still editing on a linear system; others have made the switch to nonlinear editing but may not be taking full advantage of its capabilities. In this section, we offer an approach to the editing process that can serve as a model for a new way of working. The emphasis is on process over product, a process that should feel something like the creative work of improvisational jazz. This process might not save you time, but it will enable you to create a better program.

In the linear editing world, the goal for the offline edit is to leave few, if any, creative decisions for the online edit. However, because of the limitations of the system, that goal is often unattainable.

In the linear editing model, you lay down the first shot, make sure it ends at the right place, cue the second shot, make sure it starts at the right place, then make the edit. You build the sequence sequentially, by making sure each transition is correct before moving to the next edit.

The penalty for revising an earlier shot or scene is that you have to dub the program and make the change on the next tape generation, or to use some other equally time- and quality-consuming procedure. If you've ever worked on a seventh-
generation dub, you know the pain of depending on your memory to supply the missing visual detail. In nonlinear editing, once you digitize the media you can create any number of revisions on that same "generation" of media.

When you make a cut on a linear system, you think in "words" and "sentences." You lay down a scene bit by bit. When you make a cut on a nonlinear system, you think in "paragraphs" and "pages." You can rearrange big chunks of footage as easily as a single shot.

In linear editing, you want to make as many editing choices up front as possible. It's not unheard of for a producer to create a paper edit for the linear edit which becomes — with few or no alteration — the final program. In the linear universe, change is your enemy: it slows you down; it makes life difficult. In the nonlinear universe, you can embrace change as a sign that your creative juices are flowing, that you're coming up with better ideas, and that you're working more collaboratively with your editor and more closely with your footage.

Point of View

I spent most of my career working in the linear world. It gave me a lot of discipline in terms of being able to make decisions quickly, and knowing that I couldn't change my mind without a major hassle, and that was good. But coming over to nonlinear has just been amazing — it gives you a lot of freedom, and the ability to really go in and change things. I think it's made me a much better, more creative producer.

Now I can run a documentary scene that was put together the way I wrote it, and say, "Okay, is this really working?" You might see that something just doesn't belong there. To be able to pull that out, to move it some-where else, to switch things around, has really made a huge difference. I do productions for various people, and I always have to react to their feedback. So when they say, "Oh, I'm not sure that works there," you can go back in and make a different version, and do it quickly without saying, "Okay, it's going to take us another four days to change that show around." That's where nonlinear really made a difference for me.

— *Yolanda Parks, producer*

In the linear room, it was like quarry men working at a rock face with small chisels. In other words, you'd be trying to finish each shot as you went; because when you were editing the tenth shot, it was prohibitive to add four frames on the end of the fifth shot in a 250-shot show. Just the real-time rollovers were so time-consuming that you wound up having to make a lot of compromises, and attack your problems on a priority basis. Nonlinear editing is much more like sculpture, in that we just blow blocks off the face of the quarry and go for structure. So when you start editing the rough cut, precise IN and OUT marks really are irrelevant. We can just storyboard together a basic idea, throw it into the timeline, and that's where the real cutting is done. That wasn't possible in a linear room. Non-linear editing gives me total, absolute flexibility, and a work flow that's much more reminiscent of other art forms like painting and sculpture.

— *Tom Hayes, Avid editor*

The Nonlinear Approach

We encourage you to start thinking about the process of editing in a new way. Editing on a nonlinear system provides you with the freedom and flexibility to assemble your footage in any sequence and in any duration, rearrange your sequence, edit entire chunks before you look at the details, work on a middle scene first, add or delete a shot, and extend or shorten the length of a shot. Nonlinear editing allows you to experiment with your sequence until you get it right.

Your greatest challenge is to understand the capabilities of the nonlinear editing system, and use them to full advantage. You will be challenged to:

- Plan to edit in multiple passes.

  Unlike working on a linear system, you don't have to do everything in one pass, and you don't have to get it right the first time.

- Use pictures rather than the script as the driving force.

  When you work in a nonlinear environment, you can experiment with your images and sounds much more easily than in the linear environment. Take advantage of the possibilities; don't be imprisoned by your script.

- Work more collaboratively with your editor.

  Because you can modify sequences so easily, you don't have to plan each shot precisely before you lay it in the sequence. Instead, you can discuss various possibilities and try them out.

Editing in Multiple Passes

A nonlinear system gives you an opportunity to work in an entirely new way. The editor can proceed through the edit nonsequentially, bringing the flexibility of film editing to video. You can explore new approaches that were difficult with the linear model. For example, you can edit in multiple passes as described in the following steps, or you can devise another approach that better suits your project and your way of working.

Here is one approach to editing in multiple passes:

1. Perform the rough cut.

   The editor might spend a fraction of the scheduled edit time assembling the rough cut, which consists of arranging shots in sequence using mostly straight cuts.

   This first pass may seem the most similar to traditional linear editing. However, in linear editing, this "cuts only" approach is often the one that is taken to the online suite. In nonlinear editing, this approach creates a "sketch" of the program, which needs to be refined and revised.

You do not need to attend the rough cut edit if you provide the editor with an accurate script and specific instructions. The editor's cut can easily be changed.

2. Get the structure right. Evaluate the rough cut and rearrange the program or sequence elements.

There is no point in fine cutting shots until you know where they go or even that they will remain in the program.

3. Perform the fine cut.

The editor should spend most of the scheduled edit time creating the fine cut. This pass is most similar to film editing. The tasks at this stage include: rearranging shots, trimming the length of shots, adding split edits, and laying up additional audio tracks.

The producer can attend the fine cut edit sessions or schedule regular review sessions.

4. Add effects and titles.

5. Finish the audio.

We borrow the terms "rough cut" and "fine cut" from film. We do not use them as synonyms for "offline" and "online" editing, but to capture the sense of progressive refinement of the product. Offline and online editing, in contrast, are differentiated from each other based on the quality of the image, and the relative expense of the editing system.

Point of View

I used to go from rough cut, to middle ground, to fine cut. With nonlinear, I am much more involved in my audio and my music tracks than I ever was as a producer. Because music is really critical to the rhythm of the piece, I first build the music tracks. I usually sketch them together myself as opposed to working first with an audio guy. I look for really unusual cuts of music... nothing too "corporate synthy." Then I rough together the program in Media 100 in the simplest way, by slamming in the interviews and slamming in rough titles. After I sketch the program together, I go back and make one pass after another through the show. Each pass gets a little closer to the final program. After the whole show has been approved, I go back and re-digitize.

— Rebecca Miller, producer, Media 100 editor

Nonlinear editing is very unlike the linear system, where you would go from a rough assembly, to the next stage of polishing, and then to the next stage. Now, we polish a lot as we go. The distinction between rough cutting and fine cutting is much more transparent. We actually do a lot of fine cutting while we are rough cutting. It is a different way of working. So at the end of the day there are some things that are very polished that we have worked on all the way through. That gives the unique advantage of very early on getting a sense of the flow and pacing of a show. I like very much that in the current software we can mix resolutions so we can look at a lot of the graphics files at a high resolution, while we are still rough cutting the video, which was digitized at a much lower resolution.

— Vanessa Boris, Avid editor

Editing Nonsequentially

Here are a few tasks that nonsequential, nonlinear editing enables editors to try:

- Start editing before all the footage becomes available.

- Tackle a tricky, problematic sequence first, to make sure you have it.

- Insert reshot scenes or any new footage at any time.

- Try a new way to edit a previously cut scene.

- Try two solutions to a problem, and then choose the one that works best. This is a fast, tension-free way for you and the editor to resolve conflicting ideas.

- Rearrange the order of shots, sequences, or entire program blocks.

- Remove material from anywhere in the program at any time.

- Assemble a rough cut quickly and use it for script review and approval.

Before you try a new idea, which you may or may not like, duplicate the sequence. If you don't like the change, you can always go back. (Depending on your system, you can also "undo" the changes to return to the previous version.)

Using a Picture-Driven Process

The editing flexibility of nonlinear systems lets you create a picture-driven, rather than a word-driven, program. You might base your first cut on the script, but then you can play with the sequence, freeing yourself from visually replicating the script. Seize the opportunity to creatively rethink your involvement in the edit.

Collaborating with the Editor

Nonlinear editing encourages you to develop a new relationship with the editor. As long as you can carefully explain your ideas for the program, you no longer have to attend the entire edit. Here are some ways you can work together:

- Let the editor create the first cut based on your instructions while you do something else.

- Give the editor more freedom throughout the edit. For example, you might discuss a sequence, let the editor edit it, and then you both revise it. Changes are easy to make.

- Collaborate more closely during the edit sessions. Because the editor will devote less time to technical operations, and you will be less worried about the cost of each revision, you can both contribute creative ideas.

- Once editing begins, the process moves more quickly than you may be used to. Don't expect to have time in the suite to do other work.

Just because nonlinear editing makes it easy to make changes doesn't mean you can relinquish your responsibility to convey your ideas effectively to the editor. The editor can adopt your viewpoint only to the degree you convey it.

Point of View

When I was working on the Blackside show, "BreakThrough," I just gave the editor the treatment and left him alone. He did an assembly cut of the show, just tagged a bunch of scenes together to see the story line. So early on, I won't be that involved. I tend to rely on my editor (and I developed this when I was working in a linear world) as the freshest pair of eyes to the project. It's really important for me that the editor puts his or her own stamp on the show. I like sitting down with the editor after a couple weeks and saying, "Okay, let me see what you think," and then looking at the piece. We pick it up from there and start collaborating.

— Yolanda Parks, producer

[After digitizing, I'll tell the editor,] "Assemble shots 1, 10, 11, 35, 3, 86, 4." And then I'll usually leave the editor alone with the footage for a while in order to become familiar with it. I guess the reason I let the editor sit alone for that length of time, even during the assembly (although I may come in and say, "How's it going?") is that I want the person to have a sense of ownership of the footage. I don't particularly want to be looking over the editor's shoulder at the beginning. As the editor begins to see the logic of what I'm doing, and develops her or his own relationship to the footage, it's fine with me if he/she wants to change what I'm suggesting. Then I come in as soon as it's assembled.

— Barbara Holecek, producer

[One of my favorite things is] producers who trust me. I work best unsupervised. One of the points of having an editor as opposed to just cutting your own stuff anyway is to get a fresh look at the footage. And so if they give me the script and the logs and let me run at least on my first cut, then it's going to have a fresh look. I'll build it from the ground up, and then they can go, "That's not really what I was looking for," or "That's interesting, I hadn't thought of that." You know, it makes it more interesting.

— Tom Hayes, Avid editor

Digitizing Video Footage

In a nonlinear edit, the editing system does not work with the actual physical source tapes. Instead, it uses digitized footage that contain the audio and video information captured from the source tapes.

While digitizing is primarily the editor's domain, you should have some understanding of the digitizing process, which is a crucial, and often maligned, phase of nonlinear editing.

Digitizing takes place in real time: while the tape deck plays the source material, the nonlinear editing (NLE) system digitizes (or captures) the footage into the system. A 20-minute videotape will take 20 minutes to digitize. (New DV and Betacam SX systems might soon increase this rate of transfer to four times real time.)

During the digitizing process, the nonlinear editing system converts the source footage into the 0s and 1s of digital data. Even if the footage is in digital form, such as a Digital Beta tape, it needs to be transformed into a form the NLE system understands.

The system creates a media file for each track of video and audio based on the information in the logged clip. The clip maintains an important relationship with its media files. When you play a clip, the system looks for media files that contain the video and audio.

Keep in mind that the clip does not contain the actual picture and sound data, just references to it. Clips are stored on the internal drive, and consume little storage space. Media files require substantial storage space, and thus are stored on separate, large-capacity external hard disks.

Digitizing gets a "bad rap" as a storage hog and a time waster. While we dream of the day we will be able to digitize hours of uncompressed footage onto a disk the size of a fingernail, we should be able to manage our drives so they don't become a problem. As for wasting time: if the editor is doing the digitizing, he or she can use that time to advantage by becoming familiar with the footage. And the time it takes to digitize will be more than saved when doing the first cut, which you can do in a fraction of the time it would have taken in the linear environment.

Digitizing is rarely a one-time event during the edit session. Don't feel pressured to get everything for your program in one mammoth digitizing session. You might consider digitizing scene by scene, and editing each scene before moving on. And you can always digitize a new shot if you need it, especially if you logged the shot and can find it easily.

Point of View
[Digitizing is not a waste of time.] I do all my own high resolution digitizing (or redigitizing) for the final program... For low resolution digitizing, we often have people who have to do it at night because of time constraints. When I do it myself it's a real bonus, because if I see all the footage I'm more prepared for the edit. *— Vanessa Boris, Avid editor*

And let's not forget that it's the digital nature of the media that gives it its power. Digital media enables you to easily arrange and rearrange the footage to create a "virtual master" or playlist. And it enables you to instantly locate a clip or a frame, eliminating those time-consuming hassles of linear editing: prerolls, cueing, tape changes, and timecode searches.

Digitizing Quality Audio

In audio editing, as in video, the editor invests the time saved by working in a nonlinear system into making a better product. Time is spent finding creative solutions rather than working with the technology.

Most nonlinear systems provide full digital audio with full stereo. If you optimize the audio quality during input, you might be able to finish the audio in the system, and avoid the cost of the audio post house. Some of the ways the editor can optimize audio include:

- Not compressing the audio

- Setting the audio levels properly before digitizing

- Monitoring the levels during digitizing

- Regulating the stereo balance of the speakers for each track

Point of View

Once you have your deck in place, a problem that arises is that people routinely under-record when they digitize, like up to 10 dB. They somehow think that digital audio is perfect, and so they can therefore under-record. While that's to some extent true, it's a good idea to digitize your material at full level. When you set the levels in preparing to digitize, the peaks should go right near the top of the indicator, but not turn on the overload, which will over-modulate the audio. If you over-modulate the audio, that's bad.

It's true that under-recording is probably preferable to over-recording, but you should still do it right. In computer terms, it's 16-bit audio; so to the extent that you under-record it, you are cutting down the number of bits you're using. You're basically throwing away quality. Is that quality that important? I don't know. But it would still be a good idea for people to use the full scale, without over-modulating....

If the sound has been recorded well, you should be able to set the levels so they peak near the top of the indicator, start digitizing, and leave the room. A good sound recording person will use the full level, and won't over-modulate, but won't under-record either.

— Richard Bock, rerecording mixer

One thing to consider when you are digitizing, even for the rough cut, is that the audio going into the system may be your final audio. So when you are working in low-res [low resolution] video you are actually working with online audio. For a lot of my projects, we take the audio we originally digitized for the rough cut and use that audio in the mix.

To get good quality audio when you digitize, you need to get a clean signal from the deck to the Avid. I try to monitor the levels while I am digitizing which means I don't leave a digitize unattended. As long as the levels in your final rough cut sequence are clean and consistent, that audio should be fine for ultimately outputting to the mix. When you're ready to finish the program, such as an hour-long documentary, you only need to redigitize the video at a higher online resolution. This can save you hours of online time.

— Arnie Harchik, Avid editor

Running Out of Storage

If you start running out of disk space, here are a few suggestions:

- Delete media files you no longer need.

- If someone else's project is on the drive, ask if you can delete the project's media.

- If you have not been digitizing footage scene by scene, it's time to start.

Edit your program in sections and remove unused media as you go. Make sure to reserve enough storage space for your edited program.

- Render only when absolutely necessary. If you render frequently you end up re-rendering effects multiple times which consumes disk space and also takes time away from the edit. (Any time you render an effect, the system creates a media file which takes up drive space.)

- If your editor has media management skills, he or she might have other suggestions for deleting unused media.

- Rebatch digitize the media at a lower resolution.

- As always, you can rent more drives or other storage media.

If you anticipate a storage problem before you start digitizing, and are editing a "talking head" or interview-driven program on Media Composer, the editor could digitize all the audio but only one frame of video for each clip (by selecting an option in Media Composer Digitize settings). While editing, you use the one frame of video as a reference. When you are ready to finish the program, you digitize only the video that you used in your program. (Of course, if you are running out of storage, you can also use this option by rebatch digitizing the media.)

Communicating with the Editor

Before the editor digitizes a single frame, you should convey your ideas about the style and structure of the program, and any guiding principles you'd like him or her to follow. A good editor will want to represent your perspective and sensibility in the work, and you can help by formulating and communicating your ideas as early as possible.

When you hand off the log to the editor, you should also go over how you arranged the log and any potential problems (inadequate scene coverage, an inconsistent or weak performance).

If you have not done so already, you and the editor should devise a digitizing plan, considering the following factors:

- The image quality of the digitized footage

  Image quality is determined by the resolution, or level of compression, at which you digitize the source material. The more the image is compressed, the lower the image quality.

- The audio quality of the digitized footage

  You should be able to digitize footage at CD quality (44.1 kHz) or DAT (digital audio tape) quality (48 kHz). Audio data consumes considerably less storage than video data.

- Amount of footage to store at one time

  Does the editor need to have access to all the footage during the entire edit? Can the footage be stored scene by scene?

  If your NLE system has a dedicated tape deck, you can easily digitize footage scene by scene.

You and the editor should review the compression setting you used in your log and determine whether or not you want to change it for digitizing. You want to find the best balance between image quality and conservation of storage space. Figure out the highest quality you can achieve with the available storage, making sure to keep some storage space free so you can build the program, add effects and dissolves, and so on.

Remember that the compression you choose for your edit will often be lower than the compression needed for the final program. You can cut on a low resolution, such as 20:1 compression. When you are ready to output the program to videotape, redigitize only the footage used in the program at a higher resolution, such as a 2:1 or 1:1 (uncompressed) resolution.

If you apply all your creative thinking and still cannot figure out how to store the media in your available drives, consider renting more drives.

If you logged using Avid MediaLog, the editor can correct a number of problems created in the log at this stage. Some of the settings that can be changed are: Tape Name, Tracks, Resolution, Detail, Color, Rate, and Audio Rate.

If your program includes a lot of imported graphics material and you want to offline your program at a low resolution and online on the same or a compatible nonlinear editing system, consider digitizing your footage at a low two-field resolution but import your graphics at the maximum two-field resolution. This way you can avoid the complications of reimporting graphics or stills when you reach the online stage. Use this method for systems (such as Avid systems) which do not support mixing single-field and two-field resolutions in the same sequence.

The Digitizing Process

To digitize properly, you should have the following equipment and materials:

- Videotapes (or other source material), preferably with timecode, and the correct play deck

    The NLE system keeps track of digitized footage by timecode. If you have a non-timecoded source, such as VHS tape, seriously consider transferring to a timecoded material and use that for digitizing. That's because non-timecoded material is given time-of-day timecode during digitizing, which cannot serve as a reference back to the source material if you need to redigitize at a later time. In addition, time-of-day timecode cannot be used to create an EDL (Edit Decision List) for a linear online edit or for the audio mix. If you are confident you will not need to redigitize, create an EDL, or otherwise need to reference timecode, you need not transfer the material.

- (Option) Remote cable between the play deck and NLE system, so you can control the deck remotely from the editing system

- (Option) Log of shots

Editors can digitize shots one at a time, or they can select some or all of the items in the log you created and batch digitize the selected items. Generally you will want to batch digitize large chunks of material to create the rough cut. If you need another shot later on, you can always digitize it, particularly if you can quickly locate it on the digital log.

Organizing Shots After Digitizing

To review various logging techniques, see Chapter 6.

When you logged, you may have organized your footage as separate clips in bins. Even so, your editor may reorganize bins to make the clips easy to access and to conform to his or her working method. Don't begrudge your editor the time to organize material. The time the editor spends organizing footage will save you time and money during the edit by making it quick and easy to locate needed footage. And remember, although you may be intimately familiar with each frame of your footage, the editor needs time to absorb the material.

See the Appendix for different producers' and editors' approaches to organizing clips.

The editor can organize clips, for example, by:

•   Dividing one clip into smaller units, called subclips, for easier access

    For example, you can break down a long interview clip into one subclip per question, subclip a long clip of B-roll footage, or subclip pick-up lines of a take.

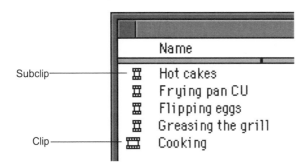

•   Moving or copying clips from one bin to another

    Let's say you digitized clips from a project into bins based on tape name: each tape is given its own bin. Two bins, Tape 001BD and Tape 006BD, have footage of food being cooked in the diner. The Tape

001BD bin contains "eggs" and "soup," and the Tape 006BD bin contains "apple pie." You can create a new bin called Food and copy these clips into it, keeping the original clips in Tape 001BD and Tape 006BD.You might worry that copying clips can consume quantities of drive space. Don't. Remember, clips are pointers to the media files and contain only statistical information about the media.

- Sifting a bin and copying the sifted clips to a new bin

Sifting and copying clips are often done together. Suppose you have a B-roll bin and want to isolate just the close-ups. First you sift the bin for CU in the Name column.

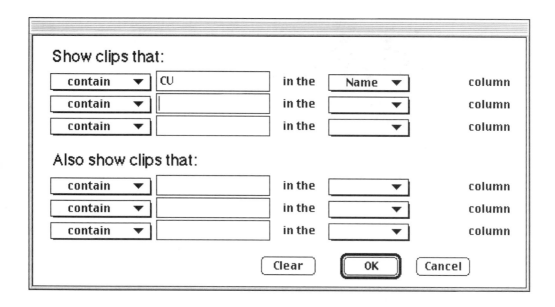

Then you copy the sifted clips from that bin to the new CU bin.

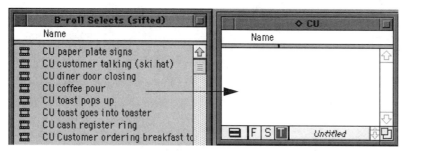

Clips will be copied from the sifted bin to the CU bin.

Managing Bins

After reorganizing the clips in bins, the editor can further manage the
bins by:

- Displaying the clips as single image frames or rows of text data.
  Most nonlinear editors have these options, including Media Composer and Premiere.

  When you display the clips in frame form, you see the first frame
  of the image, which you can change to a more representative
  frame.

  Frame view

  When you display the clips in text form, you can display
  different columns of data such as the statistical data created during
  logging and digitizing (start and end timecode,
  storage drive, tracks, and so on) as well as the custom data you or
  the editor added during logging or in this organizational stage.

Text view   Statistical columns

Name	Start	End	Tracks
CU paper plate signs	01:02:26:26	01:02:38:18	V1
MS customers laughing,joking	01:08:48:20	01:09:01:24	V1 A1
Customer: "Never trust a skinny cook"	01:11:02:24	01:11:22:23	V1 A1-2
CU customer talking (ski hat)	01:11:58:06	01:12:10:14	V1 A1
John: "over a million eggs"	01:16:22:08	01:16:36:24	V1 A1
Kenny: "hard to figure/needed calculator"	01:16:44:10	01:17:03:18	V1 A1

Creating a Rough Cut

Creating a rough cut of a sequence is simply a matter of editing together clips or segments of clips in mostly straight cuts. You should be able to follow the editor's work fairly easily, as long as you understand some basics of the nonlinear editing interface and a few main operations. The following outline of the procedure will help you follow the editor's work.

To get a hands-on understanding of the NLE editing process, consider attending an introductory course on the editing system your editor uses.

The Editing Interface

The editing interface is the area of the user interface where editing takes place. It may occupy its own monitor or share real estate with the organizing interface, which contains the project's folders and clips.

The editing interface consists of three basic components:

- Source Monitor, where you view footage

- Record Monitor, where you play the sequence

- The Timeline, where you edit and modify the sequence

Source Monitor   Record Monitor

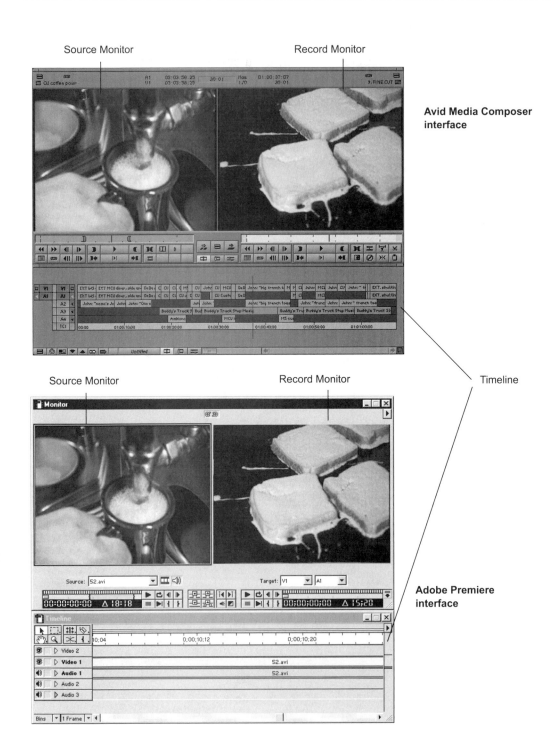

Avid Media Composer
interface

Source Monitor   Record Monitor   Timeline

Adobe Premiere
interface

Adding Footage to a Sequence

The editor can add shots to the sequence by splicing or overwriting. The editor uses *splice* to insert material and ripple the shots downstream the shots that follow, and *overwrite* to replace what's already there. These changes are reflected in the Timeline — a graphical representation of the sequence.

Splicing

Splicing has the same function in nonlinear editing as splicing in film. When you splice, material you select in the Source monitor is inserted into the sequence at a specified point. Any shots in the sequence after the edit point move down, lengthening the sequence.

For example, you could use splicing to add an interview shot in the middle of your program.

Say you have a sequence of five sync shots (VA1) and another audio track (A2) for narration or music, and you want to add a sixth VA1 shot between shots 1 and 2. (See the graphic below.)

On a linear system, this would mean covering shot 2 with the new material and re-editing 2, 3, 4, and 5 into the sequence.

The nonlinear system edits in the shot, automatically rippling the edits downstream.

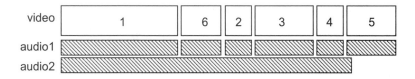

It is important to realize that with splice capabilities you also have the ability to break sync. If shot 6 were video only and you spliced it in, the sequence would look like this:

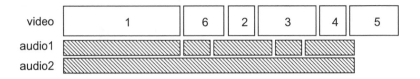

Overwriting

Overwriting is the digital equivalent of a videotape insert edit. Using the Overwrite button, the editor replaces (writes over) existing sections of the sequence with new material. Overwriting does not change the sequence's duration.

You might use overwriting to add a cutaway over an existing interview, "writing over" the interviewee with the new shot.

In the previous example, if you used overwrite instead of splice, you'd end up replacing all of shot 2 and part of shot 3 with the new material (shot 6).

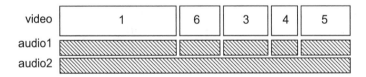

Overwrite, regardless of the tracks, does not break sync downstream from the edit. With a video-only edit, you get this result:

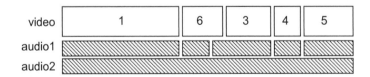

Removing Footage from a Sequence

You can remove footage from a sequence by:

- Lifting footage from the sequence, which removes material and leaves black or silence to fill the gap

Lifting, like overwriting, does not change the duration of the sequence. It is the equivalent of recording black and silence over a portion of your tape master.

• Extracting footage from the sequence, which removes material and closes the gap left by its removal

Extracting, like splicing, changes the duration of the sequence. There is no equivalent in tape editing, but it is comparable to removing frames from a film.

Changing Your Mind

When you use your word processing system and make a mistake, you can generally undo the previous action, but that's all. (And you're grateful for even that much!) Many nonlinear systems enable you to undo and redo numerous previous editing changes. Having many levels of "undo" promotes experimentation. You can try a revision that takes many steps, and simply undo them if you do not like the results.

Keeping Track of Timecode

If the editing system has a Timecode Display window that can be enlarged and positioned anywhere on a monitor, you can easily use it to keep track of source and sequence timecodes while the editor edits. Newer editing systems from Avid include a Timecode Window.

Master Timecode	M	01:00:06:19
Duration	D	1:07:08
V1 Timecode	V1	03:24:42:11
A1 Timecode	A1	03:24:42:11

Working on Program Structure

After completing the rough cut, you can look at it and evaluate program flow, duration, and impact. The editor generally uses the system's Timeline to work on structure because of the ease of working with chunks of material.

Timeline Editing and Trimming: The Power of Nonlinear Editing

Trimming and editing in the Timeline might be the most powerful operations of the nonlinear editing system. Trimming and Timeline editing are the true heart and soul of nonlinear editing. The editor will spend most of his or her time using these operations, which allow for maximum creativity, flexibility, and control.

You can be confident while editing your rough cut, because Trim mode and Timeline editing mean you can always change it later. These operations free you from having to get it right the first time, and from having to check every edit as you do it.

Walking Through the Timeline

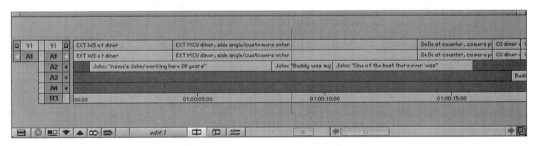

Color-coded tracks   Zoomed in on tracks

Depending on your nonlinear editing system, the editor may be able to configure the Timeline to make it easier for him or her to work and for you to follow along. Some of the capabilities your Timeline display might include are:

- Display selected information for each shot

- Display the entire sequence or only a section of it

- Display or hide a track

  Make sure you know if a track is hidden. When segments are rearranged in the visible tracks, you want to be sure the hidden tracks are not adversely affected.

- Enlarge or reduce the size of a track, or zoom in to a portion of the track

  If you need to see a track, ask the editor to enlarge it or zoom in.

- Color code the tracks

- Color code individual clips or sets of clips on the tracks

Helpful Hints for Understanding Timeline Editing

Although you won't necessarily want to know every item displayed on the Timeline and every action the editor performs, here is some basic Timeline information that will help you follow along:

- The Timeline can be customized to display various details.

- The editor might not display all video or audio tracks. Make sure you see all those necessary to supervise the edit.

- The Timeline can be scaled to show the area you are working on in more detail.

- Icons on the Timeline identify effects.

- You may also be able to record audio directly into the Timeline.

Editing in the Timeline

Most nonlinear systems enable the editor to move and edit segments in the Timeline. Moving a segment typically involves simply selecting one or more segments in the Timeline, and dragging the segment(s) to a new location.

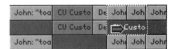

Moving segments to the right

The move has one of the following results, depending on how the editor instructs the system:

- Leaves a black hole at the original location and records over material at the destination.

Segment moved to the right,
black hole remains

- Closes the gap left by the shot being moved. This operation is often used to rearrange program elements after a rough cut.

Segment moved to the right,
leaving no gap

- The editor can just as easily delete a segment (shot or shots) from a sequence. The system extracts the selected segment from its position in the sequence. Again, you have two choices: to leave a black hole (so the duration of the sequence is unaffected), or close the gap and all the material downstream moves up (the duration of the sequence becomes shorter).

The editor can also add tracks to the Timeline and move material from one track to another. This feature is particularly useful for adding layers of audio, checkerboarding audio (moving one person's dialog to an adjacent audio track to prepare for overlapping dialog) and creating multilayered visual effects.

Trimming Edits to Create a Fine Cut

As we have seen, you create a rough cut of a sequence by simply stringing together a series of shots and then rearranging segments to get the structure right. Once you know how long the sequence runs and where it drags, you can go back to individual edits and transitions, remove shots, tighten or extend scenes, or add dissolves. The nonlinear editor uses Trim mode to make these changes and produce a fine cut.

Trim Mode

Trim mode is used to trim transitions, to remove or add frames to a shot on either side of a transition. The monitor typically displays the incoming (A) shot in the left window, and the outgoing (B) shot in the right window. The transition appears as the dividing line.

Outgoing (A) shot   Incoming (B) shot

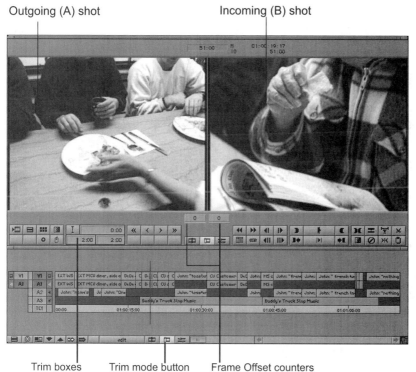

Avid Media Composer trim interface

Trim boxes Trim mode button Frame Offset counters

Adobe Premiere
trim interface

The editor can trim the incoming shot, the outgoing shot, or both simultaneously; and can explicitly select the number of frames to add or remove from the selected shot or trim dynamically "on the fly." The trimmed transition can also be played repeatedly in a loop for evaluation and for refining the trim.

The screen may have a different look for Trim mode than for Edit mode. For example, Avid Media Composer presents a Trimming interface with the following characteristics:

- The Frame Offset counters indicating the number of frames being trimmed from the incoming (left) and/or outgoing (right) shot

- The Trim Mode button highlighted in light gray at the bottom of the Edit monitor

- The trim boxes (Preroll and Postroll) under the left window, indicating the number of seconds and frames before and after the transition which are played in a loop

Duplicating a Sequence

You can easily make duplicate copies of your sequence for protection and archival purposes. If you periodically duplicate your sequence as the edit progresses, you can retrieve a previous cut at any time.

You will occasionally want the editor to experiment with an edited sequence. He or she can first create a duplicate, and experiment on the copy. If the experiment doesn't work, you can return to the original.

Duplicate early; duplicate often!

Editing Audio

Audio also benefits from nonlinear editing. The editor can edit the audio much more quickly than on a linear system, and improve the quality of the work.

Editing Audio Quickly

Editing audio on nonlinear systems is *fast*. Some of the complicated operations of linear audio are unnecessary, such as adding new audio tracks and performing audio dissolves. For example, on the Media Composer the editor can dissolve between the audio of two adjacent shots — on the same track. You no longer need to tie up two tracks to dissolve.

Be prepared: You won't be waiting for the editor to perform previously time-consuming technical tasks.

Most of the editing operations performed on the video track also apply to the audio track. You can quickly:

- Cut and trim sound

- Create split edits

- Create audio dissolves

- Correct a sequence that goes out of sync

Creating Split Edits

When you edited the rough cut, you produced a series of straight cuts, where the video and audio start and end at the same point. After creating straight cuts, you can trim the audio and video differently to create a split edit, also called an overlap cut, in which the video and audio start or end at different points. For example, you might use a split edit to cut to one person in the scene before another has finished speaking.

Split edits are used to improve pace and fluidity, provide rhythmic variety, call attention to one person's reaction to another's dialog, emphasize the relationship between one subject's audio and another's video, and so on. The ease of adding split edits is one of the significant contributions of nonlinear editing to the art of film and video.

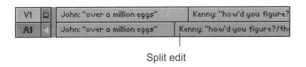

Split edit

Editing Narration

We will present one procedure for editing a narration track to show you how easy it is to perform this common procedure, and thus to demonstrate the power of nonlinear editing.

To edit narration on a nonlinear system, the editor might follow this simple procedure:

1. Lay down the entire narration on an audio track.

2. Delete unnecessary segments.

3. Drag and drop pieces of the narration to the sequence as needed.

Using Multiple Audio Tracks

Depending on your system, you may have many audio tracks (up to 24 audio tracks on Media Composer), and be able to listen to 2, 4, or 8 tracks at a time. If you want to monitor more tracks than your system allows, some nonlinear systems enable you to combine multiple tracks and mix them down to a single track. You can then hear all your sound, and still monitor new material on additional audio tracks. The mixdown is performed digitally, and is of high quality. When your tracks are mixed down, they remain separate tracks.

You can use mixed down audio tracks for playback and output to tape or for export to Quicktime or AVI movies. The mixed down tracks are not, however, represented in an edit decision list.

Ending the Session

At the end of each session, the editor will back up the Project file to floppy disk or another type of removable media. If the project is a large one, you may need to store the Project file on a Zip® or Jaz® disk. Make sure you walk away each day with your own copy. Having your own copy of project files is the best insurance policy you can have. If natural or human disaster strikes and other copies of the project files are destroyed, you can easily get back up to speed with your backup and the source tapes.

Optimizing the Effects Session

There are a few issues to consider before you add effects to your program. As always, planning ahead will save time and aggravation in your session.

Learning Your System's and Your Editor's Capabilities

Not all editing systems — even from the same manufacturer — or editors have the same effects capabilities. You are advised to familiarize yourself with your system's effects capabilities and your editor's abilities to create the kinds of effects you want in your video. Ask which third-party software packages your editor uses. Also, ask to see some effects he or she has created.

Point of View

I think that there's a huge difference between people who understand and perform effects, and people who are more traditional storytelling editors. Just like not every great effects editor can cut a beautiful story, not every great story editor can cut a complex effect for you.

A good effects editor understands the entire process of what it takes to create an effect. I can be working in the Avid and visualizing the effect, and understand what it's going to take once it goes into a Henry [a finishing system made by Quantel] to be finished. I may not be able operate a Henry, but I understand what a Henry can do, and so I can prepare for it.

Producers should look for someone who is creative within the world of effects, instead of someone who puts together an effect in a kind of technical, mechanical way. Effects can be so expensive, and everything gets so locked down, you might not think there's room to change anything. But there's *always* room for creativity.

— Wes Plate, Avid editor

See as many demo reels as you can get your hands on. They will give you ideas for effects you might want to try. Keep your eye out for effects you see over and over again; you may want to avoid overused effects. Watch and analyze television commercials; they can offer a gold mine of ideas and expand your knowledge of the possible.

Point of View

Sometimes I have a bin in front of me called "Inspiration." This bin mostly has pieces that I tape off the air and then digitize; stuff that I think is really good, especially high end graphics stuff. And I study how they did it. I try to figure it out, or I just look at it for inspiration and do it my own way. Or I'll see that a piece is much better because they slowed down a particular part of it. I also study other people's reels, especially the high-end graphics reels. When you work alone, like I do, it's always good to get fresh viewpoints.

— Rebecca Miller, producer, Media 100 editor

Communicating with the Editor

If your program calls for sophisticated effects, you must be able to communicate your needs to the editor. You should not have to use technical jargon, but you should be able to explain (or sketch) your general idea.

If you want to build complex effects, talk to the editor before the session to make sure they can be done. It's better to alter the concept or decide to use third-party software before the editing session than during it.

Point of View

Some of the best effects I've done were for effects-heavy national Home Depot commercials directed by Dale Fay. One was a spot for lumber, and this is how the client first described it to me: "A stack of wood falls down, revealing the logo, Home Depot. The stack then spins around, a saw blade goes up the middle of the stack of wood, splitting the stack of wood into two pieces so it opens up like doors. Then the camera turns to read words that are printed on the edge of the newly cut wood." I was listening to this idea and thinking to myself, "That's impossible." Because you can't cut and then all of a sudden have words printed there. I was not thinking "out of the box," like the people who wrote this idea were. Then once I let myself think about the possibility of how this "impossible" idea could happen, I started actually doing it. I started identifying problems and immediately working around them. It turns out that there was nothing about it that was impossible. It was just a limitation of my thinking at the moment. Generally, if somebody can come up with an idea, you can figure out a way to make it work.

— Wes Plate, Avid editor

This spring we experimented with MediaBrite screens. It is a type of video projection screen technology that we like to use in trade shows. You can literally shape the screen into a circle, a parabola, or whatever. When you work in Media Composer to edit a piece for eventual playback on one or more MediaBrite screens, you can work with the mattes that are shaped as you will need them to look in the final projection. It's a great previsualizing tool.

— Vanessa Boris, Avid editor

Choosing the Right System

Nonlinear editing systems offer a wide range of effects, many of which you may be used to creating during the linear online edit with specialized effects software and a DVE (Digital Video Effects) system.

Nonlinear systems generally offer varying levels of effects options. Depending on your system, you might be able to create 2D effects, DVE effects, or 3D effects, each with variations in real-time capabilities and rendering times.

If your program is effects intensive, use a system with features such as 24 video layers, unlimited key framing, and many real-time effects.

It often makes sense to build your complicated effects after solidifying the program structure. It is easier to rearrange your program before applying effects.

As an example, effects you can create on an Avid Media Composer system include:

- Simple transition effects, such as wipes and peels, in real time

- Effects applied to an image in your program, such as color correction and resizing

- Luma, Chroma, and Matte keys

- Sophisticated multilayer special effects, limited only by your imagination and the capabilities of your system

Types of Effects

Most nonlinear systems offer a wide range of effects, some of which are applied to the segment (shot) and others are applied to the transition between segments.

In the following discussion, all effects are available on Avid Media Composer. If you are using a different system, ask your editor which effects are available. It may also be a good idea to find out which effects are real time.

Transition Effects

Transition effects are used as a transition between two segments. They are similar to traditional video switcher effects. You can simply apply them to your sequence, or customize them by reversing them, repositioning them, adding a border color, and so on.

Examples of transition effects include:

- Dissolves

- Wipes

- Spins

- Peels

- Fades

Segment Effects

Segment effects are applied to an entire shot or segment. Once an effect is applied, you can customize it much like the transition effects. Examples include:

- **Mask**: Masks out an area of the image and displays it over any background color

- **Color Effect**: Applies a color to the entire image

  When you apply a color effect, you can adjust parameters such as luminance, hue, saturation, contrast, and brightness. You can use this effect for color correction, as well as for special effects such as making an image black and white or sepia tone. You can poster-ize, solarize, and control the color gain.

Color effect

- **Flop**: Reverses the camera angle

- **Flip**: Places the image upside down

- **Resize**: Resizes the image and places it over background color

Multilayer (Layered or Composited) Effects

Multilayering allows you to combine and play two or more video layers simultaneously.

Picture in Picture (PIP)

You can create PIPs in a fraction of the time possible with an online system. Feel free to use them in your sequence, as appropriate, without concern for taking up too much editing time. Two types of PIPs are:

- Split screen

- Superimposition

PIP

Keys

Keys are an important element in program production. They can be used to add a simple title or create multilayered complex commercial presentations. All keys do basically the same thing — they replace part of the keyed image with the picture(s) on the tracks below it.

When creating keys in Photoshop, make sure you find out the file format, such as PICT or TIFF, that your nonlinear system requires.

Luma key: This is the most basic key, in which a luminance or brightness level is made transparent and replaced by the picture below it. Luminance keys are useful when the keyed graphic does not have a wide range of tones or brightness values. Examples include simple titles, graphic objects, and "spotlights" over an image.

For example, let's say you are creating a video of alphabet primer for young children. You might want to key the letter "L" in purple over a shot of a lemon. To do that, you might create a PICT file in Photoshop with a purple "L." You import the PICT file into your system and use it to create the keyed effect. You can also animate the letter so it moves around the screen.

Chroma key: In creating a chroma key, a color in the keyed image is replaced by the video on the tracks below it. A familiar example is a televised weather report, where a presenter performs in front of a blue wall, which is replaced by the weather map. Chroma keys are used when the image to be keyed uses a full range of tones, but not a full range of colors.

Matte key: This effect applies a stencil to the sequence, creating a hole in the background shot that is filled with a foreground image. Matte keys are often used to create unusual blends between images and custom transitions.

To create a matte, you might import an image into Photoshop, and draw an outline around an object to create the stencil's boundary. This cutout is called the "alpha channel" (or key channel, hi-con, or matte) and is saved as an electronic file, such as a PICT or TIFF file. You then import it into your system where it is used to create the matte-key effect. Some system features that allow you to generate matte keys on-the-fly (without importing), such as the Animatte effect in Media Composer.

One of the most exciting properties of the matte key effect is that the amount of "mixing" between the images depends on the brightness of the key channel. This enables you to create transparent keying of objects such as drop shadows in titles.

Make sure you bring a disk that contains your elements for creating keys to the edit suite.

Motion Effects

Motion effects allow you to create freeze frames, speed up or slow down a shot, or create a strobe motion effect.

You can use motion effects to give your video a "film look." In Media Composer, create a motion effect at 100% speed, select strobe motion to update every frame, and select "Render 2-field motion effect using duplicated field." (Shooting your footage with a MiniDV camera heightens the effect.)

Creating Your Own Effects Library

Some editing systems, including Media Composer, enable you to save all the characteristics of an effect as a template and later apply them to other areas of video in your program. The template might consist of anything from a color correction you'll need to apply to other shots to a very intricate combination of effects.

If you are working on a Media Composer, ask your editor to add your favorite customized effects to your Project file, and copy it to a disk at the end of the project. You can then use the effects on future projects.

Creating Titles

Your editing system may have a Title tool that creates text and graphics that can be saved over a color background or keyed over video. On the Avid Media Composer, you can play titles created in the Title tool without rendering. In addition to text, you can create boxes, ovals, lines, and arrows with the Title tool.

Depending on your system, here are some of the attributes you can apply to your text:

- Font size and style

- Kerning and leading

  Kerning adjusts the space between letters; leading adjusts the space between lines of text.

- Color and color blend

- Transparency

- Outlines

  You can apply an outline to text and give it a new color, color blend, transparency, or transparency blend.

- Shadows

  You can apply drop or depth shadows to text, and select their color, width, direction, and transparency.

Changing Effects over Time

Key frames are used to alter the parameters of an effect over time (see the screen below). With this feature, the editor can animate an object or an image by, for example, moving an image across the screen, or zoom in or out on it.

Keyframe

Performing Real-Time Versus Rendered Effects

Real-time effects can be performed immediately after they are applied. Rendered effects need to be calculated ahead of time by the computer, and stored on the hard disk as a separate media file. As a result, with rendered effects you need to be concerned with rendering time and disk storage.

Two factors affect whether the effect is real time or rendered:

- System configuration

  If your system has a board with real-time effects capability, it can play many effects in real time, without rendering them.

- Nature of the effect

  For example, dissolves and superimpositions might be real-time effects, while nested effects (multiple effects added to a single segment of video) need to be rendered.

Most systems can play only one real-time effect at a time. If real-time effects overlap, the system will play only one of them in real time.

For example, on Media Composer, real-time effects overlap when dissolving from a shot using a color effect. The system will play the dissolve but jump out of the color effect while doing so. The solution is to render one of the effects. In this example, you would render the dissolve because it is shorter.

Depending on your system, you can render effects one at a time, as you apply them; or you can batch render a group of effects when you break for lunch or at the end of the edit.

Working with Third-Party Graphics Applications

In the digital age, many editors have expanded their skills to include those of the graphic designer. Software packages such as Adobe Photoshop and AfterEffects enable editors to manipulate images in ways that previously were the exclusive domain of specialized graphic illustrators and designers. This software is relatively easy to learn and use, is (relatively) inexpensive, and can be run on just about any system. So when you hire an editor, look for a combo editor/graphics designer if your project calls for graphics work.

Graphics software can be used to perform a range of functions, from fixing a problem, to enhancing an existing image, to creating an entirely new graphic element.

There is an infinite number of ways you can take advantage of the integration of nonlinear editing systems and third-party graphics programs. A few include:

- Export an image (frame) from your sequence, manipulate it in a graphics software package, and then reimport the frame. For example, you might want to do something funky to a frame of your show and then use it for the background of a title or a credit roll, or as one element in a complex effect.

- Export a shot to AfterEffects, eliminate a microphone shadow that appears in the frame, reimport the shot.

- Export an image, which you use to create a matte in Photoshop.

- Export an image to use as the basis for creating your film poster.

- Scan a photograph (transforming it into digital media), then manipulate it in Photoshop. After that, add a camera move in AfterEffects. Import it into your nonlinear software and add it to your sequence.

- Export a series of frames, import them into Elastic Reality (morphing software), stretch, bend, or otherwise morph an element of the images, and reimport them back into the sequence.

Point of View

Despite the best efforts of our editors and producers, sometimes they have to leave a jump cut in the middle of an interview. Usually a soft cut, a couple of frames dissolve, handles it for them, but sometimes it doesn't. Sometimes the move is so radical — the person that has their head up and to the right in one scene, and down and to the left in the other scene — that it really doesn't work. So we're now using Elastic Reality to morph between those two disparate cuts. And I would say that 3/4 of the time it looks as though it was shot that way.

We also use AfterEffects extensively for graphics and layering work. In the simpler range, we're replacing the rostrum camera by scanning images, and then doing the moves in AfterEffects. That gives us more flexibility. For example, with the rostrum camera, you think you need a 7-second move, but you get in your edit and you end up doubling it. It's now a 14-second move. You got a big slo-mo on there, which you'd rather not have, and you might see the steppiness of the slo-mo. Now, we'll take that same document, scan it in, recreate the move in AfterEffects, and make it the correct duration in the first place.

— Tim Mangini, production manager, FRONTLINE

You may also want to get in the act and buy a scanner and learn Photoshop and any of the other image-manipulation software packages. If you are preparing images in Photoshop or another program to be imported into a nonlinear system, you need to prepare the image properly in the third-party application so it will work in your sequence. Ask your editor about the following specifications, given that the image will eventually be imported into his or her system:

- Dimensions of the image, in terms of both the aspect ratio and the width x height, in pixels

- Resolution, in number of pixels per inch, or ppi

- File format, such as PICT and TIFF

- Color space (also called Color mode), such as bitmap, grayscale, RGB, CCIR601, and CMYK

- Alpha channel or matte: Ask whether or not you need to create one

Output

This section provides a general introduction to the three basic ways to output video edited in digital nonlinear systems: a digital cut (video-tape), a digital file such as QuickTime or AVI movie, and an Edit Decision List (EDL). The section also covers audio options and the process of doing the offline at a low resolution (high compression rate) and the online at a high resolution (low compression rate or uncompressed). The output method you choose partly depends on the image quality produced by your system.

Your choice of output method may vary from project to project. In some cases, the system's optimum image quality may be suitable for your project, and so you could use the digital cut feature. Other projects, to be finished in a linear online suite, require an EDL. In still other cases, you may decide to create a combination of output types, perhaps creating a digital cut as a reference for the linear online editor who is using your EDL to cut the job. And if you are creating a CD-ROM or website, you may output as a digital file.

Selecting the Output

You can select among the following choices for output:

- Digital cut (videotape), which is useful for:

  - Final program, if the image quality is appropriate

  - Showing the linear online editor the sequence

    The editor particularly needs to see complex and multi-layered effects.

  - Having copies of your program for review and screening

- EDL, which is useful for:

  - Conforming the edit in a linear online edit

  - Mixing and balancing the audio at an audio post house

- Transferring the offline edit from one company's NLE system to another company's online NLE system

- Digital files, such as QuickTime (Macintosh or Windows) or AVI (Windows) movies, which are useful for:

  - Creating CD-ROMs

  - Creating websites

Finishing the Audio

You can decide how to finish your audio independently of your video. If your system outputs CD-quality audio (44.1 kHz) or DAT-quality audio (48 kHz), you have three options:

- Finish in the nonlinear system.

  You finish and mix down the high quality audio onto two tracks in your nonlinear system. After that, you only need to lay down the audio tracks in the linear online, when you conform the video.

  You can record mono or stereo sound to your master tape at the proper level. Ask your editor how many tracks the system can output, and make sure it is sufficient for your needs.

- Finish at an audio post facility.

  If you plan to finish the audio at an audio post house, ask your nonlinear video editor to print out the timeline for the program's audio tracks. The timeline gives the audio editor an excellent graphic display of each audio track.

- Finish mostly in your nonlinear system, but do your final mix at an audio post facility.

  You can output mono or stereo sound to tape at the proper level. Ask your editor how many tracks the system can output, and make sure levels and tracks conform to the needs of the audio post facility. Consider arranging a meeting or at least a phone conversation between your editor and the audio mixer to discuss the best way to prepare for the mix.

Point of View

The [audio] mix involves taking all of the audio tracks and making them sound the way you, the producer, want them to sound. You set the relative levels. You also fix things that nobody heard in the edit room, because it's too noisy. For instance, in a documentary situation, you might cut from the synch interview to a voiceover. When you get into the mix room, you hear the interviewee finish the last word and go, "hh," inhaling for the next sentence. You never heard that in the edit room. So you have to go in and nudge the edit a little bit. You're doing a lot of little micro-edits in the mix. In some of the over-edited sections, where words may have been chopped because you've spliced together too many of them, you can do micro-editing here so that it sounds better.

— *Richard Bock, rerecording mixer*

Conforming on the Nonlinear System

You may want to offline your program at low resolution to store more footage for editing, and then re-input the sequence footage at a higher resolution to complete the project. This process can also be used to conform an EDL from a nonlinear offline session.

Remember to schedule time for redigitizing media at a higher resolution, re-importing graphics if necessary, and re-rendering effects at the end of the edit.

Nonlinear finishing systems, such as Avid Symphony or Softimage, are gradually replacing many linear online suites, and might save you some time while producing higher quality results as a result of easier conformity between offline and online systems, not to mention the speed and flexible of the nonlinear model which is being used for the first time in many of these online environments. These dedicated finishing systems provide sophisticated image manipulation and correction tools, along with sophisticated graphics capabilities that you won't find on any other nonlinear system.

Digitizing Media at a Higher Resolution

If you choose to redigitize your material at a higher resolution, the editor will re-input the video, re-render effects, and recreate titles. If you originally input your audio tracks at high quality, you will not need to re-input the audio.

The editor follows a simple sequence of steps to redigitize the video image after the offline edit. The editor:

1. Makes a copy of the sequence.

2. (Optional) Deletes all original low-resolution video from the hard drives to make room for new video.

3. (Optional) Performs color correction using external scopes.

   While you may not want to attend the entire color correction session, you should be present to approve the color quality of key baseline shots, particularly for flesh tones of your main characters or interviewees.

4. Re-inputs all video footage at the higher resolution, with "handles," or extra footage, at the head and tail of each shot, as appropriate.

   The system then asks for tapes required, one by one. It will record all the shots it needs from each tape. Your shots are sorted by reel number, and then by ascending timecode on each reel. Thus, the system digitizes the shots in order, progressing from the beginning to the end of the reel. This process is performed automatically, and is done for minimum tape cueing and fast input.

Point of View

We start [the onlining process] by digitizing the show through a digital color corrector. We utilize a digital processing amplifier [proc amp] to take off the tops and the bottoms (to control the luminance and blacks) and to control the chroma. We want the images coming in to be sweet, to be just right, so that what you're dealing with in the box is right in the first place. Once it's in the box, we review the show, and find that shot-to-shot there's some unevenness. So we decide in each particular instance: What's the most appropriate way to smooth this out? It may be to add a color effect inside the editing system; we generally use color effects for smaller shifts. Then if we feel that we're pretty far off, we'll go back and just redigitize those clips very quickly. So that's sort of a one-step, two-step process.

— Tim Mangini, production manager, FRONTLINE

Upon completion, the sequence will play back at the higher resolution. Several steps remain:

1. **Review the program.** You and the editor watch the program, taking notes on last minute *minor* fixes you want to make. For example, you may want to extend a dissolve or tweak the color for a few shots (using external scopes or the color correction capabilities within the nonlinear editing system).

2. **Re-render non-real-time effects**. You need to regenerate the rendered media for each of the non-real-time effects at the new, higher quality of your video image. You can avoid this step by creating and rendering effects at high resolution from the start.

3. **Recreate titles**. Titles, created at the offline resolution, need to be recreated at the higher quality. This is done automatically in Media Composer; you do not need to manually re-make each title.

4. **Add non-timecoded material.** You must re-edit into the sequence PICT files, for example, which have been re-imported at higher quality.

   Remember, in a Media Composer project, you can mix single-field resolutions together in a sequence, or two-field resolutions together in a sequence, but you cannot mix single-field and two-field resolutions in the same sequence. If your sequence has a lot of (non-time-coded) image files, digitize the offline video at a low two-field resolution, and import the images at a high two-field resolution. When you redigitize the video at the higher two-field resolution, you need not re-import the images.

After these steps, you are ready to perform a digital cut to tape.

Benefits of Onlining on a Nonlinear Editing System

The benefits include:

- You do not have to create B-roll (duplicate) footage for effects, as you would in a linear suite.

- The process is very efficient because footage can be recorded with minimum cueing of source tapes.

- You can realize the cost benefit of offlining and onlining on two different systems, performing only the online on the more expensive online system.

Point of View

When our producers finish their offline... we have them come in [for the online] and spend the first few hours of day 1 setting the tone of the show. We go to each of the interviews and find the sweet spot for each one. We see them all together, because that is the fundamental baseline of a program. Once we're happy with that, we send the producer and editor off to the mix, and we batch digitize without them. Meanwhile, the mixer has been prepping tracks. They've gone in and found out what the EQ should be for everybody, and so on. The producer goes to the mix for the rest of the day.

Then generally the producer comes back the beginning of day 2, and we review the program. Everybody makes time-coded notes on color correction (for example, this scene is too yellow, that scene is too bright) and on technical problems, such as a blanking problem or dropouts. We end up with a list of between 75 and 150 things to take care of on an hour-long program. And we spend all of the second day making those adjustments. At the end of day 2, we play the show as a final review with the producer. If they have any notes, they can either stay and watch us do them, or they fly out of here and we send them a copy the next day of the final tweaks.

— Tim Mangini, production manager, FRONTLINE

Performing the Digital Cut

When the master program is available in the nonlinear editing system at high quality, it is time to create a copy on videotape. This is called "making the digital cut."

To make a digital cut, the system performs the following steps:

1. Reads the digital video and audio for the sequence from the storage disks.

2. Converts the information into analog audio and video.

3. Records the information onto preblacked master tape.

Be sure to use preblacked tape for your master. Preblacking tapes lays down continuous timecode on the tape.

Revising the Master

If you need to revise the master tape, you can always make the changes and then recreate the entire digital cut.

To save time, in some systems including Media Composer, you can instead perform an insert edit. You can start at the point of the change and redo the output from there to the end of the program. If the change does not affect program length, you can edit IN and OUT points to retransfer only the altered portion of the sequence.

Creating an EDL for a Linear Online Edit

Conforming the video on a linear online system involves reproducing the decisions made during the offline, preferably using the Edit Decision List (EDL).

If you will finish your program in a linear online suite, your editor will create an EDL of your sequence. He or she can specify the tracks to represent in the EDL, and set other EDL options to determine the information to save in the list. The editor then puts the EDL on a floppy disk.

You can take the floppy disk with your EDL and source tapes to the edit, and the linear online editor uses them to reassemble shots on a master tape.

The software you use to create your EDL will probably support a number of EDL and floppy disk formats. It's critical for you to know the EDL format and physical disk format required by your online facility. The safest way to find out is to call the online house and ask.

If using an EDL, be prepared to redo all complex effects in the online session.

Checklist for Online Editing

When you use EDLs, you may encounter some obstacles. If your editor has generated an EDL in a particular format, for example, you may find that this particular format is incompatible with the edit controller at the online suite. Or, you may be unaware of the dupe reel characteristics you need to specify in the EDL. These problems may result in an unproductive and costly online session.

This section contains a checklist of helpful procedures and tasks that you can go over with the linear online editor to minimize these potential problems.

Checklist

Follow the suggestions on this checklist to avoid potential problems at an online edit session.

1. Call ahead to the online suite before you finish working offline and find out the following information:

   • Find out what kind of edit controllers are used in the online suite and which EDL format the controller will read.

   When you don't know which format to use, CMX 3600 is preferred. In fact, you should always take a CMX 3600 list for backup.

   • Go over the lists you will bring. For example, find out if you need to generate a dupe reel list with new timecodes or a multiple B-roll list.

   • Find out whether there is any other information required for your project that you should include as a comment in the EDL.

   • Find out if the online suite can create all the effects that are specified in your EDL. If not, you may need to adjust the options and regenerate the EDL; discuss with the online editor.

   • Find out the name of the switcher used in the online suite. If you are not sure which switcher is used, set the switcher setup in the EDL software to SMPTE.

   • Find out which disk format the online system uses. In most cases, they read 3.5-inch disks. However, some older systems only use 5 1/2-inch or 8-inch disks. Find out whether you need to use high-density or low-density disks.

2. Send a preliminary version of the EDL ahead of time to test whether it loads properly on the edit controller. You should do this at least a few days before the online edit. Don't worry if your sequence is finished.

3. When you visit the online suite, you may want to bring the EDL(s) in several forms:

   • Printed on paper (in A-mode sort for easy reference; this mode sorts the edit events according to timecode in the program)

   • On disk (3.5-inch floppy disk)

4. You may also want to bring as a helpful reference one of the following:

   • A digital cut

   • An audio layback

   • A printout of the Source Table

5. Having your EDL(s) in several forms allows greater editing flexibility. Also, if there are difficulties, you have a paper copy to refer to.

6. Make sure the EDL filenames are the correct length and type for the disk format in which they are saved. Follow these guidelines:

   • If you save your EDL to a CMX- or GVG-formatted disk, the file name must have six or fewer alphanumeric characters followed by the extension, .EDL. There can be no spaces in the file name, and no other characters except letters and numbers.

     For example: 001BD.EDL is a valid filename for GVG and CMX systems.

   • If you save your EDL to a DOS-formatted disk, make sure the file names have no more than eight alphanumeric characters followed by .EDL. Again, there can be no spaces or other special characters in the file name; only letters and numbers are acceptable.

     For example, 001BUDDY.EDL is a valid filename for DOS-formatted disks.

Avid EDL Manager is a stand-alone program that can run on a laptop to allow EDL creation in the online edit.

Exporting the Program as a Digital Movie

If you plan to output your program for use in digital form (on a CD-ROM, DVD, or website, for example), you must first export the sequence (or part of the sequence) as a QuickTime™ movie (when working through a Macintosh-based or Windows NT process), as an AVI file (when working through a Windows NT process), or as an OMFI (Open Media Framework Interchange) file. Note that OMF is gradually being supplanted by the next-generation interchange format from Avid, OMM. Some nonlinear systems offer other export formats, allowing you to go directly to an MPEG format, for example, for use in a VideoCD or DVD project.

What is OMF?

OMF Interchange is a platform-independent file format that stores both the digital media (video, audio, graphics, animation) and the information describing how the media is edited to form a final sequence. This editing information, called a composition, is the OMF representation of the sequence created in your Avid system. The OMF Interchange format is the result of cooperative efforts of many industry and standards partners and Avid Technology, Inc.

Any other program that supports OMFI can read OMFI files, even if the program resides on a different computer platform. As a result, with OMFI you can transfer among different applications on different platforms without worrying about cross-platform translations. This can be very effective for importing animation or audio files created on proprietary platforms.

Another case where digital output is important is when you want to apply effects in a third-party application such as Adobe AfterEffects before reimporting the footage back into the system.

Read the documentation covering the export process for the nonlinear editing system carefully before performing the export. There are many specific options for audio, video, movie format, and compression that must be chosen carefully depending on the purpose of the output.

The following sections provide some general guidance. For more information on the ever-growing range of development paths available for your digital exports, see Chapter 8, "New Directions for Your Video Output."

Choosing a Movie Format

The first choice the producer must make when exporting video in digital form is whether to begin working with the exported sequence in QuickTime, AVI, or some other format. Aside from your platform of choice for your own work, you must anticipate at each stage of development on the project what platforms are in use by those who will be working with the files.

When developing a multimedia title, for example, you should determine what formats the authoring tools can handle. If you intend to compress the video further — into an MPEG format, for example — you must learn what input formats are supported at the facility that will perform the compression.

For more information on the ever-growing range of development paths available for your video output, see "Digital Distribution" on page 258.

Choosing a Codec

When you choose the movie format for your digital export, your job is only half done. Within that movie container, whether it's QuickTime or AVI, another process occurs involving our old friend (or enemy as the case may be), compression.

Codec is shorthand for "compressor-decompressor." Codecs can be hardware or software-based. Most nonlinear editors include a set of codecs you can choose from when exporting the footage.

Note that in most cases the video you export from a nonlinear system like Media Composer will in all likelihood undergo further compression at some stage down the road. For example, on most multimedia projects an application called Media Cleaner Pro™ from Terran Interactive is used to compress video and audio into a variety of formats with great precision. DVD projects also require high-quality compression in the MPEG-1 or MPEG-2 format. As a result, whenever possible you should output your video project at its native resolution (the resolution used during editing in the nonlinear editor) without adding any further compression to the media. In the case of Media Composer, this involves choosing one of the codecs from Avid (the Avid QuickTime Codec or the Avid AVI Codec) without altering the source compression, which basically takes your sequence and wraps it in a QuickTime or AVI container. These codecs are also much faster on export than another codec which requires reprocessing of the images.

If you must move quickly from your project directly to CD-ROM or the World Wide Web, for example, then you might choose another codec, but in most cases this choice comes later.

For more information on the ever-growing range of compression choices for digital video, see "Compression Revisited" on page 260.

Ending the Edit Session

When you complete a nonlinear edit, be sure to take the output of your session (digital cut and/or EDL) and the disk of your Project files.

Your Project files contain your clips, sequences, and effect templates. This gives you all the information you need to recreate your session on another system. For example, from your project files alone you can output EDLs on a Media Composer system, or on any system running Avid's EDL Manager software.

Cleaning Up

When the project is finished, the post facility will want to erase your footage. You may:

- Continue to rent drives to keep the media online until final approval.

- Back up to digital linear tape (DLT) or another storage medium.

- Allow the post facility to erase the media, knowing that you always retain your field tapes and project files as backup.

The only remaining task is to go out and celebrate a job well done!

Producer's Checklist: Nonlinear Post-production

Digitizing

* Video and audio compression settings

* Disk storage capacity

* Digitizing plan

Attending the Edit

* Create storyboard edit for part or all of the program (optional).

* Review the rough cut.

* Attend the fine cut (or review in stages).

* Obtain a backup copy of all project files at the end of each session.

Remember to:

* Forget the limitations of linear editing; think "nonlinear."

* Try alternative cuts of a sequence.

* Encourage your editor to experiment.

Designing and Editing Effects and Titles

* Determine the level of effects and titles permitted on your system.

* Storyboard your effects and titles or be able to describe them.

* Meet with the editor about effects and titles.

* Create and bring a disk of all elements needed for keys to the edit.

* Request the editor to save useful customized effects and titles as templates, and copy the templates to a disk.

Creating Output

* Determine offline/online strategy for video and audio.

Option 1: Onlining on the Nonlinear System

* Obtain a digital cut.

* Obtain the Project files on disk.

Option 2: Redigitizing at a Higher Resolution

*   Obtain a digital cut of the master.

*   Obtain the Project files on disk.

Option 3: Offlining on the Nonlinear System; Onlining in a Linear Suite

*   Obtain an EDL:
    – Call post house for EDL format and floppy disk format for their system.
    – Obtain additional EDL(s) for extra video tracks.
    – Obtain additional EDL(s) for extra audio tracks.

*   Obtain a digital cut.

*   Obtain the Project files on disk.

Option 4: Creating a QuickTime/AVI Movie

*   Obtain a disk of the QuickTime or AVI movie.

*   Obtain the Project files on disk.

Audio

*   Take EDL to audio post house, if applicable.

*   Take a printout of the Timeline displaying the sequence's audio tracks.

Additional Charges to Expect

*   Preblacked tape for digital cut.

*   Creating the digital cut.

*   Rental charges for drives.

CHAPTER 8

New Directions for Your Video Output

When you output your video sequence in digital form — as opposed to a traditional analog recording onto tape — you multiply the distribution possibilities tenfold. The following sections describe some of the new paths for distributing and "repurposing" your video in the digital age.

Chapter Topics

- Digital Distribution

- The Age of Repurposing

- 24p: The Next Big Thing

- Producer's Checklist: Trends to Watch

Digital Distribution

Producers of video programming have never had so many options for distributing their work in today's markets. Digital, computer-based development and distribution methods have multiplied the possibilities beyond anything we could have imagined just ten years ago.

While staring at a grainy clip of streaming video on the World Wide Web and pondering your own personal broadcast network, you might reasonably wonder whether all this "quantity" adds up to any real "quality." You might wonder why the broadcast and cable networks would ever worry about this little window of video on your computer monitor, considering that they already control the ultimate "streaming" media in the form of high-quality broadcast signals.

Bill Gates once described these times as a kind of "Model T" era of the personal computer. In other words, like those first Ford automobiles that required the consumer to possess the skills of an engineer and the patience of a saint to keep the thing running all year round, our struggles today with incompatibilities and compression algorithms and hard drive crashes will soon give way to an era when the technologies reach their full maturity, and computers in one form or another are used by just about everyone on our communication highways.

In this environment, the smart executives are keeping their eyes on pretty much all of it, on the off chance that any one of the currently available distribution streams becomes a flood. Likewise, as a digital producer of content you should be aware of the full range of distribution possibilities, even if your own turf requires mastery of just one or two.

To that end, the following chart lays out a set of terms in a structure that provides a quick glimpse of the many distribution options available, both old and new. These concepts will be described in greater detail throughout this chapter.

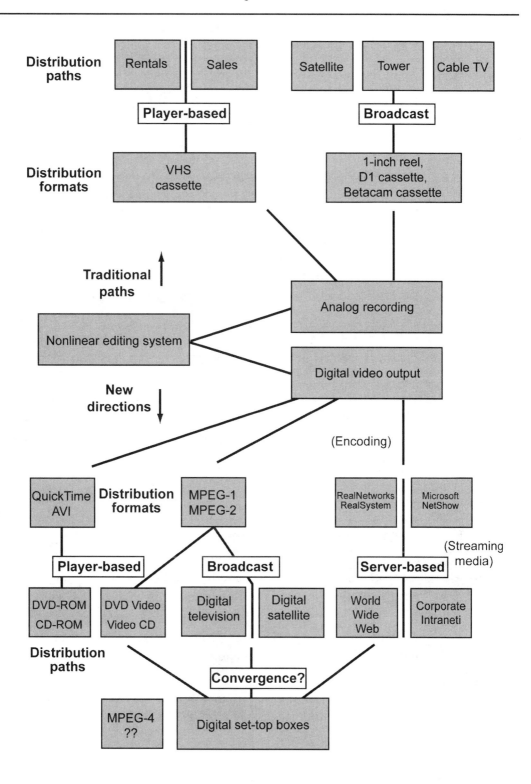

Compression Revisited

From the vantage point of the production "trenches," perhaps the best approach to all these distribution options is by way of compression. Returning once again to this fundamental concept, the form of compression you choose for your final video content defines the context in which it will be used. As mentioned in the previous chapter, you first output your digital video sequence using the source compression from the nonlinear editing system, but there is one more step. As the previous chart indicates, you determine the final distribution format of your video by *encoding* the sequence into any one of a number of possible compression schemes.

The following sections describe the most common compression schemes and their place in the flow of digital distribution.

All Things MPEG

For more information on evolving MPEG standards, visit: drogo.cselt.stet.it /mpeg

Out of the broad field of existing codecs, MPEG is quickly becoming the de facto standard for mainstream delivery of digital video. MPEG is a worldwide compression standard developed by the Moving Picture Experts Group, an organization started in 1988 by Leonardo Chairiglione and Hiroshi Yasuda with the intent to standardize video and audio for compact discs. The MPEG-1 standard, delivering near-VHS quality digital video, was adopted in 1992 by the International Standards Organization (ISO) and the International Electrotechnical Commission (IEC). The MPEG-2 standard, delivering broadcast-quality digital video, was adopted in 1994.

As this brief history implies, these two highly effective compression schemes are custom-made for digital distribution of video content. Note that in the chart on the previous page MPEG appears as a kind of "cross-over" distribution format, allowing delivery of video content both on disc (Video CD and DVD) as well as in broadcast contexts such as digital television (DTV) and direct broadcast satellite (DBS).

Surprisingly, despite all the virtues of MPEG video many of the most popular nonlinear computer-based editing systems make use of that other "PEG" of the compression world, Motion-JPEG, for storing and playing video. So why are we stuck with two different formats? Wouldn't it be better to have one universal digital video format that would require no further encoding?

One reason for the prevalence of M-JPEG on editing systems is that MPEG poses some serious problems for the engineers developing nonlinear systems. To simplify the issue, MPEG compression is *inter*frame, which means that compression frequently occurs across multiple frames. Motion-JPEG compression is primarily *intra*frame, which means that it occurs only within individual frames. As a result, it is much easier to "splice" apart frames of JPEG video than it is to produce frame-accurate cuts of MPEG video frames in which compression stretches across those frames.

The reason M-JPEG is not used for distribution is that the "interframe" nature of MPEG video compression means that it is much more effective for full-motion video, producing a higher-quality picture with less data. In small bandwidth situations, MPEG wins hands down over Motion-JPEG as an efficient means of delivering high-quality video content.

There are a handful of editing systems emerging to handle MPEG video directly from start to finish. Most of them use some variation of MPEG that makes editing easier, but also require some kind of re-encoding at various stages. Many production environments simply bite the bullet and send their final video sequences to professional encoding facilities, where they know careful attention to compression details will produce the best possible results.

A new format to watch for in all this is MPEG-4, a standard currently under development that, unlike its predecessors, takes into account the need for interactivity and world-wide-web-enabled video in the digital future, particularly when the next generation of set-top boxes begins to arrive in our homes some time around the year 2001. MPEG-4 is intended to provide a useful platform for ITV (interactive television) applications, as well as multimedia delivery over the World Wide Web.

While interactive television promises to deliver an experience more like that of a media-rich CD-ROM, there is one basic useability issue that has not been solved: unlike a multimedia title on disc, an ITV box cannot pause the linear broadcast programming when the user embarks on some interactive exploration, and then resume the show again when the user returns to the program. This problem requires full-fledged "video-on-demand" with playback of programming directly from a server, which remains some years in the future.

DVD: The Perfect Medium?

For more information on evolving DVD standards, visit: dvdforum.com

DVD is the next generation compact disc technology appearing in ever greater numbers in computer stores and neighborhood video stores around the world. It uses the same size disc (4 1/2-inch) as the now familiar CD, yet it holds up to 25 times more data and is 9 times faster.

DVD stands for Digital Video Disc, or Digital Versatile Disc, depending on whose column you are reading this week. While "Video" is the more popular term, "Versatile" is more apt. DVD was designed from the very beginning to overcome a number of limitations in the current generation of digital video technologies. Here are some of the benefits:

- Image quality: DVD makes use of the MPEG-2 video standard discussed earlier. As a result, it is the first consumer format to offer broadcast-quality video, overcoming the unimpressive video currently delivered on CD-ROM or the World-Wide-Web.

- Interactivity: The first-generation DVD-standard offers a level of interactivity previously unavailable with broadcast-quality video. In this respect, it might be the ideal medium, combining the kind of passive viewing experience the television audience is used to with the ability to stop and explore interactively at any time. DVD also solves the fundamental limitation of ITV (interactive television) in allowing the user to exploring interactive content and then return to any part of the program in progress. Today's CD-ROM (and also DVD-ROM) titles generally deliver a greater degree of interactivity, but the DVD-standard will certainly continue to evolve.

- Clear standards: The DVD standard, while still evolving, is embraced by a broad spectrum of consumer and computer device manufacturers. Unlike the piecemeal standards that have always hindered the development and marketing of CD-ROM titles, DVD titles that adhere to the standards should play effectively on any compatible device.

- Cross-over medium: Unlike CD-ROMs, which must be played in a computer, DVDs will play on DVD players in the family room as well as on any computer equipped with a DVD drive. In this respect DVDs have more in common with audio CDs, but this time with pictures. Unlike audio CDs, however, DVD titles provide a level of interactivity that is more like a CD-ROM title. In the future, we will also begin to see more "hybrid" DVD titles that integrate the World Wide Web into the experience. Versatile, indeed.

QuickTime and AVI Codecs:
Whither (or Wither) CD-ROM?

QuickTime started the revolution in digital video early in the 1990's. AVI soon followed on Windows. Will these old standards become obsolete after a mere decade?

The last section described the virtues of DVD. Here are a few reasons why CD-ROM technologies are not going to disappear overnight:

- Clear standards? Well, not quite. DVD does not yet have a unified standard for recording onto disc, for example. CD-R (CD recordable) and CD-RW (CD read-write) technologies are well established and should have a firm hold on the market for some time. There are also licensing and copy protection issues still under discussion. Audio standards for DVD are also unclear as of this writing.

- Interactivity? CD-ROM titles still display a much broader range of interactive possibilities than first-generation DVD titles. For some applications, such as complex forms of computer-based training, CD-ROM remains a superior medium. And despite its unique ability to branch seamlessly between video clips, the average DVD player cannot play video backwards.

- Limited Graphics: The subpicture feature of DVD is limited to four colors and four contrast levels at a time. CD-ROM technology allows a much greater range of graphics image display.

- Installed base: The number of CD-ROM equipped computers currently in homes ensures that the current generation of CD-ROM titles are not ready for retirement just yet.

DVD standards obviously continue to improve, as does the installed base. No doubt the DVD standard will supplant CD-ROM technology, as it was meant to do, but it won't be next year. In the meantime, here's a list of codecs you can continue to use (safely) for your multimedia projects.

Codec	Description	Uses
Microsoft Video 1	Creates files that will play with Video for Windows.	Windows-based CD-ROM development, hobbyist or home video use.
Cinepak Codec by Radius	For export at low resolution for use in contexts where high quality is not an issue, such as presentations or educational uses, or for small-screen size playback from CD-ROM or hard drive. This codec uses a compression algorithm optimized for CD-ROM playback.	Cross-platform CD-ROM development, hobbyist or home video use.
Avid AVI Codec (Avid systems)	For quick export of high-resolution AVI files in which no picture information is lost (up to 1:1 compression). Maintains the resolution of the digitized media. For high-quality export as an AVI file in which no picture information is lost (1:1). This option does not compress the file and can result in very large files.	Primarily Windows-based exchange of broadcast-quality video between AVI-compatible applications also equipped with this codec. Requires hardware support for smooth playback. QuickTime 3.0 or later also supports the AVI format on the Macintosh.

Codec	Description	Uses
Animation	For high-quality, lossless compression (in which no picture information is lost). Uses a run length coding scheme to encode each pixel, resulting in a file that is 70 to 95 percent the size of the uncompressed file.	For exchanging 2D or 3D animation between graphics, editing, or compositing workstation. Requires hardware support for smooth playback.
Avid QuickTime codec (Avid systems)	For quick export of high-resolution QuickTIme files. Maintains the resolution of the digitized media. Encapsulates media files, making them readable by QuickTime applications that are also equipped with the codec. See Using the Avid QuickTime Codec.	Primarily Mac-based exchange of broadcast-quality video between QuickTime-compatible applications also equipped with this codec. Requires hardware support for smooth playback.
Component Video	For high-quality, lossless compression (in which no picture information is lost). Uses the same algorithm as the Animation method but saves the file in YUV RLE format, which separates the luminance from the chrominance. All QuickTime applications can read this format, but only some can write to this format.	For exchanging digital video between broadcast-quality video applications, such as nonlinear editors or graphics applications.
DV-NTSC DV-PAL	For storing original or edited DV (digital video) footage in QuickTime files.	For editing or creating effects in the DV format, Mac or Windows-based.
Graphics	For export at low resolution for use in contexts where high quality is not an issue, such as presentations or educational uses, or for small-screen size playback from CD-ROM or hard drive. Uses a limited color palette version (16 colors) of Animation compression.	For use in CD-ROM titles, Mac or Windows.
H.263	For video conferencing. Optimized for low data rates and low motion.	Video-conferencing or World Wide Web streaming video.
Intel Indeo Video R3.2 Intel Raw	For export at low resolution for use in contexts where high quality is not an issue, such as presentations or educational uses, or for small-screen size playback from CD-ROM or hard drive. Files do not export at 720 x 540 and 720 x 486 frame sizes, even though these sizes are listed.	CD-ROM, video-conferencing, or video on the World Wide Web

Codec	Description	Uses
Motion JPEG A	For medium-quality, lossy compression (in which some picture information is lost) requiring much storage space and additional hardware support for real-time playback. Motion JPEG (M-JPEG) is a variant of the ISO JPEG specification for use in digital video. Considered the standard for Motion JPEG, format A is supported by chips from Zoran and C-Cubed.	Primarily for use in nonlinear editing systems. Mac or Windows.
Motion JPEG B	For medium-quality, lossy compression (in which some picture information is lost) requiring much storage space and additional hardware support for real-time playback. Motion JPEG (M-JPEG) is a variant of the ISO JPEG specification for use in digital video. Format B cannot use the markers that ISO JPEG and format A do; supported by chips from LSI.	Primarily for use in nonlinear editing systems. Mac or Windows.
None	For high-quality, lossless compression (in which no picture information is lost). Does not compress the file; results in very large files.	For final output or exchange of digital video at high quality. Requires additional compression for most playback contexts.
Photo-JPEG	For medium quality, lossy compression (in which some picture information is lost) requiring moderate storage space and data throughput on playback. Uses the Joint Photographic Experts Group (JPEG) algorithm for image compression; results in files that are 20 to 30 percent the size of the uncompressed files. Some data is lost during compression, and the export process takes longer to complete (typically six times longer than the Animation compression, for example).	Usually used for export of individual images as single frames, for graphics applications or situations where a single still frame is needed. Other formats are more effective for motion video.
Planar RGB	For high-quality, lossless compression (in which no picture information is lost). Results in large files. Encodes each image plane separately, using a run-length encoding scheme. Used primarily to support Photoshop files, which are usually stored using a planar run length algorithm. Uses the standard Macintosh compression, which takes less time to compress but does not play back as effectively as Cinepak.	For exchange of video between applications

Codec	Description	Uses
Sorensen Video	For medium-quality, lossy compression (in which some picture information is lost) at a low data rate and low storage requirements. This codec is particularly suited for Web or CD-ROM delivery.	For CD-ROM or the World Wide Web. Mac or Windows.
Video	For export at low resolution for use in contexts where high quality is not an issue, such as presentations or educational uses, or for small-screen size playback from CD-ROM or hard drive.	For CD-ROM.

Streaming Media Codecs

You can add to the table in the previous section a collection of codecs with a specialized purpose: streaming media over the web. Two of the most prominent systems at the moment are:

- Microsoft Netshow system, with service integrated into the Windows 2000 server and playback on local systems via the Media Player

- RealNetworks Realsystem G2, with the RealPlayer client

Apple QuickTime 4.0 is also making a bid in this arena, with some catching up to do.

What does "streaming" mean? Most of what we experience on the web involves pulling still image files and text off of a server somewhere and displaying them on the screen. Video poses the extra challenge of maintaining a steady stream of data over the phone lines that can be reassembled as full-motion video on the "client's" (your) computer monitor for a sustained period of time.

Even though you don't see it, non-streaming video on the web, such as QuickTime 3.0 video clips, actually download to your system's memory or hard drive in the background until enough data is assembled to start playing the video. Like a live television broadcast, true streaming video starts to play right away, with all the work being done back at the server. And like a television broadcast, streaming video presentations can be set up to form a "multicast," where anyone who "tunes in" to that web location at a certain time can see the show.

If you've ever "tuned in" to a streaming event, you probably wonder why anyone would bother. The television networks do the same trick, with much better results.

Where streaming video goes beyond the "broadcast" mentality, that's where things get interesting. Streaming video holds the promise of real "video-on-demand," allowing any number of viewers to view a program at any time of the day. And of course, unlike the big networks with their command of limited airspace, eventually anyone with a web address can be a streaming video "broadcaster."

The biggest challenge for streaming video is image quality, which requires bandwidth. For now, the broadcast networks aren't too worried: the promise of broadcast-quality streaming video is far off.

The Age of Repurposing

One of the great advantages of computer-based development tools is that you can adapt and convert images easily between different formats. Analog video required costly conversions to go from one form to another — from video through Paint Box to electronic still store, for example — whereas a clip of digital video can be instantly exported into any number of still or motion-image formats using one of the codecs described in the previous sections. If current predictions are to be believed, this flexibility of computer-based tools will soon expand to eliminate the even more costly conversions that often occur between NTSC, PAL, and HDTV video formats (see "24p: The Next Big Thing" on page 270).

We are all aware of the synergy that exists currently between the print industry and the World Wide Web. Once the web becomes fully integrated with interactive television in the years ahead, the cross-over among all forms of media will mean even greater sharing and recycling of resources.

Along with these expanding opportunities come new responsibilities. The management of numerous source materials and their various output forms is giving rise to new systems and workflows, as described in the following sections.

Asset Management

That's all we need — more acronyms. Some call it MAM (media asset management), some call it DAM (digital content management systems), and others DMMS (digital media management systems). Whatever you choose to call it, the basic concept is the same. Industries from print to broadcast news to satellite services are attempting to use computers to enact some form of this management imperative.

If you work in an environment any larger than a closet you know that managing source material is one of the greatest challenges in production. If you think about it, each time you make a backup of your project or pull a saved image off a disk, you are already conducting a small scale form of asset management. You also know that the time you might waste searching for a poorly archived visual would be better spent getting the work done.

Asset management is especially suited to the digital era. Networked computers make storage and retrieval of various assets nearly instantaneous, while digital copies avoid degradation of quality.

Various new techniques and tools of asset management are available, ranging from the inexpensive software packages for managing image files to high capacity storage devices linked up via networks for storing and retrieving massive amounts of data.

The goal of asset management is making it easier to get a hold of those files again, the next time you need them. In the age of repurposing, this is more than a luxury, it is a necessity.

Beyond that, move toward real-time access to resources. Imagine the production house or newsroom of the near future in which that old tape library is converted into a central server where new and old images are both randomly accessed as producers and editors build their pieces on the fly without touching a single plastic tape box. That's the real promise.

Collaborative Environments

Another benefit of the networked environments is collaboration during development. As an adjunct to asset management in environments where a number of people work together to complete projects, consider working out a system of sharing and distributing resources, from scripts to storyboards, graphics to sequences, budgets to meeting notes.

Also consider the possibilities of web-based collaborative setups. Beyond email, a network location for project folders, made available on a company website, can keep a production team in touch with minute details across town or even cross-country. You can also set aside an area of the website for review by the client.

You can use the Advanced Project Templates described throughout this book for project development in a networked environment, in either a client-server arrangement or over the World Wide Web. For more information, see your Filemaker Pro documentation.

On a grander scale, high-speed networking, via T1 lines or fiber-optic networks, allows greater flexibility in the transmission of live video feeds or large video sequences or graphics files. When working with Avid systems, you can use a tool like AvidNet to transfer sequences quickly among facilities.

An effective collaborative environment can cut down on the need for extended meetings, avoid confusion through lack of information, and speed up the production process overall.

24p: The Next Big Thing

Facing the rapid growth of distribution possibilities, Hollywood has begun to take seriously a new format — 24p, or 24 frames-per-second progressive — that relies heavily on the oldest format in the industry: film. In the process the production community seems to be coming full circle.

To folllow the development of HDTV, visit: web-star.com/ hdtvnewsonline/ news.html

The catalyst of this "devolution" is HDTV (High-Definition Television). HDTV demands a high quality capture format (like film) with a wide aspect ratio (like film) that can be easily repurposed for delivery around the world in multiple formats (like, you guessed it, film).

So where does the computer come in? Video producers rarely cross paths with that other nonlinear system from Avid Technology that won an Academy Award in 1999 for technical achievement, the Film

Composer. Film Composer has gradually been embraced by Hollywood as the most creative and flexible way to handle the complexities of editing feature film projects.

Based on Film Composer's unique ability to input and edit film-based material at the native rate of 24 frames-per-second, Avid has developed a system that literally takes the 24p format to heart: with a digital 24p format as the engine, the system can quickly convert and output programs in standard-resolution formats like NTSC or PAL, output a cut list for editing the film at the source, output EDLs for editing HDTV material at the source, or output wide-screen formatted material for direct conversion to HDTV. Combined with the system's ability to export using various codecs (see "QuickTime and AVI Codecs: Whither (or Wither) CD-ROM?" on page 263), this system comes close to doing it all, especially for large international projects.

Technologies like 24p, DVD, and the upcoming digital set-top boxes seem to promise that the era of ever growing complexity in digital media might soon be replaced by an era of true convergence, bringing greater simplicity to the development process, and fewer gray hairs to the producer's head. Let's hope so.

Producer's Checklist: Trends to Watch

Take note, and read carefully, when you spot the following terms in your trade journals. These are the trends that will most affect your work as a producer in the future.

The big buzzwords:

- DVD

- MPEG-1 and MPEG-2

- MPEG-4

- Digital set-top boxes

- Streaming media

- Asset Management

- Collaborative environments

- 24p formats and workflows

APPENDIX A

Interviews

Producing is an art, not a science. And much of the art is learned by trying things out, experimenting, making mistakes and learning from them, reading about what's happening in the industry... and talking to peers. Throughout this book, we have stressed the importance for you to communicate throughout the process with people in all aspects of production and post-production—to describe your ideas for the project, and to learn as much as possible from people with more specialized skills. These interviews may help open dialogs with others in your craft.

In these interviews with producers, editors, a cameraperson, and a re-recording mixer, we hope to recreate the feeling that you are sitting in a coffeeshop and having a conversation with your peers. You will notice a range of opinions about how to name your tapes and the best way to log your footage, which is as it should be in a profession that's more an art than a science. As you read the interviews, you may want to add your own point of view. And so the dialog begins....

Barbara Holecek

Barbara Holecek is an independent documentary producer, direc- tor, and writer based in Cambridge, Massachusetts; she is also a member of the Filmmakers Collaborative, a nonprofit group of inde- pendent filmmakers. She has produced many programs for UNICEF and the PBS series, NOVA, including the award-winning films, "The Business of Extinction" and "Doctors of Nigeria." Holecek recently wrote "Hopes on the Horizon" for Blackside (Boston, Massachu- setts), and she is currently developing a series, "Voices from Africa," consisting of audiovisual oral histories for schools and archives.

Digital Producer: Can you describe your process of logging?

Barbara Holecek: Logging with the MediaLog system is fabulous for me; it was actually a huge breakthrough. When I was working in film or linear editing, a production assistant used to do the logging; now I do it myself. This is how the process works: a production assis- tant or I takes minimal logs while we're shooting. After the shoot, I rent a 3/4-inch deck or a VHS editing deck and sit and look at every frame. It may take me two weeks or more to log the footage in Medi- aLog if I've shot around 30 hours of footage. But by the end, I have a fairly good idea of what the rough assembly is going to be. So by the time I get into the edit room, I really remember almost every single shot, the way an editor would. This has cut down enormously the amount of time I spend preplanning or driving an editor crazy by not knowing what I'm going to do.

DP: What information do you include in the log?

BH: Quite a bit, actually. I give each shot a number. I'm still a little bit used to a film system, so I have in my own mind shot 1, 2, 3, 4, 5, to 1,000, and the roll number. I also describe the shot: long shot, pan, holding shot, whether there's something the matter with it, along with a description of the content of the shot. And then I give the shot a pri- ority number... I mean priority in terms of what gets digitized. There's going to be way too much material, so I'll either digitize just all the #1 shots, or all the #1 and #2 shots. Or, if a shot is not good but I know I need it I may call it a #3 shot but I'll add a little star, and say this has to be digitized anyway. So that's what I take in to the editor, along with the treatment. So before they even get into digitizing, they at least know what the film is about, and have some detail about the film.

The editor (or the assistant) digitizes those shots, and actually only knows those shots. But it does lessen the time, and probably gets rid of a lot of the dreck that often happens at the beginning. And then the editor makes an assembly, based on what I've suggested, and also on what she or he has seen in the footage that might be different.

DP: When you do the assembly, do you order the shots?

BH: Yes. I'll say, "Assemble shots 1, 10, 11, 35, 3, 86, 4." And then I'll usually leave the editor alone with the footage for a while in order to become familiar with it. I guess the reason I let the editor sit alone for that length of time, even during the assembly (although I may come in and say, "How's it going?") is that I want the person to have a sense of ownership of the footage. I don't particularly want to be looking over the editor's shoulder at the beginning. As the editor begins to see the logic of what I'm doing, and develops her or his own relationship to the footage, it's fine with me if he/she wants to change what I'm suggesting. Then I come in as soon as it's assembled.

DP: When you cut interviews, do you lay down the interview first and then put in your B-roll?

BH: Yes, although even in an assembly, if I have a pretty good idea of what I want to get across, I may say, "Use take 5 of the interview, and then insert the following shots at this point." (The interviews will have been transcribed and I will have logged the different takes for the interview footage as well as the B-roll footage.) But more likely, by then I would be sitting with the editor.

DP: So if they have another idea while they're assembling, will they do both your and their versions?

BH: They might. Or they might just simply say, "What you tried really didn't seem to me to work, so I tried this." And actually, at that point usually we both know the footage well enough. It's not such a big deal. I mean, if I looked at what they'd done and saw it was different from what I'd done, I'd say, "Why did you do that instead of that?" If I didn't notice, then it almost doesn't matter.

DP: Before working in a nonlinear video editing environment, you edited either film or with linear video editing systems. What's different about digital nonlinear editing?

BH: It provides the best combination of video and film. I hated video editing when it was linear. I loved film editing. You just go to where you want to go, and cut. It was still a very arduous process, but at least you could do all the "real" editing, the fine tuning. And that is very difficult with linear editing, very irritating for everybody, because it takes so long to run through the footage and make changes.

With nonlinear editing you have little digital pieces that are essentially like little rolls of film, and you just cut. And this allows you to do it even faster. But it also allows you to do what you can do with linear video, which is to keep various versions. It's like the best of both worlds. If you're not sure, you can keep three versions of something, which in film you can't. Several times in film, I've been through the nightmare of doing something that ultimately did not work in the whole film, having to go back, put all the little tiny, tiny, tiny pieces of film back together again, reconstruct the entire scene the way it was originally shot, and re-edit it. And that is horrific. I don't need to do that any more. You can actually say, "Let's try it this way." If you have the time and the money, a digital editing system gives you the ultimate luxury in how you're going to think.

DP: What do you think of digital cameras?

BH: I like digital cameras; I think they're great. But I think it has made camera work often kind of lazy, because you can just endlessly practice and rehearse on camera. When you shot on film, you had 10 minutes to shoot usually if it was in documentary; you couldn't look at the footage after it was shot. That was both very bad and very good. If the director and cameraperson were good at what they were doing, it was very good, because you had to be so precise, you already kind of focused yourself, narrowed yourself, disciplined yourself to make sure you would get the shot. So you had camerapeople who were utterly supreme, and directors who really watched what they were doing.

Now, if you make a mistake, you can generally fix it. And what happens is that you end up with a lot more footage to edit, which is harder. It makes the editing process a lot longer. And often you don't end up with the same crispness of thinking that you had with film. I think that's the one drawback.

But I think there are also some good reasons to shoot on video or digital. Obviously, digital-to-digital is a great benefit technically — at least for television. It does allow you a greater degree of different options in the field. Certainly, you can shoot in either video or digital format less expensively and with a greater degree of independence. For example, I may be going to Nigeria this summer, and it's a tense country, and now it's still not clear how open people are going to be, because what I want to do is moderately political. So I'm just going to take in a little digital camera and shoot, myself. I learned how to shoot film in film school, but I actually can't do it very effectively any more. However, with a little digital camera, I can. I will probably hire a sound person in Nigeria. I wouldn't just use the sound on the top of the camera; I would set up a separate sound connection.

DP: What would your ideal production/post-production process be?

BH: For crisp thinking and putting together a good, clear story line, as well as for the look of the footage, I would want to shoot on film, digitize it, and then edit it on an a digital editing system, because I do think that does give you the best of both worlds. It kind of makes it the most creative world. You have your original thoughts that went into the pre-production and the shooting, but you then have many variations that you can try very quickly and very efficiently.

DP: How has your relationship with the editor changed with the use of nonlinear editing?

BH: I think it transforms the relationship of the editor and the director, without changing the balance of power. It actually makes it easier for each party to contribute equally, because you can communicate by just doing things. You don't need to have a big discussion about it, really. Working digitally, I can just say to them, "Could you try it this way?" If they say, "I don't like it that way," I don't have to say, "Well, I like it that way; that's the way we'll do it." I can say, "Okay, let's try it your way." Then we can look at both versions. We still might disagree, but we can now have a dialog over the material, in a way that doesn't take as much time and emotional energy. The energy and the emotions can be put into the creativity.

Yolanda Parks

Yolanda Parks is an independent producer/writer, and owns her own company, Dauphin Street Productions, in Los Angeles, California. She produces documentaries and documentary-style programs for both broadcast and non-broadcast venues. Among the programs she has produced is "A Delicate Balance," an episode of "Break-Through: The Changing Face of Science in America" for Blackside, Inc., Boston, Massachusetts.

Digital Producer: How would you compare working in a linear versus nonlinear editing environment?

Yolanda Parks: I spent most of my career working in the linear world. It gave me a lot of discipline in terms of being able to make decisions quickly, and knowing that I couldn't change my mind without a major hassle, and that was good. But coming over to nonlinear has just been amazing — it gives you a lot of freedom, and the ability to really go in and change things. I think it's made me a much better, more creative producer.

Now I can run a documentary scene that was put together the way I wrote it, and say, "Okay, is this really working?" You might see that something just doesn't belong there. To be able to pull that out, to move it somewhere else, to switch things around, has really made a huge difference. I do productions for various people, and I always have to react to their feedback. So when they say, "Oh, I'm not sure that works there," you can go back in and make a different version, and do it quickly without saying, "Okay, it's going to take us another four days to change that show around." That's where nonlinear really made a difference for me.

DP: When you look for an editor, what characteristics do you look for?

YP: I find myself partial to people who have come out of the linear world and who have, like me, discovered the benefits of working in a nonlinear system. I think it was a great discipline, and that people trained in linear are often just very fast, and they "get it."

I look for people who are really creative, who understand timing, understand rhythm, understand really how to cut. And it's important that they have worked on the Avid and they feel comfortable with it. I've also run into editors who can pull an Avid apart and put it back together in a record amount of time, but have no sense of storytelling. And that's the negative side of nonlinear editing: that people can think that they're good editors just because they've technically mastered the machine.

DP: How do you find an editor you want to work with?

YP: I look at a lot of his or her work, and sit down and talk with them. You know, sometimes it comes across in the interview. If somebody's just talking about, "Yeah, the new model can do this, this fast," that's a signal. I try to get back to talking about story, and showing examples, and saying, "How do you feel about this," or "What do you think the cutting was like here," or "How would you change this?"

I try to talk a lot about story and content and timing, and just the beauty of editing and making a piece that tells you something. I find that if you talk to people long enough and ask them the right questions, and get them to explain the way they like to cut, then hopefully you can see where they're coming from, if it's more from a technical point of view or a more artistic one.

Ultimately I prefer working with editors who have both skills. I appreciate technical skills because if the Avid goes down, it's frustrating when the editor doesn't understand what's going on. So the answer is really a matter of finding the right balance.

DP: Do you log, or does the editor log?

YP: Mainly, I have a production assistant do media logging. I log all the interview bites I need on paper myself, so the PA can just type them in; I'm very selective about interview bites. In terms of B-roll, I just leave it up to the assistant to log the entire tape. If I have re-enactments, I'll log most of the good takes, and maybe throw in a couple others just to be on the safe side. The editor batch digitizes the material, and that's the material he or she works with.

DP: How do you organize your project into bins?

YP: The bins I have are generally Interview, B-roll, Photos, and Archival footage. Occasionally I have a Re-enactment bin, because a couple of shows I've done have required that.

DP: How much do you collaborate with the editor?

YP: It depends on where we are in the project. For instance, when I was working on the Blackside show, "BreakThrough," I just gave the editor the treatment and left him alone. He did an assembly cut of the show, just tagged a bunch of scenes together to see the story line. So early on, I won't be that involved. I tend to rely on my editor (and I developed this when I was working in a linear world) as the freshest pair of eyes to the project. It's really important for me that the editor puts his or her own stamp on the show. I like sitting down with the editor after a couple weeks and saying, "Okay, let me see what you think," and then looking at the piece. We pick it up from there and start collaborating.

DP: When editors assemble the first cut, do they edit B-roll?

YP: Yes, I like to see the B-roll as well, just to get a sense of how they're working with the show and if it makes sense to them. It's very nice if you can find an editor you can work like that with; it's really liberating. I think it's the classic way to do it. I don't want to work with someone who feels like he or she is just a button pusher. I want somebody who's going to be a part of the process, who has good ideas and who can talk me out of some ideas that I may have had during the shoot, which now I see may not be working.

DP: How do you deal with differences of opinion, when your editor thinks he or she has a better idea?

YP: Of course, I always want editors to cut my ideas together first. But I'm also really open to looking at their ideas because they may be better than mine. I just don't like when an editor says, "Oh, instead of doing what you wanted, I thought I'd do this instead." I've had that issue a couple of times with editors, and that has led to some difficult and awkward situations. I prefer if the editor says, "Yeah, I cut it together your way, but tell me what you think of this." Then we can look at all of our options. And that's what makes working in nonlinear great.

DP: Have you shot any material on DV?

YP: Yes, mainly for some re-enactments. Instead of shooting that material on Beta SP, we shoot it on DV to distinguish it from the rest of the show. And then in the Avid, we give the footage more of a film look, to further distinguish it from the rest of the show.

Steve Stone

Steve Stone is a Senior Producer/Director at Creative Video Design and Production in Medfield, Massachusetts. He produces and directs corporate videos in scenario-based and documentary styles. Some of his clients include the Greater Boston YMCA, TJX Corporation, Allied Domecq (Dunkin' Donuts), BJ's Wholesale Club, and The Greeley Education Company.

Digital Producer: I understand you create a project book for each of your video programs. Let me ask you to describe how you create and use it.

Steve Stone: For all of my shows, I create a project book using a 3-ring binder. This book becomes my bible for all aspects of pre-production, the shoot, the edit and any re-edits or revisions. When the script is finished, I take the script file and using the computer I break the script down, giving every scene a number. The first scene is 01, the next 02, and so on. A scene is often defined by a change in location, but it may also be a different camera setup in the same location. I give each scene its own page to help me establish a shooting order when we're in pre-production and to easily switch scenes around if there are any last minute changes. If it's a scenario-based program where I'm probably going to shoot a master and reversals, then I 'll put all those scene numbers on the same page. For example, the master will be scene 24, and the reversals will be 24A and 24B.

LOCATION

SCRUB AREA

TALENT
PAUL B.
Chris C.

Scene 28 - 2 Docs Scrubbing
WE FLIP TO A SCENE OF 2 DOCS SCRUBBING UP. THE FIRST DOC
SEEMS SURPRISED TO SEE HIS COLLEAGUE AT WORK:

DOC 1   Martin! Hey, thought you were gonna be away with Jen
             this week?

DOC 2:   No, that's next week. She's already packed, though.

DOC 1:   (SMILES THEN ASKS) Hey, how'd you and Bill Fitzpatrick
             make out?

DOC 2:   (SOUNDING HOPEFUL) You know, it looks like we might
             actually be all set.

DOC 1:   You were hoping to get in over at Felton, right?

DOC 2:   As long he works with me on the rent, think it's a done deal

DOC 1:   (TRYING TO REMEMBER A PREVIOUS
             CONVERSATION): And *what* was the deal?

DOC2:   Well, rent over there is twenty bucks a square foot

DOC 1:   (SHAKING HIS HEAD) .   know

DOC 2:   But the deal is, they're going to knock it down to *twelve*, as
             long as I continue to refer my patients.

DOC 1   (WALKING OUT, IMPRESSED) Jeez, that sounds terrific!

DOC 2:   Hey, let's hope so.

28
MASTER
6/:48 - 2:35
1:41 - 2:30
2:53 - 3:43 ✔
4:19 - 5:08 ✱

28A
DOC1
6/ 7:05 - 7:46 ✔
7:54 - 6:41 ✱

28B
DOC2
6/8:47 - 9:25
9:36 - 10:24 ✱

Script Courtesy of Therese Perreault, The Greeley Education Company

DP: How do you deal with the B-roll or cutaway shots in your project book?

SS: If it's a scripted show I'll assign a scene number for every part of the narration that I think will need a corresponding visual. So, let's say the narrator is talking about the importance of proper coding in the Medical Records department. Well, you usually can't log timecode when shooting B-roll, but you do know that the shots of people coding will be scene 25, 25A, 25B, etc. and you can make some general timecode notes on that page of the script after you shoot the B-roll. Later, when I'm logging these shots, I can match them up with specific scene numbers. This method lets my editor know exactly where to place B-roll shots.

One other thing concerning B-roll: When I'm breaking down a script, on the top of many of the pages of the B-roll scenes I write the word "ditto" and then make a duplicate of that page. One copy will be for logging the narrator, and the other for logging the corresponding B-roll. So, a lot scenes will show up twice in my project book depending on the shooting schedule.

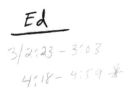

Location

Medical Records

Talent

Ed Y.

Ditto

Scene 17 - Ed - OC & B-Roll
WE FLIP TO B-ROLL, AS OUR HOST CONTINUES IN VOICEOVER:

The difference between a consult and referral or transfer of care is dependent upon the documentation provided by the attending, or *requesting*, physician. The Medicare Carriers' Manual states that a consult is a request of another physician to obtain advice or opinion on patient care .... and it is the requesting physician's responsibility to define what service is to be provided to the patient. In addition, when the referring physician orally or in writing transfers responsibility of treatment at the time of the request, the receiving physician may *not* bill a consult.

Ed

3/2:23 – 3:03

4:18 – 4:54 ✱

Script Courtesy of Therese Perreault, The Greeley Education Company

Next, I divide the project book up for each day of the shoot. For example, Day 1: Shoot — the various short dramatic scenarios; Day 2: Shoot — the on-camera narrator scenes; and so forth. I place the scenes in the project book in the order in which I'm going to shoot each day. Now if the schedule changes (which it almost always does), I can simply rearrange the pages in the book.

DP: How do you use the project book in pre-production?

SS: The project book is great for casting and scheduling talent, because now I know what my needs are for each day of the shoot. If there are any needed props or whatever for a particular scene, I include that information on the top of the scene's page.

On a recent medical project, a few days before the shoot, the hospital's public relations person informed me that we could only shoot in Critical Care on Tuesday at 2 p.m. So I rearranged the scene in my project book and called the talent agency with the new scheduling information.

The project book is great for last minute changes because now I can just change a single page rather than the entire script. It's also very easy to find a scene and make duplicates to send to my talent ahead of time.

DP: How does the client follow along during the shoot?

SS: After I break the script down for the project book, I put it back together again, eliminating the page breaks, but keeping all the scene numbers intact. I give one copy of this abbreviated version to the client, along with a shooting schedule to help them follow along. I'll keep another copy of the abbreviated version for myself and use it to help me, as well as the actors, put the scenes into context when we're shooting out of order (which we almost always do). The project book, with the individual scenes in their shooting order, is given to the tape operator and it stays with him throughout the shoot.

When we're shooting, the tape operator writes the start and end timecode numbers of each take on the scene's page, and he stars the takes that will be digitized later. When we're finished shooting, the project book is now a complete record of the shoot and it corresponds sequentially with all the footage on my rough tapes. Therefore, after the shoot, I never change anything in the book, which simplifies the logging process.

DP: So let's talk about your method of logging.

SS: When I sit down to log, I go to Day 1 in the book, and put the first tape in. Because my tape operator has already starred the best take, I can fast forward to the timecode number at 5 minutes and 20 seconds, or whatever, and put the shot with the appropriate scene number into my log. For scenario-based shows, I try not to log more than one take of anything, so I'll often watch the take just to make sure I starred the right one when we were shooting and also to give the editor fewer choices when they're cutting the show without me.

For scenario-based shows, I log using three columns, Name, Scene, and Comments. I log the scene number as the clip's Name because on our Avid the clip's Name is what shows up on the Timeline, and it helps when you're trying to do a fast search for a particular scene. Under the Scene column I log what kind of shot it is, such as: master, reversal, narrator, or B-roll. And under the Comment column I usually log which take it was, or any kind of description that will help me later. Logging doesn't take long because the project book enables me to skip over any of the unusable footage.

DP: What happens during the edit for the scenario-based show?

SS: We start by sorting the Name column, which now represents all of the scenes in the program, and we put it in ascending order. We drag the scenes into the Timeline and basically the show is there, obviously in a somewhat rough form, from start to finish.

Very often, the editor can do the first rough cut without me. If I've logged my footage properly there's very little guesswork on the editor's part, except maybe when to use a close-up or a wide shot. Most of the editors I work with appreciate the opportunity to put the program together their own way. As we get closer to the final version I spend a lot more time working with the editor. If we find that a certain shot isn't working well within the context of the program, I can rely on my project book to help me find a better shot that now needs to be digitized.

DP: How do you log interviews?

SS: For the Greater YMCA show that we just did, which consisted of interviews and B-roll, we shot about ten interviews. I had prepared roughly 10 to 15 questions ahead of time. During the interview I would slate the question number before asking the question, so I can hear it when I'm logging. This can be extremely helpful.

When I log an interview-style program, I use three columns: Name for the person's name, Scene for the question number, and Comments for a very shorthand version of what was said. So now you can sort the clips in two ways: by scene, which would be all the content grouped together, or by name, which is all the people I interviewed.

DP: What do you do if you have B-roll and you're not sure where it will go?

SS: For a documentary-style program I'll also log the B-roll using three columns: Name, Scene, and Comments. Under Name I'll identify the shot as B-Roll.01, B-Roll.02, etc. Under Scene, I'll try to place the shot in a basic category. Under Comments, I'll include a description of the shot content. When we were shooting the YMCA show, we shot about 15 minutes of these older Chinese men playing Ping-Pong. So when I logged these shots, under Scene I put "Ping-Pong," and under Comments I gave a brief description of the action. Now, when I'm cutting the show if I need a Ping-Pong shot it's easy to find.

For a documentary-style show, I'll put all the B-roll in one bin, so I can sort by Scene, which is my shot category, or by Name, which is the shooting order. (When I do documentary-style shows, I create three separate bins: Interview, B-roll, and Voice-over, which makes it easy to find the right shot.)

DP: So when you log, it's very important for you to create columns you can sort.

SS: Right. When I started using the Avid, I realized that if you log properly by making shots sortable and by using scene numbers, the scenario-based show is basically cut for you. And the documentary style show is a lot easier to cut when all your material is organized in bins, and all your clips are sortable by category and/or content. I know using the Avid has greatly improved all of our shows here at Creative Video, as well as my own productivity.

Rebecca Miller

Rebecca Miller has been producing programs since 1985. She founded Rebecca Miller Productions in 1992 (in Newton, Massachusetts), where she functions as Producer/Director/Designer/Editor of broadcast and non-broadcast video programs. Miller has worked for a long list of clients including: NBC Cable and International, Caribiner Communications, Jack Morton Productions, Panasonic, Digital, and the PBS series "Talking with David Frost." Miller recently created a video wall for Nortel Networks. She specializes in high-end programs featuring original creative ideas, well designed graphics and animation, editing, and music tracks chosen to surprise the viewer. She edits on a Media 100 system.

Digital Producer: You were a freelance producer until fairly recently; now you have your own company and produce and edit your projects. How much experience did you have as an editor before working in nonlinear editing?

Rebecca Miller: I did very little analog editing or film editing before I started editing on the Media 100. I never really considered myself an editor; if nonlinear editing had not come along, I wouldn't be editing; it's far too frustrating and not nearly as rewarding. But nonlinear editing has allowed me to do things which I would not have done otherwise.

As a freelance producer, I worked all over the country, in fact, all over the world, and I worked with some of the best editors in the world. I really learned a lot from all of these guys, but I was always telling them, "Please trim five frames here," or "Give me a ten-frame dissolve here." Once I started editing, I realized that I was able to do myself all of those things that I had been talking to other guys about and the tricks that I had learned from them.

DP: How sophisticated do you get?

RM: I think that I have turned into a pretty good editor when it comes to shaping a subject, cutting to music, doing a tremendous amount of digital and graphic effects, and animation.

DP: Can you describe one of the projects that you worked on where you had to use a number of third-party software packages?

RM: Well, yes, I just finished a seven-minute video wall using a very unusual African vocal track combined with actions shot in the studio in an unusual way and intricately shot hosts in the studio who directly addressed the camera. I also created a whole bunch of fantasy Internet stories where we invented activites that you might be able to do on the Internet in the future — like go to your computer screen and press "Feed the dog," and then the "Feed the dog" option comes up giving you a choice of two different dogs to feed. Through AfterEffects and Photoshop, I created all of these crazy scenes with people video-conferencing and people calling up and ordering things through a catalog. By using a combination of stock footage and clip art, I was able to create fifteen little stories. Then I must have done fifty pieces of animated typography that went into the show.

DP: How do you get your footage?

RM: A lot of times companies send me boxes of their footage, oftentimes junk. I slow it down, colorize, stutter, cut it, make it look as bad as possible, add a lot of sometimes sharp, sometimes grungy type over it, and the client says it looks really hip.

DP: Would you have done this kind of work in pre-digital days?

RM: It would have taken much longer to create a program like this in the online editing room. I created this seven-minute show with three sources and twenty-one minutes of final program in about two weeks in the editing room. That includes all of the editing, computer graphics, and animation.

DP: Can you describe how you digitize?

RM: My goal is to digitize as quickly as possible. It's a very time-consuming process that I always feel is a big waste of time. Sometimes I sit down with a box of forty tapes; it could take me weeks to go through it if I let it. People often go out and shoot this bad, smeary DVCam, like "garbage-cam," and then they hand me boxes of hour-long reels which may have a twenty-frame gem in the middle of it. I get stuck with this stuff constantly, so my goal is to just speed through as much as possible. I have great little keyboard commands which allow me to "buzz, buzz, buzz, grab, buzz, buzz, grab." Then I just make really minimal comments in the clip bin.

So, out of twenty-five hours of material I may end up digitizing about ten hours, from which I will edit a five-minute program. I generally have a really high ratio of material that gets digitized at a really low, low resolution.

DP: How much storage space do you have?

RM: 54 GB.

DP: What resolution do you use to digitize?

RM: I usually digitize at 10 KB/frame.

DP: What is your typical method for organizing footage once it's in bins?

RM: I have a music bin, an audio bin, an animation bin. I also have bins that are related to the footage itself: the interview bin, the stock footage bin, the good stuff, the junky stuff.

Sometimes I have a bin in front of me called "Inspiration." This bin mostly has pieces that I tape off the air and then digitize; stuff that I think is really good, especially high end graphics stuff. And I study how they did it. I try to figure it out, or I just look at it for inspiration and do it my own way. Or I'll see that a piece is much better because they slowed down a particular part of it. I also study other people's reels, especially the high-end graphics reels. When you work alone, like I do, it's always good to get fresh viewpoints.

DP: Can you talk about your editing workflow?

RM: I used to go from rough cut, to middle ground, to fine cut. With nonlinear, I am much more involved in my audio and my music tracks than I ever was as a producer. Because music is really critical to the rhythm of the piece, I first build the music tracks. I usually sketch them together myself as opposed to working first with an audio guy. I look for really unusual cuts of music... nothing too "corporate synthy." Then I rough together the program in Media 100 in the simplest way, by slamming in the interviews and slamming in rough titles. After I sketch the program together, I go back and make one pass after another through the show. Each pass gets a little closer to the final program. After the whole show has been approved, I go back and re-digitize.

DP: How do you finish the sound?

RM: If I have the budget, I go out and have it mixed. If I don't have the budget, I do the mix myself in Media 100.

DP: How do make sure that you get quality audio?

RM: I consult with engineers constantly. During the shoot I rely on my engineers to do the audio right. After that, I'm obsessed with making sure that everything goes into the system correctly. When I do the final mix, I am all over the engineer to make sure that what has come out of my system is good quality. I have to make sure that other people are double-checking my stuff all the time.

DP: What deck do you use for digitizing?

RM: I have a BVW 1800, and I use a combination of Mackie Mixer and the Media 100 input level. I make sure that the audio is zeroed all the way along.

DP: In general, how do you feel about being a combination producer/nonlinear editor?

RM: My nonlinear system has allowed me to re-invent myself in a way that I never expected. I bought the system a few months after I had a baby and now I have two little babies who are still in diapers. This system has allowed me to build the business at home and be close to my kids. It has allowed me to have a business more successful than I ever had as a freelancer.

On top of that it has allowed me to grow and develop my creative self in ways that I would never do when I was working in a highly stratified business environment. The affordable cost of this system — with loan options — combined with the incredibly high resolution, allowed me to get into the industry; I never would have been able to do it otherwise. The thing that has shocked me is that I have had my own business for only two years, and I have never ever had a problem convincing my clients that this was going to look as good as a $600/hour editing house. That includes clients who come here for high-end broadcast editing and agency work.

Vanessa Boris

Vanessa Boris is Senior Avid Editor at Wave, Inc., in Framingham, Massachusetts. She has been editing on Avid systems since 1990, and her specialty is documentary-style editing. Among the programs she has edited are: "All Bird TV" for the Discovery Animal Planet channel, "Crime Stories" for Court TV, multiple installations for the Children's Museum, Boston, and programs for many corporations, including EMC Corporation, Nortel Networks, and Fidelity Investments.

Digital Producer: How did the editing work flow change when you went from linear to nonlinear editing?

Vanessa Boris: Nonlinear editing is very unlike the linear system, where you would go from a rough assembly, to the next stage of polishing, and then to the next stage. Now, we polish a lot as we go. The distinction between rough cutting and fine cutting is much more transparent. We actually do a lot of fine cutting while we are rough cutting. It is a different way of working. So at the end of the day there are some things that are very polished that we have worked on all the way through. That gives the unique advantage of very early on getting a sense of the flow and pacing of a show. I like very much that in the current software we can mix resolutions so we can look at a lot of the graphics files at a high resolution, while we are still rough cutting the video, which was digitized at a much lower resolution.

DP: You digitize at mixed two-field resolutions?

VB: Yes, especially for trade shows, where there are a lot of graphical elements. I digitize those at a high two-field resolution, and digitize the video footage at a low two-field resolution. That way, I can rough in the video and get a good feeling for what the graphics are doing. Then once we make our decisions about the video, we can redigitize it in pieces at high res. I find that to be an incredible advantage.

DP: You digitize the video in pieces?

VB: Yes, we might finish one part of a show, redigitize just that part to a higher resolution, and keep working on the parts that are still rough. That way, clients can approve certain sections in high res as they need them. In broadcast, for example, different executives and producers have to sign off on a show at different times. So nonlinear offers some unique flexibility that we didn't have with linear tape editing or even film editing. The whole process is more fluid, and our clients are taking advantage of that fluidity.

DP: Do you have any tips for organizing bins?

VB: We always set up our bins by tape number because we have found it to be the fastest, most efficient way to digitize. Once we have everything loaded in this giant footage bin and broken it down by tape number, then we can start pulling things into work bins. That's how I do it. I actually disapprove of doing complicated logging where clips from the same tape are in separate bins because it is a digitizer's nightmare.

DP: Do you like to break down the footage into work bins yourself?

VB: Yes, occasionally I have used a very good, very focused assistant editor to help me with that, but mostly I do it myself. But like many people who came out of film editing, I am very comfortable working from different source reels. I just sort of remember that tape 11 and 12 have what I need for this section. So sometimes I don't even keep work bins.

DP: When you do make work bins, what bins do you have?

VB: I like to keep an effects bin. I keep my audio-only sources separated. I usually keep some graphical elements separate because they use different keyboard commands, and it's a little faster that way. And then I separate shots by content or relevant categories.

DP: Are you working with any new tools?

VB: This spring we experimented with MediaBrite screens. It is a type of video projection screen technology that we like to use in trade shows. You can literally shape the screen into a circle, a parabola, or whatever. When you work in Media Composer to edit a piece for eventual playback on one or more MediaBrite screens, you can work with the mattes that are shaped as you will need them to look in the final projection. It's a great previsualizing tool.

Recently I edited a multiple screen program for a trade show (we were projecting 2 separate sources onto 2 three-foot circular screens,

and I rough cut the whole thing in multiple Picture-in-Pictures. I could see both of my sources at the same time; I also applied a circle matte so that I could see them simultaneously as they would appear projected. We could preview on our system what would eventually be projected on the
MediaBrite screens.

After the rough cut stage we removed the Picture-in-Picture effects and returned to editing single sources. We continued to reposition and resize everything for optimal playback in a circular shape.

DP: Do you think digitizing is a waste of time?

VB: No. I do all my own high resolution digitizing (or redigitizing) for the final program. One of my complaints about the Avid system I use is that I don't have internal 3 x 3 color correction. Even so, in my experience it's not fast even when you do have it. So when I digitize, I go from the tape through an external 3 X 3 color corrector and into the Avid. I also have an external remote TBC (timebase corrector) so I am actually correcting the images that I am digitizing at AVR 77 [an Avid online resolution]. It's vital that I do that, because I am ultimately responsible for the quality of the video on the final master and often have to conform to broadcast standards.

For low resolution digitizing, we often have people who have to do it at night because of time constraints. When I do it myself it's a real bonus, because if I see all the footage I'm more prepared for the edit.

The one time where I think digitizing is a waste of time is when somebody says, "Well, I have these three masters, and I need to edit them all together and create a loop tape." I just go to the online room. Those are the kinds of things that you just don't do as well in the Avid.

DP: How is your working relationship with the producer different than when you worked in linear editing?

VB: Producers spend a lot more time in the room when we are offlining because the process is so much faster, although they are still making phone calls and now they work on their laptop computers. In the pre-nonlinear days, I used to edit by myself a lot. Now I find that's a little more rare because we are just moving and making decisions so quickly. Producers don't have to wait so long for things to happen.

During the nonlinear online, they spend a lot of time out of the room until it is time to put in the CG [character-generated text] or create an elaborate effect.

DP: Do you have any tips for how a producer can prepare for a smooth nonlinear edit?

VB: I think that it is really imperative that producers know their footage. That's partly because things are happening much faster now. We have overnight couriers and fax machines in a way that we didn't when I was linear editing ten years ago. But we're finding that sometimes there's not even time for the producers to prescreen in advance of the edit, so they just say, "Digitize everything and I'll sort it out in the Avid edit." I think looking at your tapes, logging them, doing some pulls and digitizing them, when time allows, is a real advantage for producers, partly because the timeline has collapsed and partly because we don't search from tape to tape to find things now that editing is nonlinear.

There are also some fabulous tools available to producers for remote on-location or desktop logging. Tools like Production Magic's Shot Logger can save producers hours of time in digitizing.

Another valuable asset for producers is to try to stay informed about "the world" of visual effects. So much more is available to producers within Media Composer and through software and hardware innovations that accompany many Avid systems. I find producers benefit from pre-production meetings with the editor in considering how to achieve an interesting look or create a specific visual effect.

Tim Mangini

Tim Mangini is the Production Manager for the FRONTLINE television series on PBS; FRONTLINE airs 30 hours of documentaries each season from its WGBH offices in Boston, Massachusetts. Mangini is in charge of a small staff that onlines and packages each weekly program on Avid Media Composers. The offline edit is generally performed in an outside facility, arranged by the individual show's independent producer.

Digital Producer: How would you characterize the advantages of a nonlinear online?

Tim Mangini: Number one is just having everything in one digital nonlinear format, coming from a variety of different places into one packaging suite. The elements of every *FRONTLINE* include the documentary itself, which is onlined nonlinearly; the packaging elements such as the *FRONTLINE* logo and lower third IDs; and any opening and closing PBS elements that have to be added. Having all of the elements in one digital nonlinear format allows us to work with them in a more seamless way, making it easier to package the program.

Another advantage is that it is much easier getting the show to time. All of our hour-long shows have to be exactly 56 minutes and 46 seconds. When you're in a linear online, you get to the end and find out you're 15 frames long or 20 seconds short. You have to figure out where to make the edits, and you make compromises, because you don't want to re-lay the whole show. So a great advantage is that it allows you to move things around easily.

DP: How do you address the issue of visual quality?

TM: Well, that's a really big question. I'll answer it in terms of image resolution or compression, and also in terms of creating a consistent visual look throughout the show. In terms of resolution, the first thing you need to decide in the digital realm is: Given the way you are distributing, what is the appropriate resolution for this program? And is that affected by the material you are sourcing from? At *FRONTLINE*, we have traditionally had large amounts of stock footage that come from less than high quality sources. Obviously, our interviews and the B-rolls shot for the program are high quality, but interviews in general don't demand low compression schemes. So we have thus far felt that the up-until-now standard of AVR 77 or 2:1-ish compression was acceptable.

We crank out a show weekly, using our own nonlinear online editing suites. For us to have D-1 machines would be impractical. For us to have some of the higher cost nonlinear systems that are uncompressed is impractical for two reasons. One is cost, and the other is that none of the uncompressed systems that were available before now had the kind of power editing tools that we need. Obviously, the advent of lower-cost, powerful, uncompressed nonlinear systems available to everyone will make a difference. We will be adding uncompressed later this summer.

The second area of quality, for me, is visual consistency. We address that in a couple of ways. We start by digitizing the show through a digital color corrector. We utilize a digital processing amplifier [proc amp] to take off the tops and the bottoms (to control the luminance and blacks) and to control the chroma. We want the images coming in to be sweet, to be just right, so that what you're dealing with in the box is right in the first place. Once it's in the box, we review the show, and find that shot-to-shot there's some unevenness. So we decide in each particular instance: What's the most appropriate way to smooth this out? It may be to add a color effect inside the editing system; we generally use color effects for smaller shifts. Then if we feel that we're pretty far off, we'll go back and just redigitize those clips very quickly. So that's sort of a one-step, two-step process.

This differs from the historical way of linear onlining and color correcting. Historically, you online your program and then you go into a color correction suite and post color correct it. This comes from the film methodology. But if you post color correct a video, even if you're in a very advanced suite (such as DaVinci), there are problems dealing with effects, whether it be just a dissolve or a wipe or a layer of some kind. What happens is that the color being applied by the color correction device gets applied to the two shots, but it also gets doubled up at the seam, and the results can look very wierd.

We just had a problem with this in a program we had to do in another country, where we had to post color correct in a linear suite. We had to go in and individually tweak all the transitions. So it ended up being fairly time-consuming, and we never quite got them to look the way they should. When you're nonlinear, that's not a problem because you're affecting the core video. So when you dissolve, you're dissolving between something that is the right color and another thing that is the right color, and the dissolve is a true reflection of a dissolve. So the nonlinear world has made that a better way of doing it.

DP: What percentage of the shots would you say need color correcting?

TM: Almost 100 percent. There's hardly a shot that we don't touch. Some of those changes are quite minute, or are done for technical reasons rather than aesthetic reasons. Occasionally we'll say, "Oh, it's just right." But in any given show, we have anywhere between 200 and 500 tapes, and we're taking a number of clips or images from those tapes. Maybe there's a few times that we don't touch a shot.

Now, there are times where producers come in, and they feel very strongly, "I don't want you to touch that. The way I shot it is the way I want it." Sometimes the creative decision-making process affects what the look should be, because obviously a look is very subjective. We have a look at *FRONTLINE* that we have the shows mold to. But if a producer has a particular vision, then we go with that vision. As long as I feel it will still fit within the *FRONTLINE* standards, that's fine with me.

DP: Can you describe the workflow for onlining a *FRONTLINE* show?

TM: When our producers finish their offline, they send us their final sequence, their audio on a hard drive, and all of their tapes. That material is due to me Monday, the week before air. The producer, often with the offline editor, comes in and onlines with us for two days, and mixes at a separate audio facility for two days. That all happens on Tuesday and Wednesday. The online and mix schedule goes like this: We have them come in and spend the first few hours of day 1 (Tuesday) setting the tone of the show. We go to each of the interviews and find the sweet spot for each one. We see them all together, because that is the fundamental baseline of a program. Once we're happy with that, we send the producer and editor off to the mix, and we batch digitize without them. Meanwhile, the mixer has been prepping tracks. They've gone in and found out what the EQ should be for everybody, and so on. The producer goes to the mix for the rest of the day.

Then generally the producer comes back the beginning of day 2 (Wednesday), and we review the program. Everybody makes time-coded notes on color correction (for example, this scene is too yellow, that scene is too bright) and on technical problems, such as a blanking problem or dropouts. We end up with a list of between 75 and 150 things to take care of on an hour-long program. And we spend all of the second day making those adjustments. At the end of day 2, we play the show as a final review with the producer. If they have any notes, they can either stay and watch us do them, or they fly out of here and we send them a copy the next day of the final tweaks. But usually we are doing very small tweaks.

Then I package the show on Thursday and Friday, adding the additional *FRONTLINE* and PBS elements that were created in another edit suite. Friday midday we finish with the master. It then gets Closed Caption encoded and dubbed to D5 at WGBH's facility, and the Master and backup tapes are shipped to PBS. Then we use Monday to create the international version, mop up, and get ready for the next show.

DP: How early in the process do you talk to a producer?

TM: I prefer to talk to producers when they initiate the project, because everything they do affects us in post, including the type of nonlinear system they edit on, the specifications and capabilities of that nonlinear system, the deck that they use to digitize, the person that they have digitize the audio... everything they do will affect me in the online. So I try to get with the producer on day 1 of their project — at the very least, talking to the person who's going to rent the nonlinear system; or, at the very, very least, talking to the editor on day 1 of their edit, so that we can make clear to them the important aspects of it.

The most important reason to talk to producers early is for audio, because in the digital age, the audio that the person hears at home is the very same audio that was digitized by someone in a nonlinear system when they were offlining. Essentially, it's the same audio that was recorded on the set. So I want to talk to my producer about: When you shoot, here's what you should be doing audio-wise; here's what you should not be doing.

For example, they might shoot large portions of their show with a conventional crew, but then they shoot chunks on a small DV camera. That's fine if you're going for a look, or you can only get something special on a small camera. But just because you're going to a smaller, more portable format does not mean that you can sacrifice audio. Generally, those more consumer-like devices have much poorer quality microphones and microphone pre-amps. So if you're going to shoot an interview with your DV camera, make sure you hang a mike.

Then, when you bring that material into your suite, make sure that it gets digitized properly. If you hire an intern and have him digitize at night, make sure that he understands what the meters are, that they digitize it with headphones on, that they're listening for problems. They can listen for and hear Dolby not being on, or double Dolby. You have to watch out for that, since whatever setting you used on the camera, you need to use on the deck. If your playback deck is set differently than the camera and you're double-decoding your Dolby, or you're not decoding your Dolby and you should be, then you have muddy audio or sibilant audio. That audio is what's going to end up in your mix, and you're going to be very unhappy.

Finally, it's a good idea to go to a mix house and talk to a mixer about how they feel about the quality of audio that's being digitized.

DP: When the producer digitizes the material for the offline, what kind of deck do you recommend, especially in terms of audio?

TM: The conventional path is shoot on Beta, playback on a Sony UVW 1800 or a UVW 1200 (which are industry-quality, not broadcast-quality decks), digitize, and so on. The problem is that the quality of the audio coming off a UVW 1800 is not as good as we would like for air.

What I tell producers is: You have a couple of paths you can follow. The highest quality method is to rent or buy a broadcast- quality deck. However, that's an expense very few producers are willing to incur. There are a couple of other options. Option number 1 is: You use the lower quality deck to digitize, you get down to the end of your project, you listen to your project with a good set of headphones or a good set of speakers, and determine if any audio is not up to your standards. Then you decide to redigitize that stuff or not. When you go to the mix, your mixer will help you out if that stuff's not good.

Option number 2 is: Use the UVW deck, and when you get to the end of the process, rent a broadcast-quality deck for a day or two, and batch digitize just the audio you need. This is what almost all of my producers elect to do. And then 19 out of 20 times, they get to the end and they say, "I don't have time to redigitize the audio. It's more important that I spend that day recutting my film and getting it perfect. I'll fix the audio in the mix." Or, "It's good enough." Or, "No one can hear those differences." But there are people who are extremely conscientious about sound; they're either doing Option 2 or getting a good deck in the first place.

Another option that a few are doing is to rent or buy, for almost the same price as an 1800, a BVW 50, which is a broadcast-quality field deck. The advantage is that you get the good quality audio, and the Avid can control it. The disadvantage is that when you do an output from an Avid, you can only do a hard record. In other words, the record tape won't have the same timecode as your sequence. However, for most of your review copies, you're doing a VHS or a crash record on Beta anyway. So for months of editing, this is a great way to go because you have a machine that has high quality audio, and you can still dub them off for people who need review copies. Just at the very end, you need to rent any kind of controllable Beta machine to do a digital cut for your mix or for your online, so when you're ready to go to online, you have a copy of the show that has matching time code to your master.

DP: What are some things you've seen go wrong with audio?

TM: Many mistakes can get made along the way: Somebody digitizes the audio wrong; somebody has the Dolby switch on the wrong setting; somebody takes audio from channels 1 and 2 instead of channels 3 and 4, or from 3 and 4 rather than 1 and 2. (That's another reason to have a broadcast quality machine from the beginning; industrial-quality machines in general give you only channels 1 and 2. Now, you can get modification kits for those inexpensive decks. But why not just use a higher quality machine in the first place?) Some sound people prefer the sound of analog tracks (1 and 2) to the AFM tracks (3 and 4). They say that analog sound is richer. Others say, "Make sure you use the AFM tracks on channels 3 and 4."

Another issue we occassionally encounter is lack of sync. This can come from a variety of areas. When digitizing audio only it is important that the digitizing device also looks at incoming video so that it can lock to 29.97 video. More often the problem is between the mix facility and our online room. We think in this digital age that sync is absolute. But as soon as the picture and sound part ways (video to the online house and audio to the mix facility) there are opportunities for sync to be lost. What we do to avoid this is to go back to a traditional film technique of adding sync pops. When the offline is locked, the editor puts a single frame of video and audio (bars and tone work well) 1 second before program start and 1 second after the end of the program. This way when the mix comes back to us we can line up the pops and verify dead sync immediately.

DP: What should producers talk to you about before the shoot, in terms of the visual quality?

TM: Well, I try not to affect their visual style. By and large, the things that shooters do that are technically wrong, I can cure fairly easily (meaning chroma over the top, or lumina over the top, or blacks that are too deep). I make sure that if they are shooting with a non-broadcast-standard format (Hi-8 or DV or some kind of smaller format), that they pay attention to the same types of things you would expect of a professional cameraman.

I try and recommend to them some new techniques that other people are using with small format cameras. There's a lot of people out there who will have a Beta rig on their primary interview subject, and they'll take their DV camera and reverse it on the interview subject. Since the interview subject is going to get a couple of nodding smiles, why spend extra money to have another whole rig there? In my color correction suite, I can make them match pretty exactly, particularly if it's lit well .

Also, some people are stacking their DV camera to get a wide shot and a close-up. Another thing that people are doing (and this is one of my favorites): One of my producers just bought a Steadicam JR, the little junior Steadicam, that he used with a little DV camera. And he got the most gorgeous, sexy stuff; it looked like he had a Luma Crane. He would do these sweeping long shots through scenes — he'd follow people through hallways; he'd come swooping into their office. Just these little things added this really nice flow to their production.

DP: What can producers do to create visually consistent images in the shoot? After all, a show is usually shot in several different locations.

TM: Our programs are shot all over the place. They're almost never shot in a single city. So if you can't bring your crew everywhere, option number 1 is: Pick up a sound man and bring the shooter. Option number 2 is: Bring the camera, and hire the shooter. But failing that, if you're going to pick up crews and you're going to be using their rig, then you need to do the best you can to get those interviews to be shot uniformly. You have to impose yourself in the process. First, get your favorite shooter to shoot something for you, even if it's an interview of you. Then, if you can, get your shooter to diagram how they do it — what lights they use, where each instrument is, how much softness they use, what the average wattage is of each lamp. Take the tape and diagram to every shooter and say, "This is what I want you to match." In the shoot, make sure you put that tape in the machine, and if necessary, say, "You know what? This is not the same." So first you have to educate yourself, and then you have to be prepared to be unpopular.

DP: What are some of the ways you're using third-party applications?

TM: Despite the best efforts of our editors and producers, sometimes they have to leave a jump cut in the middle of an interview. Usually a soft cut, a couple of frames dissolve, handles it for them, but sometimes it doesn't. Sometimes the move is so radical — the person who has their head up and to the right in one scene, and down and to the left in the other scene — that it really doesn't work. So we're now using Elastic Reality to morph between those two disparate cuts. And I would say that 3/4 of the time it looks as though it was shot that way.

We also use AfterEffects extensively for graphics and layering work. In the simpler range, we're replacing the rostrum camera by scanning images, and then doing the moves in AfterEffects. That gives us more flexibility. For example, with the rostrum camera, you think you need a 7-second move, but you get in your edit and you end up doubling it. It's now a 14-second move. You've got a big slo-mo on there, which you'd rather not have, and you might see the steppiness of the slo-mo. Now, we'll take that same document, scan it in, recreate the move in AfterEffects, and make it the correct duration in the first place.

We'll also take documents, and in AfterEffects, defocus everything but the information that we want the audience to focus on. And this can be incorporated into a move.

Steve Audette, one of our editors, has done a highlighter technique, where you can be way up above the document, zooming down, then panning over the top of the document, and highlighting (as though with a yellow hilighter) just the words you want people to read. It"s a very cool little technique.

John MacGibbon, another one of our editors, has brought a new visual style to some of our promos recently, often by using Boris Effects. For one promo called "Making Babies," which was about how technology is affecting infertility, he created water droplet effects, where concentric rings are moving in and out. On another promo, on Kosovo, John took imagery of a war-torn region, and he skewed it and sort of melted it slightly one way, and then it would sort of move in another direction. It's a subconscious thing when you're watching it, but the idea was to say to the audience, "Things are screwed up over there."

DP: How has the role of the producer changed with the advent of digital technology?

TM: I think the age of digital production has meant that a producer needs to be more of a "man for all seasons." Producers need to have a better understanding of every step of the process, because we've gone from an age of specialization to an age of generalization. We now have more shooter-editors. We also have one person in an online who's not just doing the editing, but also the color correction, making the pictures look beautiful, creating special effects, and doing graphics and titling. And audio is handled very differently as well. Producers need a broader view of the process, so that they (a) get a higher quality product and (b) don't spend more money than they need to.

DP: Any problems that you'd like to see producers overcome?

TM: The biggest problems that we have are that producers wait too long to have the client review, and then they deceive themselves about the magnitude of changes they need to make after the review. What ends up happening on almost every project is that they've got their fine cut screening one or two weeks before the show is due to me. Our executive producer walks in, watches the show. They throw the film out. They say, "Let's start again." Maybe it's not that major. Maybe they say, "You haven't covered this, so you have to go shoot a new interview." That is frequent. It's not once out of every 20 times, but one out of four times. They say, "You haven't shown the other side of the story well enough. You have to go out and shoot a couple of interviews." Or, "Put the back in the front, and the front in the middle, and the middle in the back." They essentially set off a nuclear explosion in the edit suite.

At this point, the producer goes into crisis mode, and they take their editor (who's already overworked and been doing too much overtime) and their entire staff, and they all work crazy hours for a week. And then they arrive late for the online, and there are things wrong.

One of the biggest issues is that stock footage or footage that was originally put in the offline from a VHS tape has not been replaced with its Beta time-coded source. And when they get the stock footage on Beta, the timecode seldom matches. So we have to hand-place stock footage shots, which is incredibly time-consuming. We have taken onlines that should have been two days, and they take a week. Producers will say, "It's just a couple of shots." Well, it's actually just a couple of scenes that happen to be 5 minutes long, that have 50 shots in them. And they completely discount how much time that will take.

And then they don't do the audio work that they should do, so the mix house ends up bearing the brunt of it. They come in and they just have basic tracks — no sound effects or dialog fill. So they either get less of a mix, or they spend more money at the mix than they would have.

The other problem is that after the executive producer said, "Do A, B, and C," the producer thinks to himself, "Ah, I'm just going to edit what I have better, do some of what they asked for, and then prove to them that my version is better in the fine cut." And inevitably, the executive producer goes in and says, "You know what? I asked you to make changes because my version is better." These people are at the top of their game for a reason. And it's their show.

DP: What's the solution?

TM: Get the client (or executive producer, or whoever writes the checks) to look at the program sooner, and do what they say. Make your schedule work so that you're done sooner. Don't back up your schedule to the online. Back up your schedule to two weeks before the online, and then budget for the fact that you're going to spend money and time re-editing your show. If you're wrong, the money is in your pocket — instead of you having less than a good program.

Another solution is: If you have to make significant changes in a short amount of time, diagram the resources you need to get the job done. Immediately get a lot of people involved in solving the critical path issues. Write down on a piece of paper how it will all get done. It is far cheaper to hire an extra editor to work on your system between 2 a.m. and 10 a.m., or midnight and 8 a.m., to do sound work on your newly cut sequences, or to replace stock footage.

DP: What qualities for you make a good producer?

TM: To me, preparation and trust are the keys. Prepare well, leaving as few "we'll fix it in the online or the mix" issues as possible.

One of our senior producers, Mike Kirk, almost always shoots his entire program with one guy. He spends the money to get the right guy. He has a favorite shooter, Ben McCoy, whom he trusts. His shows generally come into my box with very little tweaking, almost none.

For us, there's nothing like knowing that the producer inherently trusts us. So, find people you can trust, people who share your vision, who do things well, and who minimize mistakes, and then go with them and trust them. That's what I believe in.

Arnie Harchik

Arnie Harchik is a freelance Avid editor based in Mansfield, Massa-chusetts. He has been editing since 1986, and editing (offline and online) on Avid Media Composer and Avid Xpress systems since 1992. Harchik specializes in documentary and corporate programs. His projects include nonlinear online editing of documentaries and pro-mos for the FRONTLINE television series on PBS.

Digital Producer: Let's talk about digitizing. What do you need to do to get good audio?

Arnie Harchik: One thing to consider when you are digitizing, even for the rough cut, is that the audio going into the system may be your final audio. So when you are working in low-res [low resolution] video you are actually working with online audio. For a lot of my projects, we take the audio we originally digitized for the rough cut and use that audio in the mix.

To get good quality audio when you digitize, you need to get a clean signal from the deck to the Avid. I try to monitor the levels while I am digitizing which means I don't leave a digitize unattended. As long as the levels in your final rough cut sequence are clean and consistent, that audio should be fine for ultimately outputting to the mix. When you're ready to finish the program, such as an hour-long documentary, you only need to redigitize the video at a higher online resolution. This can save you hours of online time.

DP: Do you tend to digitize everything at once?

AH: It all depends on the project, the system, and the producer. Ide-ally, if there are ten tapes for a project, I'd like to digitize each tape in its entirety. Then I have everything at my fingertips. But usually I don't have enough drive space. For the piece I'm working on now, I just spent the last two hours logging about five tapes, all B-roll. I logged everything. I just shuttled through the shots; if I didn't like one, I still logged it, added it to my bin, gave it a name, and then moved on to the next one. I can shuttle through a 40-second shot in about ten seconds. Now that I've logged the shots, I'll batch digitize only the shots I need into the Avid.

DP: Do you prefer to log or do you prefer producers to log?

AH: I prefer to log if I can, because then I'm familiar with all the names and descriptions that I gave everything. However, producers don't always want to pay you to do that; they would rather you just come in and edit. The down side is: While I'm editing, I constantly wonder if there are extra cutaways I could use. If I had logged the tape myself, there's a good chance I'd remember what and where the cutaways were.

DP: What if the producer logged the tapes and didn't log all the footage. Then you come to a spot in the sequence and say, "I wish I had another cutaway of that person."

AH: I just open up the bin on the Avid, and see what the tape and timecode are for the B-roll shot that I have. I pop the tape in the deck and shuttle through the tape to about the same timecode. Never be afraid to go back to the tapes. Of course, when you digitize you have to make sure to enter the same tape name you've been using. Otherwise you won't be able to find the right tape to go back to.

DP: What formats do you typically work with?

AH: Mostly I work with Beta SP going in component on the Avid. You know, the Avid has two video inputs, component and composite. If you play a tape and switch from component to composite, you can definitely see a picture quality change. Component is better quality, and is used for inputting Beta SP. I hate when I go into an edit suite, and both component and composite are connected to the Beta deck. That can spell trouble. If the Video tool in the Avid is set to composite (which it is by default), you might not realize it, but for the last three days (or whatever), you've been inputting a composite signal from the Beta deck into the Avid! You're not taking advantage of the superior component signal. Rule of thumb: Connect only the cables you need for whatever you're digitizing right now, either component or composite. Unplug the other cables. Then, if you want to digitize component and you don't see an image in the monitor, open the Avid's Video tool and change the setting from composite to component. It's kind of a fail-safe method which will prevent you from digitizing composite when you want to digitize component.

DP: Are you using any digital formats?

AH: I have done a couple of projects that have incorporated some miniDV tape. We digitize directly from the camera into the editing system which means we don't get timecode. In that case, we have to digitize at high res right from the start because we can't redigitize.

We take the camera's S-video output and loop that through a Beta deck into the Avid. Doing this transcodes the S-video signal into component. The picture looks better than if you take the composite video output from the digital camera and go into composite video input on the Avid.

I also worked on another project where we had a professional DV deck that worked just like the Beta deck. You put the tape in, and the deck looked for the timecode.

DP: What kinds of changes are you seeing that reflect the differences between linear and nonlinear editing?

AH: Everything is faster. You see it in movies, in promos, and in commercials. I think that's the result of nonlinear editing. Also, people are getting more done, and faster, because they have Photoshop and AfterEffects on their Mac. Producers can hire one talented person to do a majority of what they need right on their system, rather than going to numerous specialized facilities.

I remember when I first started working on the Avid, a producer commented that he couldn't get up and walk around as much as he used to in the linear suite because things were getting done much more quickly. I'll bet if you talked to him now he doesn't remember that; he doesn't do the comparison anymore because he has been on the Avid for so long.

I don't think that everyone is taking full advantage of the digital nature of nonlinear editing. To give you an example: Recently I was working on a project and the graphics were done by a big graphics house and sent to us on Beta tape for an Avid online. I thought by now everyone would give us the graphics digitally, on a Jaz or Zip disk. Not only were they handing me Beta tapes, they were handing me Beta tapes with the mattes. I was thinking, "Wow, they could give me PICT files with real-time keys at this point."

DP: Any advice for producers regarding finishing on a nonlinear system?

AH: Just be sure you've finished offlining your show before you bring it to the online. At some point there will come a day when drive space won't be an issue and image quality will be perfect, and you can digitize the first time at high res. But right now we still have to do everything first at low res. When you go to the online system, which is more expensive, make sure you're finished editing the show.

DP: How do you like to collaborate with the producer during the edit?

AH: For the offline, I like to do the first cut alone. For the online, I like the producer to come in once in a while to look at the color correcting I'm doing. Then, after I've done most of the work, we watch it together to make sure that it's okay.

DP: How much do you help producers follow what you are doing?

AH: It mostly depends on the producer. I tell some producers everything that I'm doing, especially for something that's taking me a long time. I want them to know why it's taking me a long time. On the other hand, some producers don't want to follow along. I work with one producer who's on the phone with his stockbroker whenever I do something that takes more than thirty seconds. But when we worked together in a linear tape room, it was the same way. I'm not sure the technology has changed that aspect of post. Generally, the producer acts the same in nonlinear as in linear: If they didn't want to sit there in the linear world, they don't want to sit there when I'm working in nonlinear.

DP: It's easy to make changes on a nonlinear system. That being the case, how do you bring a project to a close and say, "No more changes"?

AH: Nonlinear's great selling point is that it allows people to tinker with the show whenever they want. The drawback is they're allowed to tinker with the show whenever they want. You used to have to spend more time talking them out of last minute changes because if the change involved taking five seconds out of the middle of the show, you just shuddered as an editor.

But the real answer to this question is the same for linear or nonlinear. Deadlines and budget decide this. I'll keep tweaking the program for as long as the producer likes, but at some point he has to let go.

Either the show has to air, or he's run out of money. Next week I'm making changes to a show that I thought I finished three months ago. Those shows with no deadlines are the most "dangerous."

Tom Hayes

Tom Hayes is an Avid editor, a self-described "Avidtaur" — half man, half machine. His company is Foglight Films, based in Columbus, Ohio. He edits documentaries, commercials, and corporate/industrial programs, and his projects include Escalator over the Hill, for the Public Broadcasting Service, and People and the Land, an independent production. Hayes has been editing since 1970, and he's been an Avid editor since 1991.

Digital Producer: How would you describe the difference between working in a linear and nonlinear editing environment?

Tom Hayes: In the linear room, it was like quarry men working at a rock face with small chisels. In other words, you'd be trying to finish each shot as you went; because when you were editing the tenth shot, it was prohibitive to add four frames on the end of the fifth shot in a 250-shot show. Just the real-time rollovers were so time-consuming that you wound up having to make a lot of compromises, and attack your problems on a priority basis. Nonlinear editing is much more like sculpture, in that we just blow blocks off the face of the quarry and go for structure. So when you start editing the rough cut, precise IN and OUT marks really are irrelevant. We can just storyboard together a basic idea, throw it into the timeline, and that's where the real cutting is done. That wasn't possible in a linear room. Nonlinear editing gives me total, absolute flexibility, and a work flow that's much more reminiscent of other art forms like painting and sculpture.

DP: And the disadvantages of nonlinear editing?

TH: Well, there is one big disadvantage. If you don't digitize your own material, you may never see all the material in real time, even once. Historically, whether you were in a linear tape room or a film room, a good part of your day was spent shuttling footage. And whether you were thinking about it or not, you were doing a lot of frame grabs with the reptilian lobes of your brain. I mean, you could be shooting the breeze with the producer, but you'd still be going, "That shot follows that shot. It's on this reel. There's six of those kind of shots." You're storing all this stuff when you're doing that. And that, to me, is the one double-edged sword of nonlinear.

DP: So how do you deal with that problem?

TH: I try not to use assistants. If the timeline is flexible enough, I try to digitize my own material. So, you might ask, what do I think about digitizing? It's probably the only time I get to see the footage, really just get to sit down and look at it.

DP: What advice would you give producers on how to log?

TH: Log loose. Don't over-select. Don't do the editor's job before the editor does it. Keep big elbow room. Because you never know. Those shots that you say, "I'd never use that in a million years," always turn out to be the shots that save the show.

DP: Can you give an example of what you mean?

TH: If there's a pan right and a pan left and a tilt up and a tilt down, and a zoom in and a zoom out, I want the whole thing, because you never know how that shot's going to break against the montage. Otherwise, I might have to go through some silly season antics with flopping a shot or adding a motion effect or something like that. And this really speaks to working in low res [low resolution] first. I run into a lot of people who are working in high res exclusively, and they're over-selecting constantly. They'll say, "We don't have time to redigitize." But what they wind up having time to do is go on these bug hunts, looking for specific shots, because they didn't get them at the front end. And that's just a big pain.

DP: Do producers tend to come in with their programs already set in their mind?

TH: I've worked with producers who are so set that they come in logged to the frame, and just to be able to use their logs, I have to increment and decrement all the timecodes in their bins, which I hate. And then I get reasonable producers who just sort of say, "Here's a bucket of this; here's a bucket of that." But the tighter it is, the worse the session is. And by the end of it, we wind up having to go back to the reels so many times.

DP: How do you get good audio?

TH: I do a final mix listening to cans [headphones] as a reference point, just to make sure that I don't have any extraneous sounds.

Because my CPU and my drives are in the room, subtle things can escape me during the edit. The only way to get heavy isolation to hear and make sure you don't have any hum, and make sure that there aren't any audible page turns or shuffled paper, and stuff like that, is to just go in the cans and listen through. You know, it's the subtle stuff that will get you.

DP: What do producers need to do before they come into the edit room?

TH: Just make sure they don't have any redundant tape IDs.

DP: Do you have a favorite way of naming tapes?

TH: Yes. Always lead with three numbers, starting with 001, and then add two alphanumerics for the project ID. That way I know that if for any reason it had to go linear in the end, I have a clean list.

DP: Do you have any advice for the shoot in terms of audio?

TH: I just say, keep the levels low. If I was talking to an audio guy, I'd say: be conservative, because if you're on Beta, you've got Dolby C in the system, so you've got lots of head room without building up noise. And split your mikes out any time you can. For example, go for the camera mike on channel 1 and then the body mike on channel 2. Keep them discrete so that you have the ability to tease one out completely if you don't like it.

DP: Is there anything that drives you crazy about producers?

TH: What I really can't take is that during the session, many producers will be reticent to try things. They're still in this kind of linear mode. The time it takes to discuss a change is going to be more than it takes me to change it. So during the session, I go, "Can we try this?" or "I'd like to try that," and they go, "Well...." And then there's the willingness to make changes during final output, when you've already rezzed it up [redigitized at a higher resolution]. And those things that you didn't try suddenly start coming back on the table.

DP: What kind of producers do you like to work with?

TH: Real sort of freewheeling brains. Just freewheeling brains. You know, it's like cartoons: There are people who hear that little devil at their shoulder that says, "We don't have time for that," and then they just say, "Get out of here!" because they can hear that little

Media Composer angel going, "We got lots of time because we can change this so quick."

My other favorite thing are producers who trust me. I work best unsupervised. One of the points of having an editor as opposed to just cutting your own stuff is to get a fresh look at the footage. And so if they give me the script and the logs and let me run at least on my first cut, then it's going to have a fresh look. I'll build it from the ground up, and then they can go, "That's not really what I was looking for," or "That's interesting, I hadn't thought of that." You know, it makes it more interesting.

Wes Plate

Wes Plate is an editor of commercial spots for Pinnacle Studios in Seattle, Washington. He has been editing since 1989, and editing on Avid Media Composer since 1995. Recently, he edited national commercial spots for Home Depot.

Digital Producer: How do you help your clients visualize ideas?

Wes Plate: Since I work with advertising agencies, the ideas are pretty fleshed out before they get to me. They usually have their concept, they bring us a storyboard and a script, and we talk about how it's going to be visualized.

DP: Do your clients ever want things that aren't possible?

WP: Yes, they want things that aren't possible, they want it quickly, and they don't have enough money to pay for it — that happens all the time. We just have to look at the situation and say, "Well, this is what you want; these are the resources we have, and here are the laws of physics." But in the end, it always works out. Sometimes we can pull off some pretty amazing things. Things that don't seem possible become very possible. On the other hand, things that seemed possible in the beginning may start to become rather impossible later on.

DP: Does the producer — or in the commercial world, the art director and the other creatives — need to know what's possible?

WP: Yes, I think so, but at the same time they can't be limited by that. One of the neat things about creative people is that they think amazing thoughts, and they don't worry about the strategy or technology needed to realize those ideas. Once they come up with the ideas, they meet with people in the effects or production industry to start figuring out how to make it work.

DP: Can you give me an example of a project you worked on where you created some good effects?

WP: Some of the best effects I've done were for effects-heavy national Home Depot commercials directed by Dale Fay. One was a spot for lumber, and this is how the client first described it to me: "A stack of wood falls down, revealing the logo, Home Depot. The stack then spins around, a saw blade goes up the middle of the stack of wood, splitting the stack of wood into two pieces so it opens up like doors. Then the camera turns to read words that are printed on the edge of the newly cut wood." I was listening to this idea and thinking to myself, "That's impossible." Because you can't cut and then all of a sudden have words printed there. I was not thinking "out of the box," like the people who wrote this idea were. Then once I let myself think about the possibility of how this "impossible" idea could happen, I started actually doing it. I started identifying problems and immediately working around them. It turns out that there was nothing about it that was impossible. It was just a limitation of my thinking at the moment. Generally, if somebody can come up with an idea, you can figure out a way to make it work.

DP: You said before that something that seemed possible in the beginning may start to become impossible later on. Can you explain that?

WP: For another commercial, we had a very simple idea that became the most complicated, nightmarish thing we ever did. This was the idea: The camera was supposed to go past lamps that were turned off, and as the camera passed them, the lamps would turn on. This is how we'd execute it: We'd shoot one pass through the house with all the lights off, then do the exact same pass again with the lights on. In the edit, we would go through and selectively mask areas with mattes to make it appear like lights were turning on. But in the shoot (which I didn't attend), they ended up shooting every single light on a different pass. So in the edit, before we knew it we had around 30 different layers, just so we could have all these lights turn on. And we had to do all these layers of compositing, adding these layers together. Then these little imperfections in each layer start adding up, and suddenly we had 30 layers, each with this minor imperfection! So it was the simplest idea that was botched in the shoot, and ended up making the post-production very difficult.

DP: So how could that problem have been avoided?

WP: That can be avoided by talking to the editor beforehand. In this case, there was obviously imperfect communication. You need to discuss what will happen in post before anything is shot, so the editor has the opportunity to say, "No, no, no, no, no. Don't do a separate pass for every single light. That's going to be a nightmare."

In general, I'm a firm believer in getting the editor involved as soon as possible. The editor can be a huge resource by being on the set, or at least being in a meeting before production. For some of my spots, I've been able to go on the set and work with the director. Those spots end up being immensely better, because instead of being in the edit room two weeks later saying, "I wish I had a close-up of her," I could be on the set saying, "You know, I could see myself wanting a close-up of her." So the sooner the editor gets involved with the producer, the easier the edit will be.

This is especially true for complicated spots with effects and compositing. There are certain features of the Avid that make my life either better or worse, so that I can kind of say, "Hey, don't shoot it that way because it's going to be a nightmare in Avid. But if you shoot it this other way, it will really make editing a lot easier."

DP: Are there any problems you see that might be avoided?

WP: Well, there are a couple of things. Sometime people shoot camera moves backwards, and then they'll plan on reversing it in post. One spot that I remember, the whole spot was shot backwards, and the client wanted to reverse the motion and change the speed. Because of the way my system dealt with motion effects, it was a huge hassle. And in that specific case, from what I could see, there was no reason to shoot backwards. The problem would have been avoided if they had discussed the plan with me before the shoot.

DP: What should producers look for in an effects editor?

WP: I think that there's a huge difference between people who understand and perform effects, and people who are more traditional storytelling editors. Just like not every great effects editor can cut a beautiful story, not every great story editor can cut a complex effect for you.

A good effects editor understands the entire process of what it takes to create an effect. I can be working in the Avid and visualizing the effect, and understand what it's going to take once it goes into a Henry [a finishing system made by Quantel] to be finished. I may not be able operate a Henry, but I understand what a Henry can do, and so I can prepare for it.

Producers should look for someone who is creative within the world of effects, instead of someone who puts together an effect in a kind of technical, mechanical way. Effects can be so expensive, and everything gets so locked down, you might not think there's room to change anything. But there's *always* room for creativity.

A good effects editor is very familiar with his tools. When I work on the Media Composer and with AfterEffects and Photoshop, I don't have to think about how to do something; the interface is second nature. All I'm thinking about is the image, the composite, and how it looks. That's really helpful, because sometimes things get so complicated that the last thing you need is to try to figure out how to do it. Instead, you want to be thinking about the end result.

I remember the first time I ever had to do an effects edit. The art director mentioned to me that he wanted five different edits happening at one time, different edits happening on different layers. And I remember thinking to myself, "Different layers? What does that mean?" Because I came from a more traditional background where there was your one video track, and that's what you used. And if you wanted two things, you had to run it through a switcher or do all kinds of complex things. I wasn't quite ready to leap into the world of layers. Of course, now I never edit on only one layer. I don't just edit from left to right across a timeline, but also up and down; a lot of things happen vertically.

DP: Do you ever have problems with producers bringing the wrong elements into the edit suite?

WP: Yes, sometimes a producer will bring in a ZIP with a Quark document on it, but I don't have a ZIP drive and we don't have Quark in this building. Or they'll bring in an image file with the wrong format, or it will be created in the wrong aspect ratio for television. That kind of thing can easily be sorted out in a discussion before the edit.

As for photographs, once in a while we shoot them with a camera. But typically we tell clients to bring them in already scanned, and we give them the specs for how to do it.

Tomorrow I have to do a credit roll. So I told the person, "Listen, between Tuesday and Friday, type up your credit roll in Microsoft Word, and I'll just paste it into the Title tool on the Avid." A lot of those kinds of things can be prepared in advance, and that saves a lot of time.

DP: What qualities do you value in a producer or creative director?

WP: The jobs that are the most fulfilling are the ones where I can speak with the creatives beforehand so they get to trust me as a creative contributor to the project. The most gratifying thing is to be able to give something to the project, instead of being there just to help the client realize their vision. I want to realize their vision, but also to try and make it better, and to put some of my own creativity into it.

DP: How do you generally finish your projects?

WP: We create an EDL, and then we edit in a linear online suite, or on a Henry. We don't use the Avid as the finishing station. We use it as the tool to identify problems, to put that whole idea together, and to start visualizing how things are going to work. In the future, we'll be able to offline and online on the same system, and have it look brilliant. I look forward to that.

DP: What do you like most about nonlinear editing and creating effects on a nonlinear system?

WP: I like the power and the flexibility to have an idea and say, "Okay, what would that look like?" And then, boom-boom-boom, do some things on the computer, wait for a render, and there it is. Then, "Great, that almost works. Now let's see what I need to fix." I like the ability to easily and quickly realize the vision.

Larry Young

Larry Young is a freelance Avid Editor/Cameraman/Producer, and owns his own company, Best Shot, Inc., based in Hopkinton, Massachusetts. He has shot and edited documentaries in the United States, Canada, South and Central America, the Carribean, and Africa; he has edited network and local news, hour-long news magazine shows, commercials, and entertainment specials. Among many other current projects, Young is editing the hour-long morning magazine program, Martha Stewart Living.

Digital Producer: Let's discuss some of the various video formats currently being used.

Larry Young: Beta SP is basically the industry standard. It is the most widely used format, period. All the major networks, with the exception of Fox, shoot Beta SP every single day. Most American television stations shoot Beta SP every day. I would say that almost everything you see on TV of videotape origin has been shot on Beta SP.

DVCPRO, by Panasonic, (along with Sony's DVCAM) is more of an industrial format, and it's cheaper. If you're doing industrial videos and you need to lower costs, you might use that. DVCPRO is being used extensively by Fox Television for news gathering, and has made some inroads into other news gathering operations, mostly because of the lighter cassette and the lower cost.

You might even see miniDV. A lot of documentary now is being done in miniDV. Editors have been telling me they've been running into it more and more. MiniDV tends to be shot by producers who are out shooting their own footage. There's the series called Trauma on the Learning Channel, which is shot in miniDV. Also, miniDV tends to be used for the "fly on the wall" type of stuff, because the cameras are smaller, and the producer can shoot with it by himself.

Digi-Beta is also used extensively, but tends to be used only in high-end productions for commercials, entertainment specials, that type of thing, where the budgets are much larger.

DP: If a producer is weighing shooting in analog versus digital format, what are some things he or she should think about?

LY: In tests that I've done with DVCPRO, it really does look good. Although it's considered lower end, I really couldn't fault it. DVCPRO 50, which was introduced at NAB [National Association of Broadcasters] this year, is more comparable to Beta SP. I think Beta SP still looks great. I think Digi-Beta looks better, but most people can't afford to shoot Digi-Beta. With HDTV, hardly anyone can afford to shoot it; the camera is prohibitively expensive at this time. Until it gains wider acceptance, until it's being broadcast into homes, you won't see a lot of people using it.

A word on quality: DVCPRO doesn't experience the dropout that Beta SP does. Beta SP is horrible in its dropouts.

But Beta SP is still the standard. It's been out since the mid-eighties and has very deep market penetration. It's pretty much what broadcast producers are going to demand. If I'm doing an industrial shoot, it can go either way, Beta SP or DVCPRO; but in my experience, producers still want to use Beta SP. It's easier for the post facilities to handle. It's easier to get into an Avid (in terms of finding a post suite equipped with Beta SP machines for record and playback). At the end of the nineties, we can see that Beta SP is now what the 3/4" format was throughout the seventies and early eighties... a real work horse.

DP: Is anyone shooting in 16x9, the aspect ratio for HDTV?

LY: There is some program origination in 16x9, but not much, although the BBC has been shooting a lot in 16x9. Very few shows are actually shot in HD; these tend to be very high-bucks productions. If people want to have a show in 16x9, they shoot Digi-Beta in the 16x9 aspect ratio, and then uplink to HDTV. So all they're doing is a standard conversion. It's a cheaper way to do it, and you really can't tell. It's very, very acceptable.

In the early eighties, we used to do the same thing with 3/4" tape. We'd just shoot it and edit it on 3/4", and we'd bump it up to 1" for the master. We broadcast it on 1", and nobody could tell the difference.

Another thing: Let's say you're shooting in a 16x9 aspect ratio, because you think your show will have a long shelf-life and you'll eventually want to broadcast it on HDTV. But first, you'll need to broadcast the show in a 4x3 aspect ratio for standard definition television. You have to realize that those are two different framings. It means that when you shoot, you have to shoot everything towards the center of the frame, which is a shame. It wastes the 16x9 frame; it's not taking advantage of the wonderful aspect ratio, the wonderful depth of field of 16x9. If you don't center the shot, you have to optically pan and scan, and then it will look really terrible, like all the old movies that have been panned-and-scanned for television.

DP: Do you have any advice for producers who are buying miniDV cameras and going out and shooting their own footage?

LY: Light, light, and light. My biggest complaint about anything I've seen on miniDV is that producers are treating it like home video. It ain't home video. Although producers are capturing the action they want, you often can't see faces. The picture then has to go through extensive color correction in the edit. This can cost big bucks, just to get it to look right.

Granted, in a lot of the situations where you want to use miniDV, you can't put in a lot of light. But when you're doing a sit-down interview, even the most minimal light would help fill in the faces and bring the foreground out from the background. And don't shoot the interview subject against a window. If you do that, you get a silhouette.

Furthermore, if you're going to do an interview, put a lavalier mike on the person and plug it into your camera. Don't use the mike on the camera.

Once I worked on a project, and the producer had shot the footage on miniDV. He had the camera on autofocus, and he was letting the camera average itself so the backgrounds were blowing out (in other words, the whites were too hot) and the clipping wasn't set correctly on the camera. On top of that, the autofocus was focusing on the background instead of the foreground. Producers need to make sure that they know how to operate their cameras before they go out and shoot.

DP: You're a cameraperson and an editor. What would you tell another cameraperson (or a producer shooting miniDV) that would reduce problems in the nonlinear edit room?

LY: Don't record time-of-day timecode. Record continuous run time. If you turn the camera off and then turn it on again, make sure you hold the last shot for several seconds before you turn the camera off, and then hold the first shot for several seconds after you turn the camera back on, so you have room at the head of the shot you want. If you have plenty of roll-in and plenty of roll-out, the tape deck will have enough time to get up to speed during digitizing, and there will be enough footage to make a dissolve on the first or last shot.

Also, do not shoot non-drop frame, especially if you're going for NTSC broadcast. Non-drop frame run times are not accurate in a broadcast world.

DP: When you're shooting in a digital format, do you have to consider anything different in terms of crew, the equipment that you need, or the preparation for the edit?

LY: No, it's just another format. The average cameraman can shoot any format. There is a difference in cost, going down from HD, to Digi-Beta, to Beta SP, to DVC, and finally to miniDV, which is the cheapest.

DP: What qualities do you value in a producer, when you're shooting?

LY: I like producers who can really describe what it is they're doing, who have a good handle on their subject, who know what they're looking for, and who know what they've already shot (if I'm one of several cameramen on a project) and can explain it to me. Or if I'll be shooting the whole project, I like it if they can give me an idea of what they want their project to look like so I can design lighting and camera moves. I like it if we can figure out what's practical, and what's not practical; what will work, and what won't work. We need to know all these things, and you can't if there is no communication. The problem with television traditionally has been that it's a communication business where nobody communicates. The producer doesn't communicate with the director. The director doesn't communicate with the cameraman. And then finally it's all dumped on the editor, who has to make chicken salad.

DP: Now I have some questions for you as an editor. What's the best way for a producer to prepare for a smooth nonlinear edit?

LY: The best way is, know your footage. Don't walk into the edit room with three boxes of tape and expect to digitize everything onto the system, knowing that you're not going to use half of it. Before the edit, log and screen your footage. Pick out your interviews and the basic shots you think you're going to need. Figure out what you want your show to look like.

DP: Do you like producers to have very detailed logs?

LY: Yes. I want to know what the shots are by looking at a one-line description for each clip that's logged in a bin. I also appreciate a Digitize column in the bin that tells me what to digitize, or some other indication of what to digitize.

DP: Do you want to say anything else about digitizing?

LY: The numbers that you enter into the nonlinear editing system should exactly match the numbers you wrote on the tape boxes during the shoot. You should always use the following system: The first tape is numbered 01. The 500th tape is numbered 500. Every tape has an individual number, period. I know somebody who's cutting a 5-hour series on women in rock and roll. They have 900 tapes. The first tape number is 01 and the last tape number is 900. The only exception is a multi-camera shoot. So if I have four cameras, I'll have tape 01A, 01B, 01C, and 01D. And that's the way all the editors I know work.

DP: How do you familiarize yourself with the material on the tapes?

LY: I look at it.

DP: When do you do that?

LY: I usually do that as I'm logging. Or if I have an assistant log it or if the producer logs it, I go back and review it. I think it's important to take that time, because it makes me a better informed editor. There may be a shot that I need for continuity that nobody else thought of. Or a producer may request a shot that I don't think is very good, and I want to be able to explain why and offer an alternative.

DP: How do you assemble a show?

LY: Generally I do a sound cut first and then come back and work on picture. That's a pretty traditional way of editing.

DP: Do you have any general advice for producers who are preparing to go into a nonlinear edit suite?

LY: Realize what nonlinear can and can't do. It doesn't work miracles; it's still an edit system. Think about what kind of system you need. Don't plan on doing an edit on a system that can't do much with graphics if you know you want to fly graphics back and forth.

Don't expect to walk into an edit room and say, "I've got 60 tapes, and I want to be able to put all 60 tapes onto 18 gigabytes of storage." It ain't happening. Plan your storage accordingly. If you don't know, ask an editor.

DP: You know the old adage, "We'll fix it in post"? Do you think it's gotten worse with nonlinear?

LY: Yes, absolutely. "We can fix it in post." It's an editor's joke, but it's become a producer's reality. In the linear world, there were a lot of things you couldn't fix on tape, and now all of a sudden there's this digital manipulation of an image. "Oh yeah, we can fix that." But it costs you $12,000 to make a 2-second fix — and it could have been shot right in the first place. And it would have made you $12,000. Then at the end of the edit the producer will invariably say, "Why was this post bill so high?"

Richard Bock

Richard Bock worked for 18 years as a rerecording mixer at WGBH, in Boston, Massachusetts. He is now an independent mixer, running his own business, Richard Bock Sound Production, in Cambridge, Massachusetts. He won a News and Documentary Emmy for mixing the show, "Renegades," a segment of the WGBH series, Rock & Roll. Bock mixes on DigiDesign's Pro Tools.

Digital Producer: I'd like to go over the workflow for audio, from shoot through post-production, and talk about how producers can get the best quality audio.

Richard Bock: First, you want to get the best quality audio at the time of the shoot that you possibly can; I think that's by far the most important thing. There are two basic ways to mike for quality sound during the shoot. Probably the most popular way is to pin a lavalier microphone onto a person; that's the way many interviews are done. As a subset of that: Is it a visible or a hidden microphone? If it's a visible microphone, like you see on TV news people, the mike is clipped to a man's tie or or to a woman's blouse.

There are a lot of people who don't like looking at lavalier microphones, and so they try hiding them, which can be a disaster. If you hide a microphone, you're now subject to clothing noise; and if the person moves, you might hear a swishing sound which can drive people crazy. The sound can also be quite muffled if you put it under clothing.

The other way to record sound is to use a boom, which is basically a mike on the end of a stick. In most cases, that is the best way to record sound, as long as you position the boom correctly. The trouble is that because you have this thing sticking out pretty close to the shot, you have to deal with boom shadows. And you have to have somebody there to hold it. The appealing thing about a lavalier is that one person can go and set the camera up, clip the microphone on, and just plug it into the audio input. With the boom, you have the potential to do some really good stuff, but it probably requires another person. These are the tradeoffs.

DP: What about recording onto two tracks in the shoot?

RB: In an interview situation, you can record with two mikes (most video recorders are two-track). You might use one microphone on the person being interviewed and a second microphone on the interviewer. But most of the time, the interviewer's questions are not used. Or, you might record with a lavalier and a boom, and then decide later which sounds better.

In a non-interview situation, two tracks let you use stereo, which is very nice. And there are other possibilities. If you have multiple people on camera, you could put each of them on a separate track.

DP: What about recording audio using built-in camera microphones?

RB: I have mixed stuff that was shot on the built-in microphone on the DV camera. I did a short non-broadcast show a few weeks ago, and it had a couple of shots of walking into a classroom. The sound is wonderful, and it was only coming from the built-in camera mike. You heard the classroom open up as the camera person walked in the door, sound coming from all around, and it was really nice.

You could have made that same scene sound really horrible by burying a radio mike on one of the people in the room. You would get no sense of sound perspective at all. The point is that you have to understand what you're doing. There are no rules, in that sense. If you took that same camera mike and went outside with it, and there was a breeze blowing, the audio would probably not be usable because the wind would blow it away. So there's the same situation, the same mike. It did a nice job in one place, and would do a very bad job in another place.

DP: When you record on two tracks, do you need to communicate that to the editor?

RB: Yes, everybody downstream has to understand that there are two separate tracks here. Also, a lot of information gets lost when you go from the shoot to the edit, so that what the sound recorder intended never gets to the editor. This happens all the time.

DP: So what may happen as a result?

RB: Editors may end up digitizing one track, to save media space. And that's a problem because once you digitize it, you're kind of locked into the fact that this picture now is associated with one sound track as opposed to two. Of course you can fix the problem by digitizing the second track, but it's annoying.

DP: I wanted to ask you about recording to channels 3 and 4, versus channels 1 and 2. Do you recommend one over the other?

RB: With analog Beta decks, you can record on analog tracks (tracks 1 and 2) or hi-fi tracks (tracks 3 and 4). In my experience, tracks 3 and 4 are more reliable. Because tracks 1 and 2 are analog and because they are Dolby encoded, you can get into a host of playback problems if the decks aren't set up correctly. (A simple explanation of Dolby is that it basically records a signal that pushes up the frequencies that later get rolled off.) Tracks 3 and 4 are not Dolby encoded.

The biggest problem (and this affected television sound for 15 years) is that there was a switch: Dolby on, Dolby off. The digitizing deck has to be set the same way you set the record deck during the shoot. When you digitize, you really have to listen carefully to tell whether the original tape was Dolby on or Dolby off. Editing rooms are always noisy, with disk drives, tape machines, and air conditioners, so editors can't hear everything. If you could use tracks 3 and 4, which don't have Dolby, you could eliminate all that. And it was my experience with a lot of years of this, that if you use tracks 3 and 4, you are in much better shape. You have to have a deck that plays back 3 and 4, which not all of them do, especially low-end decks.

DP: Has the problem with the Dolby On/Off switch been eliminated with Beta SP, which automatically switches Dolby on.?

RB: Yes, that's largely true; but it's something you have to be aware of, because every so often a field producer recycles old tapes and throws in something that's not Beta SP. If the Dolby switches aren't set correctly, you hear something that sounds unnaturally muffled or hissy. If that happens, you have to redigitize.

DP: Do you think there's a noticeable difference in audio quality between an industrial-quality and a broadcast-quality Beta deck?

RB: Once you deal with the Dolby issue and set up the deck correctly, I don't think that an industrial-quality deck (such as the UVW 1800) is an inherently inferior playback deck. Once you account for all the other possible problems, either type of deck should play back fine.

DP: Are there any other issues regarding digitizing?

RB: Once you have your deck in place, a problem that arises is that people routinely under-record when they digitize, like up to 10 dB. They somehow think that digital audio is perfect, and so they can therefore under-record. While that's to some extent true, it's a good idea to digitize your material at full level. When you set the levels in preparing to digitize, the peaks should go right near the top of the indicator, but not turn on the overload, which will over-modulate the audio. If you over-modulate the audio, that's bad.

It's true that under-recording is probably preferable to over-recording, but you should still do it right. In computer terms, it's 16-bit audio; so to the extent that you under-record it, you are cutting down the number of bits you're using. You're basically throwing away quality. Is that quality that important? I don't know. But it would still be a good idea for people to use the full scale, without over-modulating.

DP: So should the person digitizing sit and watch the audio meters the entire time?

RB: If the sound has been recorded well, you should be able to set the levels so they peak near the top of the indicator, start digitizing, and leave the room. A good sound recording person will use the full level, and won't over-modulate, but won't under-record either.

DP: After the original recording and digitizing, what can the producer do to get good sound?

RB: Don't mess it up too much in the editing. Don't over-edit interviews. Let's say you're editing the sound of an interview, to use as voiceover for something else. Editors start cutting words together that were never said together. You should make sure the audio sounds natural and pay special attention to intonation.

DP: What do you do in the mix?

RB: The mix involves taking all of the audio tracks and making them sound the way you, the producer, want them to sound. You set the relative levels. You also fix things that nobody heard in the edit room, because it's too noisy. For instance, in a documentary situation, you might cut from the synch interview to a voiceover. When you get into the mix room, you hear the interviewee finish the last word and go, "hh," inhaling for the next sentence. You never heard that in the edit room. So you have to go in and nudge the edit a little bit. You're doing a lot of little micro-edits in the mix. In some of the over-edited sections, where words may have been chopped because you've spliced together too many of them, you can do micro-editing here so that it sounds better.

DP: How is the audio delivered to you for the mix?

RB: There are editors who digitize all their material, and bring in the media. There are others who output an EDL, and give the sound house the EDL and the tapes. Then the sound house batch digitizes. In that case, if you have non-timecoded material, you should have it transferred to a timecoded medium for the edit, or else at least make it very clear where it came from.

DP: What tools do you commonly use?

RB: I use EQ [equalization] a lot. EQ removes or attenuates a specific frequency or range of frequencies of the audio. You often use equalization to fix what sounds like bad sound. If you're in a room you can get air conditioner noise; if you're using a boom microphone you can get a lot of handling noise; or you can get wind noise. A lot of that is down in the very low frequencies. One of the things I do almost without even thinking is roll off the extreme low frequencies.

I use reverberation for special effects. You can also use it to try to match a room sound, but that's a little tricky. I tend to use reverb as an obvious effect.

DP: When you get the audio tracks, do you care if the editor has micro-adjusted the audio levels?

RB: I care only if they get disappointed that all the work they did has just gone out the window; because once you start mixing, those levels change. But of course, you have to set levels in the edit in order to do reviews and digital cuts.

DP: Do you have any advice for producers on how to have a productive mixing session?

RB: Communicate. Talk. Get involved as early as possible.

DP: How early?

RB: Before the shoot, if possible. Get the sound person to talk to the editor. So if the sound person is recording two tracks of sound from two different microphones, tell the editor. Is there one track that I should take? How do I find that out? Is it actually written in the log someplace? It's much more satisfying if you can get involved much earlier than just having the person walk in the door and say, "Here, mix this." That can be very frustrating.

DP: What are some ways a producer can communicate stylistically what he or she wants from the mix?

RB: Some things to think about are: Do you want a hot mix? Do you want the effects and the music to be really pushing the voice all the time? Lots of people want that, because they think it's a much more contemporary sound. Other producers don't want anything to compete with the voice. They want it to be absolutely easy to understand, even if that means playing all the music and effects way low. You have to understand what the basic purpose of the particular project is. If it is to convey information, then you should not make it difficult to understand by pushing music and sound effects.

DP: How much can you fix things in the mix?

RB: The mix is usually the last creative step; it tends to take place after the picture is finished. You can fix lots of things in the mix, but a producer needs to know what a mixer can and can't fix. And that takes experience. So before you say, "Fix it in the mix," you'd better be sure you *can* fix it in the mix.

DP: And what makes a good producer at the mix?

RB: An educated one. Somebody who understands what's possible. A few producers, because it's the last step, come in and realize the show doesn't work. They try to make it up in sound. And you can see them totally at their wits' end, but there's not much you can do for them, because the sequence either works or it doesn't work. Sound certainly helps, but it can't make a sequence work.

I also think a producer who understands the whole production and post-production process is a better producer. Everyone needs to understand the whole process. People get wrapped up in their little part of it. You have to understand the whole thing. That seems to be extremely important.

DP: How would you compare analog versus digital source material: quarter-inch analog tape versus DAT and CD audio?

RB: Certainly there's nothing inherently inferior about analog. Analog is just more expensive and harder to do. Some people think analog is definitely better, because you haven't digitized anything. You've kept the signal as an analog signal. You are subject to a whole bunch of problems that are well known, but if you have the money and the expensive equipment it takes, you can probably get better results in analog. However, digital is easier, and it's a whole lot cheaper.

The original source is not such a big issue. It's an issue only if the composer delivers the music for a show on quarter-inch analog tape, and there's no quarter-inch playback deck.

Also, if you have a digital source, bring it in digitally. More edit rooms should have DAT machines for handling audio sources. If you have a DAT machine and a CD player, you can take both of those into an Avid digitally. And that is a very good idea; more people should do that.

DP: How are HDTV and digital television affecting choices for audio?

RB: Because of high definition television (HDTV) or digital television, there is now a new standard for sound. That standard includes up to 5.1 channels; those channels are left, right, and center speakers, two surround speakers, and a sub-woofer, which is the .1 channel. This is a high quality digital delivery system. So any project now mixed for television (and this would also apply to DVD, because DVD has the same formats) can be mixed in multi-channel, and can be played on digital TV.

You now can, in your home, have sound that's identical to what you hear in a theater, because theatrical sound on motion pictures is Dolby AC-3. And that's the format that now is going to be broadcast on digital TV and also DVD. Essentially, you will not get any better sound in a theater or in the mix room than you could get at home, if you put in big enough speakers and so on. The high quality signal is being delivered to you. You can play it back on the cabinet speaker, or you can go out and buy whatever you want to play it back on. You're no longer limited by the delivery system; you're limited only by the playback system, which is the way it should be.

DP: What would you say to people who don't think they need to worry about getting quality audio.

RB: That might have been true 25 years ago, but all that's changed now. First of all, stereo television is now the standard. Lots of people also broadcast in Dolby Surround. The Simpsons, for instance, is in Dolby Surround. I don't know what percentage still watch television on a 13-inch set with a speaker on the side. Now, you can get separate TV tuners, you can plug the TV into your stereo system, and hook good speakers up on either side of the television. You can hear basically exactly what's being broadcast. And what's being broadcast is extremely high quality at this point; it's as good as FM radio.

DP: What kind of sound do you prefer?

RB: I'm still very fond of just basic stereo. I think that's a wonderful experience, and also it's a more intimate experience. And television is basically an intimate form.

Index